PEARSON   ALWAYS LEARNING

Comprehensive Guide to Brain-based Literacy Instruction

Roxie Sporleder, Ed.D.
Indiana Wesleyan University
Marion, Indiana

Pearson Learning Solutions, 501 Boylston Street, Suite 900, Boston, MA 02116
A Pearson Education Company
www.pearsoned.com

Printed in the United States of America

1 2 3 4 5 6 7 8 9 10 V036 16 15 14 13 12 11

000200010270738663

CY/LD

ISBN 10: 1-256-34255-6
ISBN 13: 978-1-256-34255-7

Table of Contents

Preface

My passion is that all students would become proficient readers. To reach that goal, I found it was necessary to look at *all* research that pertains to reading, learning, and students, rather than at just one particular field of research. I had to understand research on how the brain processes and stores words, how learning occurs, how to achieve transfer of learning to the real world, and what is required to support the learning styles of students. Integrating this research produced the Framework for Teaching Reading that has resulted in unparalleled results. You will read the stories of students and whole classrooms that achieved outcomes beyond anyone's expectations.

This book is a comprehensive guide to literacy based on this framework. It addresses all areas of literacy through the lens of scientific research, from learning the alphabet to reading comprehension. Every strategy and principle has been proven to obtain results. You will see methods you currently use, learn why they are important, and see how they fit into a brain-based research model. In every chapter, you will also see strategies you have never seen before. They have been selected because they have achieved unprecedented results.

Some strategies that you currently use will become more important; others will not be important or will not be supported at all by research. I can't name how many strategies I "threw away" because they did not produce the kind of results I wanted. At the same time, I would see the extreme importance of another strategy and intentionally use it more and in better ways.

How is this book organized? In the first section, you are introduced to the critical knowledge needed to teach reading. Some of this may be information you did not learn in your teacher preparation program. You might want to use some chapters as reference until this material becomes a part of your knowledge base. The second section introduces methodology in teaching reading based on scientific research. Principles that expedite the transfer of learning, student progress, and inductive inquiry form the basis of reading instruction. The third section explores research and strategies for comprehension and writing. The last chapter provides general principles proven to achieve the highest learning results possible.

Scientific research has given us the tools to produce proficient readers. There is enormous hope for all readers of all ages, no matter how much they have struggled in the past. This book identifies and integrates that research into a framework for teaching reading that is capable of producing extraordinary results.

Part I

Critical Knowledge: What You Need to Know to Teach Reading

Chapter 1

We Have the Tools

The time is now. The possibility is here. After more than 30 years of scientific research using brain imaging, control groups, and statistical analysis, researchers around the world have discovered and established key principles and practices that produce remarkable reading achievement. Most of these findings have been so well documented that there is no argument as to their value. We have been shown the tools for reading success.

However, there is a caveat. Although the principles and practices for successful reading instruction have been identified, widespread use in the classroom has faltered. Application, for the most part, has been piecemeal, misunderstood, or nonexistent. Although this fact is disturbing, we must be aware that it often takes 30 to 70 years for research to be implemented. Examples are found in every area of scientific research. During the mid-1800s, the importance of hand washing to prevent the spread of germs was discovered. Louis Pasteur pleaded for the practice in 1876, but hospitals did not use hand washing until 1910. A full 60 years lapsed from discovery to implementation. Although seatbelts were invented in 1895, it was not until the 1930s that several physicians equipped their own cars with them, urging manufacturers to provide them in all new cars. However, they did not become standard on cars until 1962.

So, why does it take so long for research to become practice? It takes more than understanding the research; it also requires a change in the way we think. This is true for reading also.

Right now, we face multiple issues in bringing reading research into the classroom. First, the process has been slowed by a lack of understanding of that research. Teachers must grasp concepts and processes that have never been a part of teaching reading. For example, teachers have never had to understand phonemes or how they are processed in the brain. That was the turf of linguists. Now we are told this new concept impacts reading acquisition. If we misunderstand it, we cannot accurately implement it.

Even when teachers understand these new concepts, little direction has been given on how to implement that research into the classroom. Which methods and strategies are most appropriate for students of a particular age or for students with particular needs and learning styles? Which methods will produce the best results? We are just beginning the process of identifying those effective strategies.

Figure 1.1 How to Design a Balanced Approach

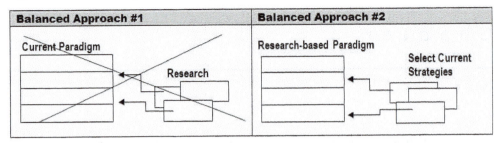

One of the largest hurdles is the conflict between the philosophical framework for reading that has been in place for 100 years and the framework suggested by researchers. Although during the past 100 years there have been variations of the framework, the basic philosophy on how we learn to read has remained the same (Balmuth 2009). We have a way of thinking about reading so when research tells us that phonemic awareness is important, the first instinct is to add it to the old framework. However, some of the concepts of the old framework contradict concepts in the research-based model, rendering the research-based strategies less effective.

In order for research in reading to make the impact it should and could have, our way of thinking must change. Instead of adding the new strategies to the old model, we need to do the reverse. We need to take strategies from the old that are effective and add them to the new framework. The balanced approach does not come by adding the new to the old, but the old to the new (see Figure 1.1).

The time has come to make a full commitment to learning and implementing what scientists have already discovered. It will require understanding the research, but it will also require a change in the way we think about reading.

The Crisis We Face

The time is now. We can't wait. Our nation has a literacy crisis. Every year since 1992, when the National Assessment of Educational Progress began tracking reading scores, 65 to 70 percent of our students leave school reading *below proficient* level. In other words, they cannot read well enough to read an article or story, make inferences, and draw conclusions. And it has been that way every year for almost 20 years (NAEP 2011).

In Figure 1.2, you see that the reading scores for both fourth grade and eighth grade have remained largely consistent over this period. Far too few students are reading proficiently. In a class of 30 students, only 8 or 9 would score at the *proficient* level. The 38 percent of fourth-grade students who are reading *below basic* cannot read well enough to participate in grade-level classroom instruction. That means more than one-third of the students in a classroom cannot perform at grade level.

One of the issues in addressing the problem is that almost all poor readers in our schools do not fit the criteria for learning disabilities or qualify for other special education services (Moats 2004). In my own experience working with a wide range of struggling readers of all grade levels, approximately 95 percent fall into this category. They have no identifiable special needs, and yet they cannot read well or read at all. These students

Figure 1.2 National Reading Report Cards for Fourth and Eighth Grade

Percentage of 4ᵗʰ Grade Students in Each Category

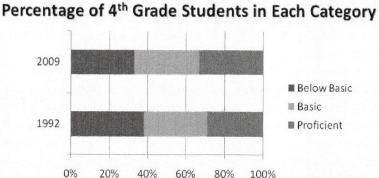

Percentage of 8ᵗʰ Grade Students in Each Category

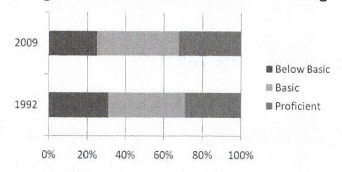

Data retrieved from NAEP at http://nationsreportcard.gov/reading_2009/

fall through the cracks, receiving no extra help unless the individual school implements a program funded through grants. Since these programs are grant-dependent, they are sparse and sporadic. And the problem persists.

The Impact on Society

The toll on our society is devastating. The impact of poor literacy ripples through every segment of our culture and costs billions of dollars a year. It not only affects the poor reader but also affects the entire society (National Center for Educational Statistics 2011).

Let's follow a poor reader from fifth grade to adulthood. By fifth grade, he hates school and hates himself. Every day he is asked to perform tasks that are impossible for him to complete. Who would willingly subject himself to such anguish? He is sure there is something intrinsically wrong with him. It appears others can do this. Shame overwhelms him, and low self-esteem is generalized to every area of his life. The anxiety and depression that permeate his being leads to aggression, juvenile delinquency, and drugs. When he is 16, he drops out of school, free to leave an environment that tore away at his soul. He can't read anyway, so what is the point?

Now finding a job becomes a problem. He doesn't have the skills that businesses require, and getting an education is not an option. Unemployment and poverty overtake him. He is not sure what services are available to him. He can't read a bus schedule, fill out a job application, or operate an ATM by just reading the instructions. He cannot read well enough to gain medical information or learn how to take care of his health. Unnecessary hospitalizations or errors in implementing health instructions may occur because he can't understand the directions of a physician. And how will he care for a family?

The consequences are profound for all of us. Every 2½ years we could fill a city the size of Chicago with individuals just like him who have dropped out of school (Learning Stewards 2011). Our economy, our health care system, our mental health system, and our criminal justice system are impacted by low reading achievement. Individuals who cannot read well are at risk for crime, unemployment, and poverty. The relationship to crime is so well documented that many states determine the number of prison cells needed based on fourth-grade reading scores. There is no argument that low literacy rates have a negative impact on an entire society.

We have a national literacy crisis. Understanding the research and how to implement it into the classroom *must* be a priority. The time is now to address this emergency.

What Do the Facts Tell Us?

What we are doing is not working.

We look at the ongoing statistics on reading achievement, and it tells us that what we are doing is not working. That does not mean some of the strategies we use aren't effective. But it does tell us some or many of them are not successful. It is difficult for any of us to let go of our favorite approaches or activities, but to change the tide of illiteracy, we must be willing to lay down those strategies and pick up only those that have been proven effective in research. We don't want to throw away time-proven strategies, but we also do not want to hang on to those that have no basis in research or are counterproductive to the reading process.

Teaching reading must be a priority.

The facts also tell us that teaching reading must be a priority. Reading is a gateway skill for all other learning; in fact, it is a gateway skill for a productive life. If an individual cannot read well, there is little hope and a bleak future. But if that individual can learn how to read well, the possibilities become endless. Every teacher must be aware of the reading level of each student, and if there is a problem, it needs to be addressed. If you give a student the gift of reading, you give the gift of hope of a bright future.

We have the tools.

More than 30 years of research has provided enough information that we truly have the tools to teach students of all ages how to be proficient readers. We will look at the research, build the knowledge base to implement the research, and explore strategies that have been proven in classrooms to produce skilled readers. These methods have been researched, formally tested, and demonstrated to help all students kindergarten through twelfth grade read proficiently unless they have some type of severe disability. Even those improve beyond expected levels. You will meet some of my students and the students of teachers with whom I have worked. Only the names have been changed to protect their identity.

My Quest

I began my teaching career as a first-grade teacher. On the first day, my mentor, who was a wonderful teacher, wanted me to be aware that some of the children would not be able to decode any words for about four months. Their reading skills would proceed slowly. My heart sank because I knew the long-term consequences their failure would have. They would be at least a half year behind, unable to read at grade level by the end of the year. Later, I would discover statistics that stated that where a student stands in relationship to age-mates at the end of the first year of school is roughly where one can expect to find that child to stand at the end of seventh or eighth grade. Poor readers tend to remain poor readers, while good readers tend to make continued gains in reading skills (Juel 1994a, 1994b). It felt like a death sentence for these students.

An urgent quest began for strategies that would enable these first-grade students to read at grade level and above by the end of the year. I did find strategies, and they all finished at or above grade level. But I had not yet seen all the problems students could have.

Each year, whether I was teaching first, second, third, or fourth grade, I continued my research, discarding strategies that didn't seem to make much difference and implementing strategies that worked well with a broad spectrum of student abilities and needs, including those with learning disabilities, communication disorders, and hearing impairments. My goal was to have every student reading at or above grade level by the end of the year. And unless students had a severe cognitive delay, they reached that goal.

It then came time to scientifically research these strategies. I found a school district other than my own that was willing to participate. It had nine first-grade classrooms that we divided into three groups, assigning each group particular strategies to use for 30 minutes each day in addition to the regular reading program. All aspects of the research were carefully planned so each group had the same type of students and the same level of teacher experience. A new reading program was adopted that year so no teacher had previous experience with the curriculum. For the designated 30 minutes a day, Group A used word families, Group B used traditional phonics, and Group C tested the research-based strategies.

After 21 weeks of instructions, formal tests showed that age, gender, and socio-economic status (SES) were not differentiating factors. However, Group C scored significantly higher in basic reading skills, total reading ability, and spelling achievement. Figure 1.3 shows the results. What did Group C do that the other groups did not do? They used the strategies explained in the rest of this book.

After that research, I collected data on 42 struggling readers in grades 4 to 12 from five different schools. After 45 hours of instructions spread over six months using the research-based strategies, all students gained at least two to six grade levels

Figure 1.3 First Grade Reading Achievement Results. Comparison of nine first grade classrooms on the Woodcock Reading Mastery Test–R using the psychometric scale of 90 to 110, with 100 representing average. Group A used Word Families, Group B used Traditional Phonics, and Group C used a Brain-based Approach.

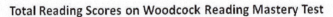

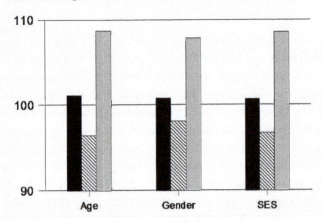

Figure 1.4 Grade Equivalent Reading Scores of Struggling Readers.

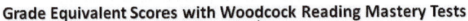

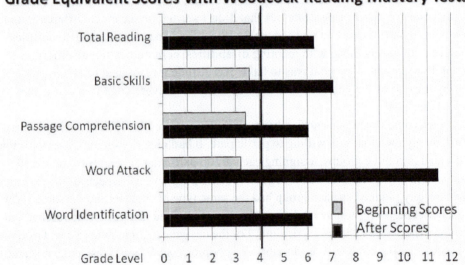

in reading, some as much as nine grade levels. Most students gained four to six grade levels. Figure 1.4 shows that most students scored *below* fourth grade level in all areas before instruction. As we will see later, fourth grade is a watershed year.

This study confirmed the principles for teaching reading are valid for all ages.

> Every individual has the potential of reading at grade level. It's never too late.

Meet My Students

John

John is a good example of a bright student who couldn't read. When I first met him, he attended a small, private school that catered to students who had learning difficulties. Although he was classified as a junior in high school, he was struggling with fourth-grade work in all subjects. Reading was difficult for him, and he could not spell even the simplest words. Probably the most notable characteristic of John was his persistent vocalizing: "I can't." Whatever he was asked to do, his immediate response was "I can't,"—and most likely, he couldn't.

At the end of 45 hours of instruction spread over six months using the research-based strategies, John was reading at a ninth-grade level rather than the third-grade level. When he realized he could read, he changed his career goal from massage therapist to lawyer. However, he had a problem. He had virtually lost all of his years of schooling because he was unable to read.

In the fall of his senior year, he called me, asking what he should do since he wanted to go to college. I suggested he go to the local university and enroll in a program that supported the acquisition of a high school equivalency diploma. They would identify areas of weakness and provide classes to prepare for the test.

Three weeks later he called me, "You'll never guess. They tested me and said that in Language Arts and Reading, I have no weaknesses. I am reading at a post-college level." Once he had learned the necessary skills for reading, he had continued to grow in his abilities. Within three months after completing my reading program, he was reading at a post-college level and preparing to go to college to become a lawyer.

Temica

When Temica entered second grade, the specialists told her teacher, "Don't be overly concerned about the progress Temica is making. *She is not capable of learning her letters and sounds.*" And so she entered second grade below kindergarten level, not even knowing the letters of the alphabet or the sounds they made. However, the teacher and others working with Temica began implementing the principles found in this book. And she made progress.

Just eight months later in April, I visited Temica and taught her a lesson. Not only was she reading at grade level but also she was rapidly and accurately spelling words such as *place*, *wage*, *huge*, and *budge* and adding prefixes and suffixes to those words. The prognosis was not accurate when principles and practices were used that fit her needs and learning style.

Tyler

Tyler was a special education student in sixth grade who spent most of his time in the special education room, joining the regular classroom only for Social Studies and Science. When I tested him in reading using the Woodcock Reading Mastery Test, a reliable and valid individual standardized test in reading, he scored in the 0.1 percentile in all areas—Word Identification, Word Attack Skills, Passage Comprehension, Total Basic Skills, and

Total Reading Skills. That means 99.9 percent of students his age would score above him. He could not even read a first grade primer since he only knew a handful of words.

After 45 hours of instruction using the research-based strategies, he could read at a fourth-grade level. The second year, he went through the 45 lessons again at a higher reading level and was reading at grade level. Tyler, the special education student who could only read about eight words in sixth grade, graduated from high school with his class and went on to college.

Insights from Brain Research

None one of these students could learn to read with the methods currently used in most classrooms across the nation. But they were successful, when the principles of reading found in research were implemented. What are those principles? What insights can research give us that will change the way we teach reading? Read on and discover how to build a framework for reading based on brain research that will produce unprecedented results with your students. These principles apply to beginning readers as well as struggling readers of all ages.

Chapter 2

The Discovery That Changes Everything

For 100 years, it was assumed that we read by seeing and remembering words. The Look-Say method in the *Dick and Jane* series, the Whole Language movement, and the strategy of spelling words by the shape of the letters all reflect that understanding.

Although some facets of each of these trends differ, the basic philosophy is the same: Students are taught to look at the word as a whole and remember it (see Table 2.1). The whole word is treated as a logogram, or a symbol, that stands for a specific word or phrase. Rather than giving attention to the individual letters or sounds, the reader visually remembers the shape of the word in the same way one visually remembers the form of any object, as illustrated in Figure 2.1 (Goodman 1986). "In the whole word method, the whole sound of the word is associated with the total visual appearance. . . A word is not a sum of letter-names, anyway, nor even merely of letter-sounds. Its visual appearance, indeed, is not a sum of letter-appearances, but has a character of its own" (Huey 1908, p. 272). When Huey's 1908 book *The Psychology and Pedagogy of Reading* was republished in 1968, Frank Smith, one of the leaders of the Whole Language movement, noted the reason it was republished was "not as a monument but as a book whose time has come." He refers to it as "brilliant" and "a milestone" (Balmuth 1982, p. 197).

Important strategies that accompany this philosophy are the use of predictable texts that contain multiple repetitions of words and phrases, memorization of sight word lists, use of context clues such as pictures to identify words, and teacher reading the text aloud to students before they attempt it. Curriculums that use this philosophy may teach kindergarten students to read words before they have even learned the alphabet. Attention to letters, sounds, and phonics is usually incidental and only used as a reference to help students when all other strategies fail. With the advent of research in reading, more phonics-type activities have been added to the curriculum, but the basic philosophy of how we learn new words remains the same.

We did the best we could. We had no way to see inside the brain to know what was going on. We made our best guess. Then, with the advent of brain research with its imaging techniques, we discovered that is not how we read at all!

Table 2.1 Comparison of Whole Word and Whole Language Approach to Reading

Similarities	Differences	
Basic philosophy: We learn new words by the visual appearance, remembering what the word looks like with minimal regard for letters or sounds.	**Whole Word 1800s–1960s Dick and Jane—1926–1960s**	**Whole Language 1967–Present Similar to early whole word methods of the 1800s**
• Memorization of whole words • Repetition to learn new words • Minimal use of phonics • Predictable text (repetition of words or phrases); no decodable texts • Use of sight word lists	• Used repetition to learn new words.	• Uses context and meaning as clues to identify new words.
	• Taught isolated skills—reading, spelling, writing were taught separately.	• Integrated skills—writing is related to reading; spelling not taught.
	• Controlled vocabulary; grade level texts were determined by vocabulary.	• No controlled vocabulary; Leveled readers are based on length, sentence structure, and concepts.
	• Workbooks, drill, skill sequences.	• Original writing; no workbooks or skill sequences.

Figure 2.1 Example of Spelling Words by Letter Shape

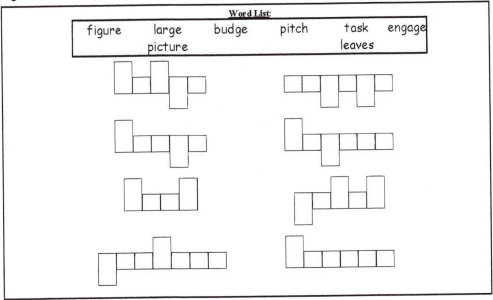

How the Brain Processes and Stores Words

So how *do* we read? Sound by sound. Accomplished readers perceive every letter in every word. The brain does this so rapidly, averaging five or more words per second, that it recognizes phrases and words at almost the same time it recognizes individual letters (Adams 1990; Shaywitz 1996). By observing the activity in the brain using functional MRIs, researchers have been able to identify the processes used by both proficient readers and those who struggle with reading. Although research on the brain is relatively young, it has provided us with extraordinary information on the reading process. With this knowledge

> Efficient reading takes place in the languages centers on the left side of the brain. Reading instruction must support the development of those structures.

> Many children who have had experience with print have memorized a significant number of words visually (without phonological record) and through reading beginning material, they will memorize more. However, they cannot learn enough words in this manner to read the bulk of material they will eventually encounter, and retrieving the word from memory will also be slower than if they had phonologically recorded it.
>
> —Bill Honig (1996), p. 62
> *Teaching Our Children to Read*

> There are several widespread misconceptions about how skilled readers actually read. For example, it is commonly believed that skilled readers do not need to read letters or even words because that would slow them down. But according to extensive eye movement research, even accomplished readers look at virtually every word, although they sometimes skip short function words such as and, to, the, or of. They accurately perceive every letter in those words, not linearly, but in chunks.
>
> —Marilyn Adams (1990, pp. 100–102
> *Beginning to Read*

of the brain along with the results of scientific causal and correlational studies, we are able to construct a framework for teaching reading that is effective for almost all learners.

Scientists around the world have discovered that proficient readers process words mainly in four language centers found on the *left* side of the brain (Shaywitz 1996, Shaywitz et al. 2004; Moats 2009). Neural pathways connect each of these areas with lightning speed and produce understanding of the printed word. In contrast, poor readers of all ages activate networks on the *right* side of brain (Moats 2009, Papanicolaou et al. 2003). However, when struggling readers are taught a research-based approach to reading, the activation switches to the networks on the *left* side of the brain (Simos et al. 2002; Shaywitz et al. 2004). What does this tell us? That efficient reading takes place in the languages centers of the left side of the brain and reading instruction *must* support the development of those structures.

The Four Language Centers Located on the Left Side of the Brain

What are these language centers, and what do they do? How does the brain process words? Figure 2.2 shows the functions of these four areas of the brain.

Speech Sound Center (Word Analysis)

Located in the left front of the brain, this area catalogs and recognizes the individual speech sounds of a language, called *phonemes*. Although this region has many tasks, including the production of speech, it also analyzes the individual sounds in written words.

Figure 2.2 Language Centers of the Brain Involved in Reading

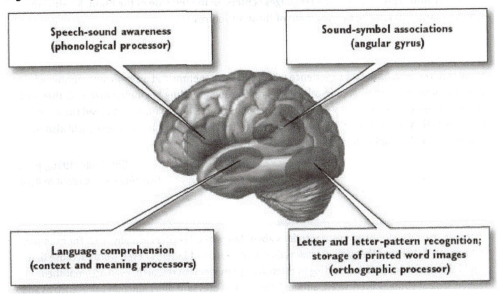

Reprinted with permission, Cambium Learning-Sopris.

This information is neurally linked to the symbols stored in the Sound Symbol Center of the brain and supports word recognition in the Word Form Center.

Sound Symbol Center (Word Analysis)

Located in the left middle of the brain, this area stores the symbols of speech sounds, called *graphemes*. For example, the grapheme for the sound /t/ is represented by the letter t and the grapheme for the sound /th/ is represented by the letters th. The brain rapidly associates the individual sounds of a word with the representation of those sounds. When learning new words, this area is active in "analyzing a word, pulling it apart, and linking its letters to their sounds (Shaywitz 2003, p. 79). This area communicates with the Speech Sound Awareness Center and the Word Form Center to support word recognition.

phoneme—a single sound of speech.
grapheme—letter or combination of letters that represent a single phoneme.

Word Form Center (Storage of Printed Word Images, along with All Associated Data)

Located in the left back of the brain is a complex area that stores printed words and all the information associated with those words, including letter–sound associations, spelling, pronunciation, and meaning. It provides recognition of all parts of the word, including suffixes, prefixes, and any Latin and Greek roots. After a word has been read several times and the reader has processed the word using the first two language centers, it is stored in this area for instantaneous retrieval.

> After a child has analyzed and correctly read a word several times, he forms an exact neural model of that specific word. The model (word form), reflecting the word's spelling, its pronunciation, and its meaning, is now permanently stored in this system. Sub-

sequently, just seeing the word in print immediately activates the word form and all of the relevant information about the word. It all happens automatically without conscious thought or effort (Shaywitz 2003, p. 79).

Beginning readers show strong activity in the word analysis parts of the brain (Speech Sound Awareness Center and Sound Symbol Center) but as they become more and more skilled in reading, the Word Form Center becomes the most active region. It is not necessary for the brain to continually analyze words already processed because all of the data associated with those words are permanently stored in this area and instantly retrieved with the word.

Context and Meaning Center

Located in the middle of the left brain is an area that connects with the middle and back areas of the brain to produce meaning and context for words that have been analyzed for sound symbol associations and spelling. This information is stored with the word form in the Word Form Center and is activated during reading.

How Do Poor Readers Process Words?

Quite differently than skilled readers. When they see a word, the brain attempts to connect to the language areas, but there is little activation except in the left front region where speech sounds are stored (Moats 2009). It is an attempt to pronounce the word. As these readers reach adolescence, this front area becomes overactive:

> It is as if these struggling readers are using the system in the front of the brain to try to compensate for the disruption in the back of the brain. . . . One means of compensating for a reading difficulty . . . is to subvocalize (say the words under your breath) as you read, a process that utilizes a region in the front of the brain responsible for articulating spoken words (Shaywitz 2003, p. 81).

By pronouncing the word, the reader is more aware of the sound structure and therefore can read, although more slowly than if the Word Form Center were functioning properly.

Brain imaging shows the left hemisphere language centers do not function properly, especially the Word Form Center found in the posterior of the brain where skilled readers store words for instantaneous retrieval (Simos et al. 2002, Shaywitz et al. 2002, 2003, 2004). Instead, networks on the right side of the brain are established and words are processed through these centers (Papanicolaou et al. 2003). Words are not stored with the letter-sound associations, spelling, pronunciation, and meaning as they would be in the Word Form Center, but as logograms or pictures (see Figure 2.3). Because struggling readers do not understand the underlying sound structure of the word, only the shape of the word and meaning is stored. Retrieving this information is inefficient at best.

The good news is that after instruction using a research-based approach, brain-activation pathways in the left side of the brain become normal and the right side networks diminish (Simos et al. 2002; Shaywitz et al. 2002, 2003, 2004). Struggling readers can become skilled, proficient readers with the proper instruction (see Figure 2.4). This explains the incredible progress of John, Temica, and Tyler that you met in Chapter 1.

Figure 2.3 Areas of the Brain Activated During Reading

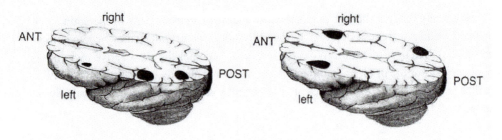

Proficient, Nonimpaired Reader   Poor, Impaired Reader

The nonimpaired reader on the left activates three main neural systems that are mostly in the back of the left side of the brain. Notice there is no significant activation on the right side. In contrast, the struggling reader, on the right, activates systems on the right side and in the front left of the brain. Words are stored on the right side, causing these individuals to be slow, poor readers because words cannot be efficiently retrieved from these areas.

Reprinted from *Overcoming Dyslexia: A New and Complete Science-Based Program for Reading Problems at Any Level* (2003), Vintage Books, a division of Random House.

Figure 2.4 Effective Reading Intervention Results in Brain Repair

Impaired Reader Before Intervention   After Appropriate Intervention

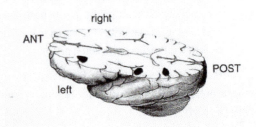

With instruction that supports the way the brain reads, the struggling reader can become proficient. This figure shows how the brain of the poor reader activates after appropriate instruction. The language centers of the brain have begun processing words, storing them in an area where they can be efficiently retrieved. Notice how the left side shows the same patterns as a proficient reader with no stimulation on the right side.

Reprinted from *Overcoming Dyslexia: A New and Complete Science-Based Program for Reading Problems at Any Level* (2003), Vintage Books, a division of Random House.

What Does This Research Tell Us?

The implications are profound.

This is the discovery that changes everything. It changes how we look at words, how we look at the reading process, and how we look at methods for teaching reading. Many approaches that have been used in the past 100 years may even be counterproductive to the reading process.

Let's identify the implications of this research. Instruction that develops each of the language areas of the brain will produce proficient readers. The following specific knowledge and skills are needed:

- ***Speech Sound Center*** *(Word Analysis)*. Students need to be able to hear the individual sounds in speech so that words can be analyzed by sounds. If they cannot hear the individual sounds in speech, they will not be able to analyze words using this center.

- ***Sound Symbol Center*** *(Word Analysis)*. Students must know the graphemes (letters) that represent those sounds. This means knowing more than just the alphabet and its sounds. Our language has 44 sounds that can be represented with about 76 commonly used graphemes.

- ***Word Form Center*** *(Storage of Printed Word Images along with All Associated Data)*. Students must know how to add prefixes and suffixes to words so these patterns can be stored along with the words. They also need to recognize the patterns of Latin and Greek roots. Students must engage in extensive reading since it takes at least 4 to 14 repetitions to put analyzed words into this area of the brain for instantaneous retrieval.

- ***Context and Meaning Center*** *(Meaning Processor)*. Students must engage in meaningful conversations about experiences and text. Extensive reading supports vocabulary, background knowledge, and understanding of text structures.

These critical instructional pieces must be a part of an effective reading program. They are not optional or secondary. To become a proficient reader, a student must be able to do all of these things well.

In addition to the identification of the essential components of a reading program, there are three other implications that will affect methodology:

1. *Methods chosen to teach new words will impact how words are stored.* In order to store words properly, students must be taught all of the phonological information that goes with those words. If they must read words for which they have no phonological information, they are unable to process them through the language systems of the brain. That means they must use other, less efficient systems to remember and retrieve words. They can only memorize them. The method of instruction has dictated how the words are processed and stored.

2. *Where words are processed and stored affects fluency and speed.* There is a difference between storing a word as a picture or symbol and storing a word with all of the phonological data. They are stored in different parts of the brain and they are retrieved differently. If a student memorizes words without attention to the underlying sound

structure, then the words will *not* be stored in the Word Form Center and *cannot* be efficiently or instantaneously retrieved. Both fluency and speed will suffer. However, if the word is stored with all of the associated data, both fluency and speed will progress toward optimum.

3. *Meaning is activated last by the brain rather than first.* Other models of reading suggest meaning is the first system readers should use. However, brain imaging shows just the opposite. Analysis of the underlying sound structure of the word must come first so it can be processed properly through the language centers of the brain. Meaning is activated last.

Identifying the Unique Characteristics of Struggling Readers

We now have a basis for developing a framework for teaching reading founded on scientific research. Before we do that, let's find out more about struggling readers. What unique characteristics do they possess? How do those characteristics make it more difficult for them to learn to read? We need to know how to teach them in a way that they learn best.

Summary

Language Centers of the Brain		To Become a Good Reader, One Must:
Speech Sound Center (word analysis)	▶	Be able to hear the individual sounds in speech.
Sound Symbol Center (word analysis)	▶	Know the letters that represent those sounds. This is more than just the alphabet.
Word Form Center (storage of printed word images)	▶	Understand how to spell and add prefixes and suffixes. Be able to spell and use Latin and Greek roots.
Context and Meaning Center (meaning processor)	▶	Engage in extensive reading.

Chapter 3

The Forgotten Learner

Why do some students fail to become proficient readers although they have no obvious disability? There is a large group of poor readers that have average or above average intelligence but struggle to learn to read.

As a reading specialist, I would receive calls from schools and parents asking me to help students who were struggling to read. They described the problem the student was having, when it started, and how it progressed. It was almost the same in every case.

So what was the typical profile? The student usually progressed "okay" during kindergarten through third grade. By grade 4, they were showing significant difficulties in reading and general school work, but both teachers and parents felt the situation would turn around. By fifth grade, the student crashed. It was obvious there was a serious reading problem. Most of the students I taught were fifth or sixth graders.

Of course, there were variations. Some students manifested problems with reading during grades K–3, but dramatically crashed at grade 4. Other students limped along until middle school or early high school. They never did well in school, disliked reading, but they survived. Only a small percentage of all poor readers had hearing and speech impairments, cognitive delays, or were just learning the English language. Almost all were students with no identifiable disability.

The interests and gifts of these students also had remarkable similarities. These abilities usually revolved around the creative and physical arts. Most liked music, art, drama, sports, computers, and/or mechanics. Science was also a favorite subject if it were taught with discovery and experiments. In addition, one or more parents of these students were usually coaches, mechanics, electricians, artists, musicians, or health club owners.

This profile of struggling readers generates two important questions. Why is fourth grade such a critical turning point? What is the significance of the gifts and interests?

Why the Fourth Grade Crash?

Josh, my third-grade student, performed well in the classroom. He produced excellent work and showed no signs of any kind of learning problems whatsoever. For this reason, I was stunned to learn that by fifth grade he could not read well enough to complete his school work and had to receive remedial help in reading. What happened?

Figure 3.1   Before and After Reading Scores of Struggling Readers

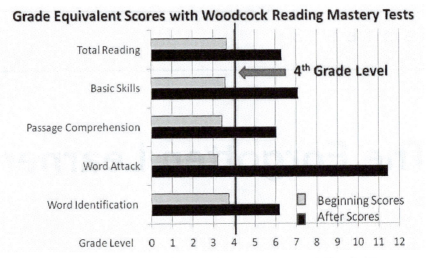

Grade Equivalent Scores with Woodcock Reading Mastery Tests

Remember, the 42 struggling readers from Chapter 1? Their beginning scores did not reach fourth grade level in any areas of the Woodcock Reading Mastery Test (see Figure 3.1). All of them would have struggled at the fourth and fifth grade level.

In conversations with teachers, I have heard this phenomenon described many times. As one third-grade teacher said, "I couldn't believe it! She was just fine in my class. How could she suddenly not be able to read?"

To find the answer, we have to revisit how the brain reads. Proficient readers have processed words through the language centers of the brain and have finally stored the word form with all of the associated data in the Word Form Center where it can be instantaneously retrieved. In contrast, the language centers of poor readers are not activated during reading. Instead, right brain networks compensate for the inability to analyze and process words properly. They have not stored words with all of the associated sound and structure data, but have stored them as logograms, or pictures.

Compensation Skills of Poor Readers

If we could crawl into the mind of these readers, we would be amazed at the compensation skills used to read texts. Since early childhood, they have been exposed to the concept of *story*. Even if parents never read to them, they have watched movies that have characters, settings, and plots. Each story has a problem and then finally a resolution. They understand *story*.

When they read a story and cannot process words through the language centers of the brain, they use other compensatory methods to read the words. Most primary texts include pictures that provide clues. That, along with their understanding of sentence and story structure, aids them in reading. If the teacher reads the story first, they have even more to help them.

You will be amazed how easy it is for you to read the following story. The only words that will trip you up are ϱϱαvδ oτηεϱ and Sπαvιση. You will guess at ϱϱαvδ oτηεϱ and come close on Sπαvιση. You are stumped unless you are familiar with horses. But because all the other words are within your knowledge base and vocabulary, you will do a good job at guessing and reading. Remember, the struggling reader has not processed words through the language centers so individual letters are not that significant.

Ηορσε

The hορσε is ρυννινγ. The hορσε wαντs to go hoμε.

This hορσε βελονγσ to a youνγ girl thατ lιϖεσ doων the στρεετ fρομ my γρανδμοτηερ. This hορσε is a Σπανιση σταλλιον.

Would you classify this as reading? But you *did* read. The picture helps and the text is a familiar structure.

Now the student has entered sixth grade and must read longer and more complex texts without pictures. What are the differences in reading the following text and the story about the horse? If you were a student attempting to read this, what feelings and thoughts would be going through your mind?

ψδρογεν and hελιυ

How does hψδρογεν turn into hελιυμ and give off ενεργψ? Four νυχλει of hψδρογεν join together to form one νυχλευσ of hελιυμ . . . We say that the νυχλει of hψδρογεν fυσε to form a hελιυμ νυχλευσ. This fυσιον happens only at a τρεμενδουσλψ high τεμπερατυρε such as εξιστσ on the sun. When four hψδρογεν νυχλει fυσε to form on hελιυμ νυχλευσ, a little of their matter δισαππεαρσ. This matter that δισαππεαρσ is turned into ενεργψ.

The concepts and the vocabulary are beyond the everyday experience of the student. In order to read to learn, one must be a proficient reader. As students enter fourth grade, they are suddenly faced with informational texts with technical vocabulary. If they do not have the ability to process words in the language centers of the brain, they will flounder. They will not be able to memorize enough words to keep up with the demands.

Why Some Poor Readers Don't Crash at Fourth Grade

How do some students survive longer with their poor reading skills than others? Although, poor readers do not process words through the left brain language centers, no matter what the age, some do better than others. One of the factors that contribute to better success is vocabulary development through exposure to a wide range of experiences and conversations. If one knows the concept and the vocabulary, then the chances of figuring out a text with those words and concepts is more likely. As students grow older, they seem to function fairly well, even though they may have struggled in reading during the early years. However, brain imaging reveals that these individuals are still not processing words in the language centers of the brain, even though they are accurate, albeit slow readers (Shaywitz 2003).

Another factor is an incredible memory. One of my colleagues completing her doctorate degree confessed to me that she could not figure out a word on her own, but if someone told her the word, she remembered it forever. Kevin, a student who had just finished his junior year in high school, struggled to maintain Cs. The school had determined he did not have a reading problem because he was an adequate reader and so labeled him "writing disabled" due to the deficiencies in that area. However, the Woodcock Reading Mastery Test, along with other tests explained in Chapter 9, revealed he was reading at a beginning sixth-grade level, three grade levels below his grade. To do as well as he had in school, he had memorized thousands of words and could conceptually understand the contexts of those words. With appropriate reading instruction, he became a proficient reader, maintaining As and Bs his senior year.

The Gifts and Interests of Many Poor Readers

The second mystery is the unique set of gifts and interests many of these poor readers possess. They aren't alone. What do these individuals have in common?

- Hans Christian Andersen
- Alexander Graham Bell
- Thomas Edison
- Walt Disney
- Albert Einstein
- Henry Ford
- Nelson Rockefeller

They are brilliant, creative, and have vivid imaginations, but they struggled with school. Notice how these individuals have the same areas of strengths observed in the struggling

---

Hans Christian Andersen was born on April 2, 1805, in Odense, Denmark. His father was a shoemaker, and his mother earned money washing other people's clothes. His parents spoiled him and encouraged him to develop his imagination. At the age of 14, Andersen convinced his mother to let him try his luck in Copenhagen, Denmark, rather than studying to become a tailor.

For three years Andersen lived in one of Copenhagen's most run-down areas. He tried to become a singer, a dancer, and an actor, but he failed. When he was 17, a government official arranged a scholarship for him in order to give him a second chance to receive an education. But he was a poor student and was never able to study successfully. He never learned how to spell or how to write in Danish.

After spending seven years at school, mostly under the supervision of a principal who seems to have hated him, Andersen celebrated the passing of his university exams in 1828 by writing his first narrative. The story was a success, and it was quickly followed by a collection of poems. Andersen's career as an author had begun, and his years of suffering were at an end.

Excerpt from Hans Christian Andersen Biography
Encyclopedia of Word Biography
Retrieved from http://www.notablebiographies.com/A-An/Andersen-Hans-Christian.html

readers with whom I worked: music, art, drama, sports, mechanics, and/or science, if it were taught with discovery and experiments. The experience of Hans Christian Andersen, who wrote stories for children such as *The Ugly Ducking* and *The Little Mermaid,* is representative of this group of learners. School was a disaster for him, and yet his imagination and creative abilities eventually led him to success in an unexpected field, writing.

Davis (2010) pinpoints the strengths of these poor readers in *The Gift of Dyslexia*:

- They are creative.
- They are highly aware of the environment.
- They are more curious than average. They ask *Why?*
- They think mainly in pictures instead of words.
- They are highly intuitive and insightful.
- They have vivid imaginations.

These individuals are some of the most brilliant in our society, but the way they process information differs from the rest of the world. And because of that, some are labeled with dyslexia, an inability to process graphemes and sounds, or with a learning disability, an inability to learn in a typical manner. However, most just fall through the cracks at school, struggling to read and write.

In the early 1980s, when computers were not common in schools, a small, rural school brought in computers for a week to introduce both teachers and students to basic functions. In that same school, six fifth-grade students who struggled with every aspect of school work spent most of their time in the Resource Room. However, that week, who went from room to room, teaching both teachers and students how to run the computers? The six fifth-grade students from the Resource Room. They "got it" easily when most of the others didn't. They definitely had gifts in an area where others lacked.

Insight from the Four Sensory Modalities

Understanding the four sensory modalities in learning will give us insight into the needs and gifts of these poor readers (see Table 3.1). To learn, we use all four modalities but usually lean on one or two more than the others. As you read these descriptions, notice the type of learner who most closely describes the poor reader. Also, decide your own areas of strength and weakness.

Visual Learners: I must read it to understand it.

We all know this kind of person. Maybe you are one of them. These individuals can hear an explanation, listen to instructions, or be shown how to do something, but they have difficulty processing information unless they can read it themselves. They need written instructions, a textbook, or a written list. In lecture classes, these students must take notes in order to have some kind of written record to read later.

My daughter says, "Listen to this paragraph. What do you think about it?" I'm not much help unless I can read the paragraph. It is as if my mind won't hold those spoken words long enough to process them and make a judgment.

Table 3.1 The Four Sensory Modalities

	Body	*In Order to Learn*	Supportive Activities
Visual	eyes	*I must read it to understand it.*	<u>reading</u>, watching
Auditory	ears	*I must hear it or talk about it to understand it.*	<u>listening</u> and talking
Tactile	small muscles (hands)	*I must write it to understand it.*	<u>writing</u>, drawing
Kinesthetic	large muscles (arms, legs, body)	*I must do something to understand it.*	writing at chalkboard, use of manipulatives, demonstrations, experiments, acting out, moving about the classroom

These individuals usually do well in school because it centers on written information. They often are independent learners because they do not need to hear explanations or be shown how to complete a task. They can read and understand. These are also the individuals who usually learn to read well in spite of the way they have been taught. They make the connections between the letters and sounds and process words in the language centers of the brain.

Auditory Learners: I must hear it or talk about it to understand it.

These individuals can read information, but not understand it well unless there is a discussion or a lecture. If there is no auditory explanation of some kind, they may resort to talking to themselves. In college, they dare not miss a lecture class because they would be left trying to understand the information from the textbook on their own. Small-discussion groups of various types support this kind of learner.

Tactile Learners: I must write it to understand it.

These learners must take notes of some kind in order to process knowledge. It might be a formal outline or random words on a page that look like doodling. When these individuals listen to a lecture, sit in a meeting, or read a book, they write. An interesting fact about these learners is that they may never read what they have written. The process of writing is what brings understanding, not reading it afterward. Sometimes a lecturer will say, "Just listen. Don't take notes." That is death to understanding for this type of learner.

Tactile learners also benefit from any activity that requires the use of the fine muscles such as picking up or touching objects. Manipulation of cards or objects that require both fine motor and gross motor skills will benefit both tactile and kinesthetic learners.

Kinesthetic Learners: I must do something to understand it.

These individuals, if they are strongly kinesthetic, do not learn well by reading, listening, or taking notes. That makes school as we know it a huge problem. They must engage in activities that require the use of the large muscles. In the classroom, this can include any

activity that uses the full arm, such as writing at a white board, manipulating flash cards or game components, or using a computer with a mouse. Obviously, activities that require movement from one area of the classroom to the other, demonstrations, experiments, or acting also support this type of learner. It is interesting that visual diagrams and pictures also aid these individuals in understanding because it organizes the information for them, something the centers in the left side of the brain usually do for other types of learners.

These learners are forgotten and left behind in the classroom. Traditional classrooms, including reading instruction, focus on reading, listening, and writing, but these students do not learn well with these modalities. They are often brilliant, and if not discouraged, do go on to do great things, but most likely they become defeated, ashamed, and even drop out of school.

Thirty-nine out of the 42 struggling readers in the research data found in Chapter 1 exhibited characteristics of kinesthetic learners. The other three had some kind of identifiable disability.

Characteristics of the Kinesthetic Learner

What are the strengths of kinesthetic learners? The list is similar to the one Davis (2010) provides for struggling readers. Perhaps, it is because kinesthetic learners usually *are* the struggling readers. By understanding the characteristics and needs of the kinesthetic learner, we can begin to design reading instruction that supports them.

- **They are usually good at art, music, athletics, computers, mechanics, and/or science.**
  These individuals are creative and imaginative. They often think "outside of the box."
  They enjoy working with their hands. You will often see them drawing or doodling during class. By the time they get to high school, we have "sorted" the kinesthetic learners into a program all of their own, usually leaving them out of college prep courses.

Table 3.2   High School Courses Categorized by Sensory Modality

Visual, Auditory, Tactile Learners	Kinesthetic Learners
English	Sports
Math	Technology Ed
Science	Agricultural Ed
History	Music
	Visual Arts
	Drama
	Industrial Arts

- **They think in pictures, not words.**
  They process the world about them in pictures and not in words. This is an asset when you are an architect, artist, mechanic, or other individual in the creative arts. To perform well, they must be able to visualize the whole as if it were completed.

  Another aspect of thinking in pictures is the depth and breadth of ideas communicated through a single picture. "A picture thinker could think a single picture of

a concept that might require hundreds or thousands of words to describe. Einstein's theory of relativity came to him in a daydream in which he traveled beside a beam of light. His vision lasted only seconds, yet spawned scores of textbooks to explain it" (Davis 2010, p. 100).

- **They usually think in three dimensions.**
Unless you are kinesthetic, it is difficult to grasp visualizing everything in three dimensions (see Figure 3.2). One scientist said, "I see the x, y, z axes in mathematics in three dimensions. I can turn it around in my head in any direction." She was searching for a computer program that would represent the three-dimensional physics model she was developing as she saw it in her head.

Figure 3.2 Two-Dimensional Thinking versus Three-Dimensional Thinking

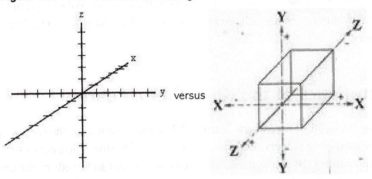

Two-dimensional thinking   Three-dimensional thinking

Imagine, then, going to school and having to read and write in a two-dimensional world. How do you place the letter *b* on paper? In your head, you can turn it in any direction, even upside down, but what is the correct direction on a two-dimensional piece of paper? It does not come naturally. You will need cues to remind you how to do it until it becomes automatic. It is not because you are deficient. It is because you are a brilliant, three-dimensional thinker!

- **They are curious and need to know *why*.**
They are usually "out of the box" thinkers. They want to know *why* things are like they are. Many students just want to know "how" to do things. That is not how kinesthetic individuals look at the world. *Why* is more important than *how*.

   They need to see the big picture because they process new and difficult information globally. Bits and pieces of information given in a step-by-step fashion are difficult for them to organize and understand (Honigsfeld & Dunn 2009).

- **They often can't sit still.**
They like to be active *unless* they are engaged in something that interests them. They *must* use the large muscles of their body. Linksman (2011), the director of the National Reading Diagnostics Institute, observes:

   Many children seen at the National Reading Diagnostics Institute have received a diagnosis of Attention Deficit Hyperactivity Disorder (ADHD). Yet in-depth reading evaluations of these youngsters often reveal that rather than having an attention disorder, they are simply kinesthetic learners. They need to engage in gross motor

(large-muscle) activity to learn best. Once they are given the opportunity to learn through the proper methods, their ADHD-like behavior often disappears (p. 1).

They might tap their pencils, shift their legs and body, or get up out of their seat. They *must* move.

- **They are often highly intelligent.**
Their lack of ability to function in a traditional classroom has nothing to do with intelligence. In fact, some of the most brilliant people I know are kinesthetic.

What Kinesthetic Learners Need

What do kinesthetic learners need in the classroom to learn? They must be engaged in activities that use the large muscles. It does not have to be the full body; using the full arm is just as effective. They also need to see the big picture and understand why. They need ways to organize the bits and pieces of information into a whole and a means to visualize concepts. The strategies they need are familiar but often not used, especially in reading (see Table 3.3). As you plan, intentionally incorporate these into all subject areas.

To prevent squandering the intellectual capital of these students, we must design instruction that meets their needs.

Dr. Grace Fernald, a researcher and professor at the University of California, successfully helped thousands of students learn how to read at grade level using kinesthetic methods (*Reading by Touch,* 1948). She did not have the advantage of the brain research, but

Table 3.3 Strategies to Meet the Needs of Kinesthetic Learners

Strategies	How It Meets the Need
• Writing on white boards • Manipulating flash, activity, or 3×5 cards • Manipulating objects • Performing demonstrations and experiments • Working on the computer • Engaging in small group discussions • Dramatizing • Playing games	• Uses large muscles (Remember, the *student* manipulates the cards, not the teacher.)
• Developing diagrams • Designing graphic organizers • Viewing and analyzing pictures	• Helps them see the big picture • Helps them organize bits and pieces
• Engaging in problem solving • Evaluating	• Satisfies need to know why
• Completing creative projects	• Satisfies need to be creative
• Investigating objects • Participating in field trips • Engaging in simulations	• Helps them form a three-dimensional picture in their mind of the concept

> It seems that most cases of reading disability are due to blocking of the learning process by use of limited, uniform methods of teaching. These methods, although they have been used successfully with the majority of children, make it impossible for certain children to learn because they interfere with the functioning of certain abilities that these children possess.
>
> We do not claim that all cases of reading disability are due to the use of methods that <u>omit kinesthetic factors</u>, but merely that such cases exist and that under our present system of education, a large percentage of the cases of extreme disability are due to the above . . .it seems also to be true that many cases of partial disability are due to the same general situation, though the individual is not so dependent on kinesthetic factors as is the individual of total disability.
>
> —Grace M. Fernald
> 1943

she understood the needs of these learners. She attributed most cases of reading disability to the omission of kinesthetic methods of teaching.

Although, kinesthetic learners comprise the largest percentage of individuals who cannot read proficiently, students with particular disabilities or intervening circumstances may also have difficulty learning to read. However, most of these also benefit from instruction that focuses on the kinesthetic.

What Do We Teach?

We now know the necessity of using kinesthetic methods to prevent reading failure for many students. Next, we need to look at *what* to teach students. Brain imaging and scientific causal and correlational studies not only inform us *how* we read, but also tell us the critical *content* necessary to learn to read. Traditionally, we have introduced students to letters and their sounds and then had them begin reading. That process misses two of the most critical components of reading instruction. What are those critical elements? Why are they necessary for proficient reading? We will explore these two components in the next chapter.

Meet My Student

Jared

Jared reminds me of Hans Christian Andersen. He is creative. His gifts lie in writing, but you would never have guessed it when he was a junior in high school. His scores on the Woodcock Reading Mastery Test showed he was reading at beginning fourth grade level, higher than most students with whom I work, but his word attack skills were barely second grade level. School was an immense struggle for him.

After 45 hours of research-based reading instruction that spanned over seven months, Jared was reading at grade level. That is an increase of seven grade levels. The most amazing part of his story is that he went on to college, maintained a grade point average above 3.0, and graduated with a degree in journalism. Today he is a voracious reader and prolific writer.

Summary

Characteristics of the Kinesthetic Learner
• They are usually good at art, music, athletics, computers, mechanics, and/or science.
• They think in pictures not words.
• They usually think in three dimensions.
• They are curious and need to know *why*.
• They often can't sit still because they like to be active.
• They are often highly intelligent.

Methods Required by Kinesthetic Learners	
• Writing on white boards	• Graphic organizers
• Manipulating flash, activity, or 3×5 cards	• Pictures
• Manipulating objects	• Problem-solving
• Performing demonstrations and experiments	• Evaluating
• Working on the computer	• Creative projects
• Engaging in small group discussions	• Teacher brings in objects
• Dramatizing	• Field trips
• Playing games	• Simulations
• Diagrams	

Speech Sounds: The Foundation of Reading

B rain research shows what is important to teach and what has been missing. In Chapter 2, we identified four distinct areas of the brain activated by proficient readers. Each area has a particular task (see Figure 2.2 on page 14):

1. *Speech Sound Center* analyzes the individual sounds in written words, called *phonemes*.

2. *Sound Symbol Center* associates the individual sounds of words with the representation of those sounds, called *graphemes*.

3. *Word Form Center* stores printed word images along with all associated data after words have been processed by the previous two centers. It also stores the context and meaning of the words.

4. *Context and Meaning Center* connects meaning and context for words that have been analyzed for sound symbol associations and spelling.

The most significant research finding is the central function of the Speech Sound Center in processing new words. It was unexpected. It is the discovery that changes how we look at the reading process and how we look at methods for teaching reading. If students are to be able to process words, they must *hear* the individual sounds that make up those words. In the spoken word *map,* they must be able to hear the three individual sounds /m/, /a/, /p/ in that word. During conversation, we only attend to words as a whole, but to be a proficient reader, we must be able to segment the spoken word into the individual sounds called *phonemes*. The ability to segment and manipulate the individual sounds in speech is called *phonemic awareness*. This provides the foundation for analyzing the sounds of a written word. *This ability to hear and segment the individual sounds of speech is the critical precursor to proficient reading.*

The ability to hear and segment the individual sounds of speech is the critical precursor to proficient reading.

There is a second important finding. The Speech Sound Center analyzes the individual phonemes in words and the Sound Symbol Center associates those phonemes with their symbols, called *graphemes*. That means students must know how to represent all of the sounds in the language. It is not enough to merely learn the alphabet because it represents only a fraction of the sounds and symbols of our language. The reading process breaks down if readers do not know the symbols for that sound even if they can hear and segment all of the sounds in a word, They need to be able to do both. The two most critical components for skilled reading are the ability to hear and segment the individual sounds in a word and to know the symbols for those sounds. In this chapter we will look at the sounds of the language and the representation of those sounds.

What You Need to Know about Phonemes

The ability to hear and manipulate the phonemes of our language is a critical component of proficient reading—but what is a phoneme? The initial response of teachers is to associate it with the similar word *phonics,* but it is not phonics. In fact, it has nothing to do with the written language. It is a linguistic term that has been traditionally unfamiliar to teachers. Now it has been brought into education.

What a Phoneme Is

It personally took me two years to understand what a phoneme was because I kept associating it with letters and phonics. Hopefully, the following explanation will illuminate you more quickly:

- **A phoneme is a single sound of speech. It is *not* the sound of a letter.**
  The brain distinguishes between an individual sound of speech and the representation of that sound. They are processed in separate parts of the brain. A phoneme has to do with the sound and not the representation. This is the most common misunderstanding of the phoneme.

- **A phoneme is represented on paper with a letter or group of letters called a grapheme.**
  To differentiate between a *phoneme* and a *grapheme,* we use slash marks such as /a/, /b/,/m/, and /r/ to represent a phoneme and letters such as *a, b, m,* and *r* to represent the grapheme. The word *map* has three phonemes, /m/, /a/, and /p/, represented by the three graphemes, m, a, and p.
  Some phonemes are represented by a single letter. For example, the sound /b/ is represented with the letter b. Other phonemes are represented by a group of letters. For example, /ch/ is represented by the letters ch or tch. A phoneme is a single sound but it can be represented by one or more letters.

- **Our language has approximately 44 phonemes.**
  The number of phonemes varies by one or two, depending on the area of the country in which you live. For example, if you live in areas of the northeast, you will pronounce the short /o/ sound differently than the /au/ sound, producing the /au/ lower in

the throat in some words. However, in most areas of the country the short /o/ sound is identical to the /au/ sound.

- **Phonemes differ from language to language.**
The number of phonemes in a language varies from 20 to 60. Some languages may have some of the same phonemes as English. If you study a different language, you know there may be sounds in that language that are *not* found in English, and vice versa. The Spanish language has no phoneme /th/ in the language, so when individuals whose native language is Spanish speak English, they often use the /t/ sound. Some languages are difficult to learn because one must be able to produce the phonemes of the language. Speaking with an "accent" reflects the inability to precisely produce the phonemes of a particular language. If you have students who are learning English, they will need to learn both the phonemes of our language as well as the representation of those sounds.

- **The same phoneme may be represented in different ways.**
The way a phoneme is represented is unique to the language spoken. For example, the phoneme /p/ may be expressed with a different letter or character. In English, it is depicted with the letter *p*; in Greek it is represented with the letter π. The grapheme, or representation, may change, but the phoneme remains the same.

  Even in our own language, many of the phonemes can be represented in more than one way. For example, the phoneme /sh/ can be depicted with the graphemes sh, ti, ci, si, or ch.

- **The same grapheme may represent different phonemes.**
My grandfather, Johannes Jens Jensen, immigrated to the United States from Denmark. In Danish, the grapheme j represents the /y/ sound, unlike English, where it represents the /j/ sound. He always pronounced his name Yohannes Yens Yensen. He never learned how to say the /j/ phoneme of English.

  Likewise, the grapheme r represents a different phoneme in English, French, and Spanish. If you are learning these languages, you must learn how to pronounce the different phonemes represented by the grapheme r.

- **There are languages that have no graphemes.**
All languages have phonemes, but some have no graphemes to represent them. They have no written code.

- **One or more phonemes together make a spoken word.**
Spoken words are made up of phonemes. The word *cat* has three phonemes: /c/-/a/-/t/. The word *sing* is also made up of three phonemes: /s/-/i/-/ng/. The last sound is a nasal sound made by placing the back of the tongue against the throat opening.

  We speak so quickly, blending phonemes together, that we usually don't stop to think about the individual sounds that make up those words. However, to become a skilled reader, we must develop the ability to segment the sounds of a spoken word into the individual phonemes.

- **Phonemes are learned during the first year of life.**
Up until approximately 6 months old, an infant is capable of producing almost all of the phonemes of the world's languages. When you hear an infant babbling, they are practicing many of these phonemes. By 10 to 12 months, the infant drops the

phonemes not needed to speak the language or languages that surround them and retains only the ones they will need (Kuhl 1992, 2006).

- **Phonemes need to be pronounced carefully, without any extra sounds.**
  Be careful not to add /uh/ to these phonemes: b, c, d, g j, k, ,w. Do not say *buh, cuh, duh, guh, juh, kuh,* and *wuh.* Instead, say the pure sound, which is abrupt. Otherwise, it will hinder the ability of the student to easily and correctly blend sounds together into words.

What a Phoneme Is Not

Although the terms *phonemes* and *phonemic awareness* are used throughout education, these are still often misunderstood. It is important that teachers have the knowledge to evaluate standards, curriculum, and specific activities to determine if these terms are being used correctly. Following are some of the misconceptions that are still widespread:

- **A phoneme is *not* the sound of a letter. It is an individual sound of speech.**
  This is tricky. If we try to relate phonemes to something we already know and teach, our first mistake is to say a phoneme is a sound of a letter. The idea that a letter has a sound comes from phonics and is a valid, but an extremely limited idea. For example, what is the sound of the letter *a?* The letter *a* does not have one particular sound. In fact, the letter *a* can represent several different phonemes in our language. Teaching reading using this approach is confusing to many students.

- **A phoneme is *not* the smallest meaning-bearing unit in a word.**
  Although phonemes are sometimes described in this way, a phoneme is NOT the smallest meaning-bearing unit in a word. It is true that changing a grapheme in a word does change the word, but the phoneme itself does not carry semantic meaning. The smallest meaning-bearing unit in a word is called a *morpheme.* We will talk about those later.

- **A phoneme it is *not* another word for phonics.**
  Phoneme or phonemic awareness is *not* another word for phonics. A common misconception is that if you are teaching phonics, you are teaching phonemes. However, it is like comparing baking an apple pie with the apples used in the pie. Although they are both necessary for completing the task, they are not even in the same classification. One is a process while the other is an ingredient. A phoneme is a single sound of speech, while phonics is a method of teaching reading. Although being able to hear phonemes in speech is a precursor to good phonics instruction, phonics can be taught without regard to phonemes. Table 4.1 will help make the distinction between the two words.

Table 4.1 The Difference Between Phonemes and Phonics

Phonemes	Phonics
A sound in speech	A method of teaching reading
• Has to do with sounds	• Has to do with letters
• Concerned with the *spoken* word	• Concerned with the *written* word
• Precursor to good phonics instruction	• Often taught *without* reference to phonemes, to the detriment of the learner

Identifying Phonemes in Words

The ability to hear and manipulate phonemes in spoken words is the critical precursor to reading and is a skill all teachers of reading must have. If you are a proficient reader, you have phonemic awareness, but you may not have had practice segmenting words. The following activities will hone your skills.

Activities

1. Right now, say some phonemes in the English language out loud. For instance, say the sounds /s/, /b/, /k/, /ng/, /l/, and /th/.
2. Activity 4.1 will give you practice segmenting words. You will find the answers at the end of this chapter.

    - What are the individual phonemes in these words? Remember to use slash marks to indicate a phoneme. For example, /m/ is the phoneme, m is the grapheme. The word *cat* would be represented with /c/ - /a/ - /t/.
    - How many phonemes are in each of these words?

Activity 4.1 Segmenting Words

Word	Phonemes	Number of Phonemes
string	/s/-/t/-/r/-/i/-/ng/	5 phonemes
computer	/c/-/o/-/m/-/p/-/u/-/t/-/r/	7 phonemes
nicely		
think		
stronger		
nation		
departmental		
tricking		

What You Need to Know about Graphemes

Graphemes are the representation of the sounds of a language. The ability to associate the sounds of speech with their graphemes is a critical component for proficient reading. There are 76 common graphemes of our language, with about 40 that occur less frequently. If students can hear the individual sounds in words and know the graphemes that represent these sounds, they can read virtually anything.

> If students can hear the individual sounds in words and know the graphemes that represent these sounds, they can read virtually anything.

- **A grapheme is one or more letters that represents a phoneme.**
  Graphemes represent the individual sounds of speech. They can be one letter such as *b* that represents /b/, two letters such as *ch* that represents /ch/, three letters such as *igh* that represents the long /i/ as in the word *light*, or four letters such as *ough* that represents the long o as in the word *though*.

Preschool to Kindergarten	Grade 1	Grades 2 to 3	Remedial Readers
Basic alphabet	Review alphabet	Review all graphemes	Learn all graphemes
Common graphemes	All graphemes		Usually know alphabet

As students are introduced to graphemes, they begin to see the letters as a whole representation rather than as individual alphabet letters. For example, when they see the grapheme th, they will know it represents /th/ rather than trying to pronounce it /t/- /h/.

- **If you are a proficient reader, you know all the graphemes.**
Skilled readers wonder how they could possibly know all the graphemes in our language, but they do. If you are a capable reader, you are able to list all of them because that is the way you have processed and stored words in your brain.

- **Students need to be taught all of the graphemes as quickly as possible.**
Teach the 76 ways to spell the 44 phonemes to all students, including first-grade children. These students can learn all of the graphemes in 26 to 32 weeks. Older students can learn all of the graphemes with about 42 hours of instructions (see Table 4.2). Without this knowledge, they cannot reach proficiency.

- **Provide visual access to the graphemes.**
It is beneficial for students to visually see all of the graphemes so that as they read and write, they can refer to them. A poster, wall sound cards, or individual sheets with the graphemes will help students learn these. Table 4.2 shows all of the graphemes.

- **The alphabet is essential but not the whole story.**
To be efficient at learning all of the graphemes, students need to be taught the alphabet with the basic sounds of each letter. This traditional approach will be a solid foundation for learning all of the graphemes of the language. But it is not enough.

There is a mismatch between the phonemes of our language and our alphabet. There are almost twice as many sounds as there are letters in our alphabet. Other alphabetic languages may have a one-to-one correspondence between phonemes and graphemes, but English does not. We have 26 letters in our alphabet, 44 phonemes, and over 76 common ways to represent those phonemes.

The Three Structural Layers of English

In teaching our language, it is important to understand the structural layers of words because this is the way words are stored and retrieved in the Word Form Center of the brain. A simple demonstration shows how the brain "pulls apart" words in retrieval. If you have read a word many times, you will instantaneously recognize it. However, if it is a word you do not read very often, your brain processes the word according to your understanding.

Table 4.2 Graphemes: The Spellings of the Phonemes

Spellings in gray are less common. Those in a box come only after a short vowel.									
a	e ea	i	o	U a e o	a a_e ai ay eigh ei ey	e e_e ee ea __y _ie/_ei _i_ ey	i i_e igh _y _y_	o o_e oa ow ough ou	U U_e _ew
b	c k ck ch qu-	d	f ph gh	g	h	j ge gi gy -dge	l _le _al	m _mb	n kn gn
p	qu	r er ir ur wr ear rhy our yr ar or	s ce ci cy ps	t	v	w	x	y_	z _s
wh	ch tch	sh ti ci si ch	th	th	oi oy	oo U U_e ue _ew ui	U oo	a a(l) a(lk) au aw augh	ou ow
ng n(k)	_s_	ar							

Reprinted by permission from Word Workshop C. Sporleder, R. L., 2007.

Try it. Pay close attention to the process you use in reading these words. You will know the word in milliseconds, so try to decipher the steps your brain takes. What do you see first? Second? How do you go about reading the word?

mismanagement

misrepresentation

If you have read these words many times, you instantly knew them. However, you may have looked at the prefixes and suffixes of the word before recognizing it. You may have seen mis, ment, manage, and then put it together, or the mis, tion, and represent. These parts of the words are called *morphemes*.

Now pay close attention to the process you use in reading these words. What do you see first? Second? How do you go about reading the word?

ostentatiously

preposterously

If you have read these word many times, you instantly knew them. However, you may have first seen the suffix *ly*, but that was not enough for you to read it. You may have had to break the word apart into chunks, called *syllables*. You may have seen *os-ten-ta tious-ly* or *pre-pos-ter-ous-ly* and then quickly put the word together.

If you are a beginning reader, you will have to break apart a word even more. You will have to look at each individual grapheme. You will be activating the Sound Speech Center and the Sound Symbol area of the brain. If you cannot segment individual sounds in spoken words and/or do not know the grapheme representation for that sound, you will not have the resources to decipher the word. You will have to depend on memory and the shape of the word. It might look like this to you.

μαναγεμεντ

There are three levels of language that a reader must penetrate to gain understanding of a word (Brady & Shankweiler 1991).

Level 1: Morphemes

Level 2: Syllables

Level 3: Phonemes

When we read a word, we automatically begin to break it apart at the level we need for understanding. If we do not instantaneously recognize the word, we pull it apart by morphemes. If we do not recognize the word at that level, we pull it apart even more into syllables. If we have difficulty at that level, we pull it apart into the graphemes that represent the individual phonemes (Calfee & Henry 1996).

Outer Level: Morphemes

Morphemes are the smallest units of a word that carry meaning. Word roots, suffixes, prefixes, contractions, and compound words are all examples of morphemes. You can remember the term by thinking of the Greek root "morph," which means transforming into something else. For example, you can transform the tense, number, or part of speech of a word by adding suffixes such as _ing,_ ed, _ly, and _est.

Bound morphemes are those that cannot stand alone. Prefixes, suffixes, and contractions are all bound morphemes. Free morphemes are root words, whole words, or compound words before any prefixes and suffixes are added. They have meaning by themselves.

The importance of recognizing morphemes cannot be underestimated. As a skilled reader, you relied on morphemes to help you read words such as mismanagement and misrepresentation. If you did not have that knowledge, you would have had to break the words apart even further. In order to be proficient, students must be able to recognize morphemes in words. They need to be taught how to add prefixes and suffixes from the very beginning of reading instruction. They must know how to combine words to form contractions and compound words. All this information is stored in the Word Form Center as part of the data associated with words to expedite efficient retrieval of words.

CAUTION: Without the ability to hear the sounds in words and to connect them to the graphemes that represent them, learning the morphemes is reduced to rote memory. Students must use their knowledge of phonemes and graphemes to form the morphemes.

Second Level: Syllables

A syllable is a unit of pronunciation that contains one vowel sound and most likely one or more consonants. For example, the word *institution* contains four syllables: in-sti-tu-tion. Unlike other alphabetic languages, English cannot be handled efficiently at the level of syllables. It has over 8,000 syllables compared to less than 1,000 in other alphabetic languages. To put this in perspective, it only takes 4,000 Chinese characters to read their daily newspaper. Those who consider English irregular are trying to teach reading at this level. Many phonics programs formulate rules to manage all the variations in syllables and end up with more than 100 rules. This is the reason many educators just gave up teaching phonics. It was so complicated.

Inner Level: Phonemes

A phoneme is a single sound of speech. This is the level at which English must be understood and taught because this is the way the brain processes words. Beginning readers quickly need access to all of the graphemes that represent the phonemes in order to become proficient readers.

Levels of English: Ways to Look at Words

Think about the ways we look at words. Do we see letters, morphemes, syllables, or graphemes that represent phonemes? In Activity 4.2, look at each word and determine *how many* of each is found in the word. The answers are found at the end of the chapter.

Activity 4.2   How Many of Each?

For each word, indicate how many letters, morphemes, syllables, and phonemes are in the word. What patterns do you see? What does this tell you?

Word	# of Letters	# of Morphemes	# of Syllables	# of Phonemes
1. strung	6	1	1	5
2. unthinkable	11	3	3	9
3. precisely				
4. phantom				
5. constitution				
6. apartment				
7. bedroom				
8. singer				
9. wages				
10. exploded				

Preschool to Kindergarten	Grade 1	Grades 2 to 3	Remedial Readers
Basic alphabet	Review alphabet	Usually know alphabet	Usually know alphabet
Common additional graphemes	All graphemes	Review all graphemes	Learn all graphemes
Some prefixes and suffixes	Common prefixes and suffixes	Most prefixes and suffixes	All prefixes and suffixes

Developing our Understanding of Phonemes

The phoneme and the grapheme are essential components of the reading process. Understanding what they are is just the beginning. How do these fit within a reading program? How do we teach them? You will learn more about phonemic awareness in the next chapter.

Summary

What You Need to Know about Phonemes
• A phoneme is another name for a single sound of speech. It is *not* the sound of a letter.
• It is represented on paper with a letter or group of letters called a grapheme.
• Our language has approximately 44 phonemes.
• Phonemes differ from language to language.
• The same phoneme may be represented in different ways in different languages.
• The same grapheme may represent a different phoneme in different languages.
• There are languages that have no graphemes.
• One or more phonemes together make a spoken word.
• Phonemes are learned during the first year of life.
• When pronouncing phonemes represented by consonants, do not add /uh/ to the sound.
What a Phoneme Is NOT
• It is *not* the sound of a letter.
• It is *not* the smallest meaning-bearing unit in a word.
• It is *not* another word for phonics.
English Has . . .
• 26 letters (5 vowels).
• 44 sounds (phonemes), 15 are vowel sounds.
• Over 76 ways to represent the sounds (graphemes) + 40 addition graphemes for unusual spellings.
• Over 8,000 syllables compared to less than 1000 in other alphabetic languages; Chinese uses 4,000 characters to read a newspaper.

Answers to Activity 4.1

string	/s/-/t/-/r/-/i/-/ng/	5 phonemes
computer	/c/-/o/-/m/-/p/-/u/-/t/-/r/	7 phonemes
nicely	/n/-/i/-/s/-/l/-/ē/	5 phonemes
think	/th/-/i/-/n/-/k/	4 phonemes
stronger	/s/-/t/-/r/-/o/-/n/-/g/-/r/	7 phonemes
nation	/n/-/a/-/sh/-/o/-/n/	5 phonemes
departmental	/d/-/e/-/p/-/ar/-/t/-/m/-/e/-/n/-/t/-/l/	10 phonemes
tricking	/t/-/r/-/i/-/k/-/i/-/ng/	6 phonemes

Answers to Activity 4.2

Word		# of Letters	# of Morphemes	# of Syllables	# of Phonemes
1.	strung	6	1	1	5
2.	unthinkable	11	3	3	9
3.	precisely	9	3	3	8
4.	phantom	7	1	1	6
5.	constitution	12	2	4	11
6.	apartment	9	3	3	8
7.	bedroom	7	2	2	6
8.	singer	6	2	2	4
9.	wages	5	2	2	5
10.	exploded	8	2	3	8

Chapter 5

Refining Our Understanding of Phonemic Awareness

P honemic awareness is the ability to hear and manipulate the individual sounds in *spoken* words. If I have phonemic awareness, I am aware of the sounds in words. I no longer just hear "whole" words as one sound. I realize that some words begin the same way, some words end the same way, and some words have the same middle sounds. If I pay attention, I can hear all of the individual sounds in a spoken word.

> Phonemic awareness is the ability to hear and manipulate the individual sounds in a spoken word.

The Critical Predictor of Reading Success

Phonemic awareness is the pivotal skill in learning to read. The function of phonemic awareness in reading acquisition is one of the most researched areas in reading. Through a multitude of causal and correlational studies as well as brain research, it has been firmly established that phonemic awareness is the critical predictor of reading success (Ball & Blachman 1991; Bradley & Bryant 1983, 1985, 1991; Velluntio & Scanlon 1987).

Individuals with phonemic awareness are *significantly* more successful at both reading and spelling than those who do not have phonemic awareness *no matter what the age*. Good readers have it and poor readers don't. Adults who do not progress beyond a fourth-grade reading level lack phonemic awareness (Read 1985). They do not know how to segment or blend parts of words.

> Phonemic awareness is the critical predictor of reading success. Those who have it learn to read and those who don't are at risk of failure.

What This Means

When teaching reading, the first question we need to ask is, "Does this individual have phonemic awareness?" This is particularly important with all students in grades K to 3 even if they appear to be able to read. This is an absolute must with all poor readers and with those who struggle with school no matter what the age. Remember, the fourth grade crash? Students may be able to memorize enough words to get by, but they are not activating the language centers of the brain. By addressing the lack of phonemic awareness, they can begin to progress in their reading skills.

> Always assess for phonemic awareness.

Phonological Awareness or Phonemic Awareness?

Phonological awareness and phonemic awareness are often used interchangeably, which may generate confusion. So what is the difference? Phonological awareness is the broad term that describes different types of sound processing such as distinguishing rhymes, syllables, and phonemes (Wagner & Torgesen 1987). Students progressively become aware of the phonological structure of spoken language, with awareness moving from larger units to smaller units of sound (i.e., from words to phonemes). The most advanced level of phonological awareness is the ability to manipulate oral language at the phonemic level.

Phonemic awareness is *one type* of phonological awareness and is the only form of phonological awareness that is the critical predictor of reading ability (see Table 5.1). An individual can be aware of words, rhymes, and syllables and yet have difficulty reading. These types of phonological awareness may be beneficial to the learner, but without phonemic awareness, the individual is at risk for reading failure.

Awareness of Rhyming Words

Certain tasks may appear to require awareness at the phonemic level, when in fact they do not. Illiterate poets who have no phonemic awareness can perform rhyming tasks (Goswami & Bryant 1990). We also know that children who categorize by rhyming do no better than those who categorize words by semantic relationship (Bradley & Bryant 1983). On the one hand, research studies report failures to demonstrate a significant relationship between rhyme-based abilities and later reading abilities (Morais 1991; Yeh & Connell 2008). Being aware of rhyming words is not a predictor of reading success.

On the other hand, awareness of rhyme is valuable in the overall growth of literacy skills and should be a part of early reading instruction. Developmentally, rhyming ability

Table 5.1   Three Types of Phonological Awareness

Awareness of Rhyming Words	Awareness of Syllables	Awareness of Phonemes
The ability to hear and identify rhyming words	The ability to hear and break apart syllables in words	Ability to hear and manipulate the individual sounds in speech

may be a precursor to phonemic awareness although in itself it does not require the ability to hear individual sounds in words nor does it guarantee that phonemic awareness will develop (Bradley & Bryant 1985).

Awareness of Syllables

Awareness of syllables is the ability to break words apart into syllables. This poses little difficulty for most children. Even young children can usually separate words into two, three and four syllables by clapping the number of syllables (Liberman, Shankweiler, Fischer & Carter 1974). When the teacher asks, "How many parts do you hear in the word *middle?*" most students can easily divide the word into the two parts (*mid-dle*) by clapping. It does not require the ability to hear the individual sounds in words and it does not guarantee the development of phonemic awareness.

However, being aware of syllables in words is a necessary skill needed for decoding and reading words. In the Word Form area of the brain, words are stored with all of the relevant data, including the chunks called syllables.

What You Need to Know about Phonemic Awareness

Why is it important to clearly understand what phonemic awareness is and is not? We teach many skills that are essential to literacy development such as the names and sounds of letters, identification of objects that begin with those sounds and letters, hearing rhyming words, and clapping syllables. However, students can be able to do all of these and be at risk for reading failure.

Phonemic awareness is the critical predictor of proficient reading and we need to be able to choose activities that ensure this develops. If we mislabel an activity as phonemic awareness, it is possible to think we are teaching phonemic awareness, when in fact, we are not. It is possible to completely miss teaching any phonemic awareness.

Six Levels of Phonemic Awareness

There are six levels of phonemic awareness.

Phonemic awareness is not a "have it" or "don't have it" skill. It has various levels of understanding that develop over time. As a teacher, you need to know and understand each of these levels so you can monitor student growth in phonemic awareness. At all times, you need to know at which level each student is functioning.

Level 1: Hear Beginning Sounds in Words

Students as young as three years old can develop this level. When orally given a word, they can isolate the sound at the beginning of the word and respond with that sound. For example, given the word *stand,* they can tell you the beginning sound is /s/. Students entering kindergarten or first grade may have phonemic awareness at this level.

This is usually the easiest sound for students to hear in a word, but sometimes children who have hearing problems hear the end sound rather than the beginning.

This is often the only sound older struggling readers will hear in a word. For example, in the word computer, the /k/ sound is the only sound they can distinguish.

Level 2: Hear End Sounds in Words

In short words, the end sound is the next easiest sound for students to hear. Once they hear the beginning sound, they need to start listening for the end sound. Students may want to give you the end rhyme rather than the end sound. For example, given the word *rake,* they may want to tell you /_ake/ rather than the end sound. They need to be able to segment the last sound from the word and tell you /k/.

In longer words, such as *tremendous,* struggling readers may find some of the middle sounds easier to hear than the end sound. In identifying the sounds in words, they will know the first two or three sounds and then have no idea what sounds come after that.

Level 3: Hear Middle Vowel in Words

At this level, students hear the beginning, end, and now the middle vowel of words. However, they still may not hear all of the sounds in a word. For example, given the word *stand,* they can tell you the middle sound is /a/, but they do not hear the /t/ in *stand.*

If the middle sound is a short vowel, students may have difficulty distinguishing between the sounds, such the difference between the short vowel sounds in *pen* and *pin.*

Level 4: Hear All the Sounds in Words with Four or More Phonemes

At this level of sophistication, students hear and can segment all of the phonemes in a word. They hear each individual sound in words like *slant* and *perfect.* For example, given the word *stand,* they can tell you each individual sound in the word.

Older struggling reader find longer words such as *fantastic, predicament, penetrate,* and *foolishly* difficult to segment at first. However, with practice, they can hear each individual sound in the word.

Level 5: Manipulate Phonemes (Adding and Deleting Sounds)

At this point, students understand how adding or deleting sounds in a word changes it to a new word. They can both hear and manipulate the sounds in words. This skill usually comes quickly after Level 4. They are able to understand the relationship between *wage* and *stage,* seeing the need to only change the beginning graphemes. They can change *sand* to *stand* to *bland* or change *split* to *spit* or *beg* to *bed.*

Level 6: Blend Phonemes

This skill is used in spelling words. Students hear or think of a word and are able to segment the sounds and then blend them back together to say the word again. They understand how phonemes blend together to form words.

Table 5.2 Levels of Phonemic Awareness

Six Levels of Phonemic Awareness
Level 1: Hear beginning sounds in words.
stand = /s/
Level 2: Hear end sounds in words.
stand = /d/
Level 3: Hear middle vowel in words.
stand = /a/
Level 4: Hear all the sounds in words with four or more phonemes.
stand = /s/–/t/–/a/–/n/–/d/
Level 5 Manipulate phonemes (adding and deleting sounds).
stand → sand → band → bland
Level 6 Blend phonemes.
stand = /s/+ /t/ → /st/+/a / → /sta/+/n/ → /stan/+/d → /stand/

Teaching Phonemic Awareness

Although some children come to school with full phonemic awareness, most do not. It is important to help students, no matter what the age or grade, to reach mastery. In the early elementary years, phonemic awareness instruction can be a part of the classroom routine. For older remedial students instruction will take place in groups.

What Phonemic Awareness Is

- **All types of students benefit from phonemic awareness instruction.**

  It was once a widely held belief that children with dyslexia and other learning disabilities needed different instruction than other children. What we know now is that all children benefit. . . . This instruction is effective for young readers as well as older readers who are still struggling with reading acquisition. It works for advantaged as well as disadvantaged children (Uhry 2005, p. 98).

- **Phonemic awareness is most effective when taught in conjunction with graphemes.** The Speech Sound Center and the Sound Symbol Center of the brain work together to analyze words (see Figure 2.2 on page 14). Both the phoneme and the grapheme that represents it are necessary for efficient analysis and eventual storage of the word in the Word Form Center of the brain. In addition to brain studies, there is a large body of research that demonstrates it is best to teach phonemic awareness *in conjunction with the graphemes* that represent the sounds.

  Activities that require students to hear a spoken word and then identify the graphemes that make those sounds is a powerful way to make the connection between spoken words and written words (Ball et al. 1991; Bradley & Bryant 1985; Shankweiler 1991). For example, the teacher says a word and asks students to find the card from a group of six or eight cards that shows the grapheme representation. The teacher says, "Show me the sound you hear at the beginning of *catch*." Students then respond by choosing the card with the grapheme c. This activity can be done for beginning, end, and middle vowel sounds. Students have to listen to the word and be able to segment the particular sound away from the whole word. More activities will be discussed later.

CAUTION: If you begin with the *spoken* word and have students identify the letters and letter combinations that represent those sounds, you are supporting the learner in acquiring phonemic awareness. However, if you begin with the *written* word and ask students to identify the individual sounds in the word, you are teaching the sounds of letters and are *not* helping the learner gain phonemic awareness. This distinction is important.

- **Phonemic awareness taught in conjunction with graphemes develops understanding of the alphabetic principle.**

The alphabetic principle is the understanding that individual speech sounds are represented on paper by specific graphemes. Individuals who do not have phonemic awareness almost always fail to understand the relationship between spoken words and the words on the paper. As far as they are concerned, the letters on the page are arbitrary and the words must be memorized as shapes.

Brad was a 15-year-old that was reading at a third-grade level. After only four lessons, he jumped out of his seat, "I get it! I get it!" What did he get? He understood that the letters on the page represented a sound of speech. For the first time, he "got" that in the word *stamp,* the speech sound /s/ was represented by the s, the speech sound /t/ was represented by the t, etc. He had no idea that letters had a purpose or any relationship to the spoken word until that moment.

CAUTION: The alphabetic principle is sometimes confused with knowing letters and their sounds rather than knowing the relationship between the phonemes of our language and the graphemes that represent them. Brad knew the alphabet and he knew the basic sounds of the letters of the alphabet, but he did not understand the alphabetic principle.

- **Phonemic awareness needs to be taught using kinesthetic activities.**

There is a misconception that because phonemic awareness is an auditory skill, it needs to be taught using auditory methods. The principle of good instruction that requires using all four sensory modalities must be applied here. The students who need the most help with phonemic awareness need tactile and kinesthetic methods.

Many phonemic awareness activities merely require an oral response from the group. "What sound do you hear at the end of *hat?* The class orally responds as a group, "/t/." Sometimes an action will be included with the response. However, if activities require only an oral group response or an oral response plus an action, kinesthetic learners either don't respond at all or only copy the response of others without understanding. To add the kinesthetic component, you will need to have students show their response with letter tiles, objects, white boards, or flash cards. Using tactile and kinesthetic responses not only provides these students with an effective way to learn, but also gives the teacher an opportunity to know how every single student is doing with this skill. These types of activities will be explained later.

What Phonemic Awareness Is NOT

- **Phonemic awareness is *not* the ability to categorize words by initial sounds.**
  The ability to identify and say the initial sound in a spoken word is sometimes confused with the ability to categorize words by initial consonants (Goswami & Bryant 1990). For example, the teacher asks students to find all the pictures of objects from a set of objects that begin with /d/.

  In the categorization activity, the teacher is the one who segments the initial sound and then asks the student to find objects beginning with the sound. This is in contrast to a phonemic awareness activity where the student must segment the initial sound from the spoken word. Although categorizing initial sounds is an important task in learning to read and should be taught, successful performance does not reflect phonemic awareness.

  An example of the difference can be found in the DIBELS® Initial Sound Fluency assessment for Kindergarten (Good, & Kaminski 2007). In this assessment, students are shown a set of pictures and then asked a set of questions.

This is tomato, cub, plate, doughnut (point to pictures).

1. Which picture begins with /d/?
2. Which picture begins with /t/?
3. Which picture begins with /k/?
4. What sound does "plate" begin with?

Items 1, 2, and 3 are categorization activities because the teacher has isolated the sound for the child. This is an important skill for children to have, but it is not indicative of phonemic awareness because the child did not have to hear or isolate the individual sound in the word. Item 4 requires phonemic awareness at Level 1. Given the word, the child must isolate the initial sound in the spoken word.

- **Phonemic awareness is *not* the ability to break a word apart into syllables or hear and identify rhyming words.**
  Phoneme awareness has to do with the ability to hear *individual* sounds in spoken words. The ability to hear syllables in words is a type of phonological awareness, but it is *not* phonemic awareness. Syllables usually have more than one phoneme and hearing the syllables does not require the ability to hear the individual sounds.

  The same is true for rhyming words. In research, it has been discovered that individuals, children and adults, who can hear and make rhyming words, but who cannot hear the individual sounds in words, are at risk for reading failure. However, it does need to be taught because it develops phonological awareness, which is a step toward phonemic awareness.

- **Phonemic awareness is *not* the ability to represent sounds with the correct letter.**
  Phonemic awareness is the ability to isolate individual sounds in *spoken* words. If the teacher has already isolated the sound, it no longer demands the awareness of phonemes. For example, the teacher says, "Write the sound /d/." This only requires knowledge of the letters and sounds, an important skill to know and be able to do, but it is not phonemic awareness.

When We Usually Gain Phonemic Awareness

Phonemic awareness usually develops in the first five or six years of life. You have heard young children "play" with words in several different ways:

- They will repeat a word over and over and over again, and laugh because it sounds so funny. Usually, the "whole word" doesn't sound funny; it is the combination of sounds that make it funny.
- They will make up a string of nonsense words, usually changing the beginning sound. For example, mat, sat, rat, tat, dat, shat, lat, gat.

Hindrances to Phonemic Awareness Development

Many children come to school with some level of phonemic awareness, but some do not. About 20 to 30 percent of children come to school *without* any phonemic awareness.

Despite these deficiencies, we can teach these students through systematic, direction instruction using kinesthetic methods. Whether hindrances come through environmental factors, physical issues, or learning style, we now have the tools to teach these students phonemic awareness. Later, you will be introduced to ways to assess and teach so all students can learn.

The following is a list of hindrances that might prevent a student from developing this skill.

Ear Infections during the Early Years

Ear infections hinder the child from hearing the sounds, a discriminating task. All types of phonological awareness develop over time, and if the child is not able to hear the sounds well during the preschool years, the development stalls.

Other Hearing Impairments

Hearing problems can cause lack of exposure to sounds in words. However, deaf individuals can and do develop phonemic awareness.

Speech Impairments

Some speech impediments can be due to hearing problems and others can be due to some physiological problem. Either way, the child may not perceive the sounds properly.

Lack of "Live" Language in the Environment

Phonemic awareness develops through conversation and interaction with others, particularly adults. If there is a lack of exposure, then there is a lack of opportunity to develop all types of phonological awareness, including phonemic awareness.

Lack of Knowledge of English and the Language of Origin

If vocabulary is limited in both languages, the child does not have enough exposure to words and does not develop phonemic awareness. However, if a child is immersed in the language or origin, phonemic awareness develops for that language. The bridge between English and the native language is more easily spanned when this occurs. The child only has to learn the phonemes unique to English.

Lack of Literacy in the Home

Phonemic awareness not only comes through conversations, but through interactions with books. Many preschool books contain repetition and rhyme that develop all types of phonological awareness. When selected books are read repeatedly, children begin to notice the individual sounds in the words and begin to develop phonemic awareness.

Tendency toward Right Brain/Kinesthetic Learning

Kinesthetic learners can be immersed in a rich, literate environment and not develop phonemic awareness because they are not attending to words or the sounds in words. They are busy creating, moving, and solving problems.

Choosing Phonemic Awareness Activities

Identifying high-quality phonemic awareness activities requires some discernment. One of the cautions is to make sure it is a true phonemic awareness activity and not some other form of phonological awareness or phonics activity. Since phonemic awareness is a relatively new concept to education, it is not surprising that there are many activities available to teachers that are labeled phonemic awareness, but are not. Many of these activities may be valuable for your students, but do not teach phonemic awareness. The following guidelines will help identify the best activities:

- **Words are given orally.**
  Any activity that provides students with a written word or letter is *not* a phonemic awareness activity. All phonemic awareness activities are oral.

- **Students must segment the sound.**
  Any activity where the teacher segments the sound from a spoken word for the student is *not* a phonemic awareness activity. For example, a categorization activity where the teacher isolates the beginning sound in a word and then asks students to find objects beginning with that sound is *not* a phonemic awareness activity. All phonemic awareness activities require the student to isolate the sound.

- **Students are asked to listen for individual sounds in words, not groups of words.**
  Any activity that asks students to listen for rhymes, syllables, or other groups of sounds is *not* a phonemic awareness activity. A phonemic awareness activity will *always* ask for individual sounds in words.

- **Students respond individually in a tangible way.**
  The strongest phonemic awareness activity will require an individual, tangible response in addition to the oral reply. When the teacher says a word, students will say the isolated sound *and* manipulate cards, objects, or write on the white board to show that sound. This provides immediate feedback to the teacher as to what each individual

student understands and does not understand. Phonemic activities that only require an oral response or a group kinesthetic response will not provide the information you need to know about each student's progress. In many cases, however, these activities can be "tweaked" to include a tangible response.

- **Students use all four sensory modalities.**
  If students are using white boards, tiles, or sound cards, they are using all four modalities. They hear the word and say the sound, see the representation of the sound, and respond using tactile and kinesthetic methods. This addresses the needs of the kinesthetic learners, the very students who need this instruction the most.

- **Students identify the grapheme that is represented by the sound.**
  Phonemic awareness is best taught in conjunction with the grapheme representations. If students respond with sound cards, tiles, or white boards, they are identifying the grapheme that is represented by the sound, strengthening the association between the Speech Sound Center of the brain and the Sound Symbol Center.

Teaching Phonemic Awareness to Older Readers

Readers in grades 2 and up usually know most of the letters and sounds and have memorized many words. For this reason, they will attempt to depend on their letter knowledge rather than listening for individual sounds in words. Phonemic awareness is best developed by having them segment sounds in spoken words using game chips *without reference to the grapheme*. Additional phonemic awareness activities that associate the phoneme with the grapheme can be used for the grapheme representation they do not know such *as au, aw, oi oy, ou, ow,* and *ph.*

Phonemic Awareness Games

The following phonemic awareness games have been carefully selected to develop several levels of phonemic awareness using a kinesthetic approach.

Game One: Sound Card Games

This game is intended to be *fast-paced,* taking only a few minutes to respond to several words. It requires students to hear the individual sounds in words and to connect that sound to the grapheme representation. It focuses on Phonemic Awareness Levels 1, 2, and 3.

The Sound Cards

What is on each card will vary. They are about 2½ × 3½ inches.

Kindergarten: Single letters

m	t	d	s

Grades 1 and up: All the spellings of a single phoneme

oi oy	a au aw augh	ar	ou ow ough

Grades 2 and up: Single spellings of single phoneme

er	ir	wr	ur

Purpose	To connect the sound in a spoken word with the grapheme representation.
Materials	Students are given a set of two to eight cards. They lay these out in a single or double row. These are only the sounds and spellings they have learned. Manage cards by placing the appropriate cards in a plastic bag for easy distribution.
Procedure	The teacher says a word and asks for the beginning, end, or middle sound. The student finds the card that represents that sound, picks it up, and holds under his/her chin, and when the teacher says "Sound," says the sound. As students advance in their skills, the teacher may also ask, "Which spelling?" if the cards have multiple spellings on them.

Sample Sound Card Game

"Show me the sound. . ." (The teacher says the sound and has students find the correct card, show, and say the sound of each of the following sounds.)

/m/. . ./h/. . ./r/. . ./s/. . ./t/. . .

"What sound do you hear at the beginning of. . ." (The teacher says the word and has the students find the correct card, show, and say the sound of each of the following sounds.)

dog. . .hate. . . moon. . . took. . . race. . . mattress

dry. . . try. . . so. . .hook

Choose the cards and the variation of the game that is appropriate for the needs of your students. Older struggling readers benefit from the cards that have the vowels, vowel diphthongs, the consonant digraphs, and the single spellings of each of these, but they usually do not need to use the other types of cards.

Game Two: Chip Game

This game is designed for students in grades 2 and up and is not recommended for younger students because it does not connect the phoneme with the grapheme representation. Colored chips are used to represent the sound in order to force these older students to listen to the sounds in spoken words and not lean on their knowledge of spelling. It focuses on Phonemic Awareness Levels 4 and 6.

Purpose	To hear each individual sound in a spoken word.
	In the process of segmenting, most students also begin blending the sounds.
Materials	Colored counting chips, two colors, ten each; one color to represent consonants and the other color to represent vowels.
Procedure	Say a word and have the students put down a chip for every sound they hear in the word. Once every student has finished lining up the chips for the word, have one student slowly "read" the sounds while all students point to each chip. If a chip is incorrect, have students correct it.
	Then have all students together say each individual sound while pushing each chip up.

Sample Chip Game

"The _____ (name the color) will be the consonants."
"The _____ (name the color) will be the vowels."
"What are vowels? What are consonants?"
If the student does not know, then tell them they can use any color.
Put down a chip for every sound you hear in the word *destination*. You will *not* be spelling the word. Only putting a chip down for every sound.
destination
● ○ ● ● ○ ● ○ ● ○ ● (What the chips will look like)
● ○ ● ● ○ ● ○ ● ○ ●
d e st i n ati o n

Activity 5.1   Are These Phonemic Awareness Activities or Not?

Evaluate these activities.

1. Is it a phonemic awareness activity?
2. If not, what kind of skill is being taught?
3. If so which of the levels of phonemic awareness is being targeted?
4. Which of the four sensory modalities is being used? Remember, visual is reading.

Answers are found at the end of the chapter.

Activity #1	
Teacher:	I have given each of you one Dd and one Mm letter card. I will say a word and then you say it back to me. If the word ends with the /d/ sound, hold up the Dd letter card. If the word ends with the /Mm/ sound, hold up the Mm card. Say the sound when you hold up the card.
Teacher:	ride
Children:	ride
Children:	(Hold up the Dd letter card and say the sound /d/)
Words to use:	

groom	add	greed	odd	seem
grade	need	roam	hide	room
home	food	foam	rude	time

Activity #2

Objective: To be able to match a picture that rhymes with the picture on the activity sheet.

Materials needed: Activity sheet with six pictures with a row of blank boxes below each picture, A set of six pictures to cut out. Students cut out the pictures and paste each one under the picture that rhymes with it.

picture	picture	picture
picture	picture	picture

Activity #3

Objective: Student is able to identify the correct picture that begins or ends with the sound the teacher gives.

Materials Needed: A set of six or eight pictures

Teacher: Which picture shows an object that begins with /t/?

Student: table

Teacher: Which picture shows an object that begins with /l/?

Student: lamp

Activity #4

Materials Needed: Colored counting chips, two colors, ten each

Procedure: Give the chips to the student

Teacher: The ___*red chips*___ (name the color) will be consonants;

   The ___*blue chips*___ (name the color) will be vowels.

   What are vowels?

   If a student has no idea, let him/her use any color he or she wants.

   I will say a word and you will put down a chip for every sound you hear in the word. You will not be spelling the word—only putting a chip for every sound.

   If it is a consonant, put down ___*red*___ (color).

   If it is a vowel, put down ___*blue*___ (color).

Then have the student say each sound as he/she points to the appropriate chip.

If the chips are incorrect, help the student correct it.

mathematics	title	motivation	brother
●○●○●○●○●●	●○●●	●○●○●○●○●	●●○●●

Activity #5

Teacher points to a picture. The students say the word together. Then students clap the number of sounds they hear in the word.

Teacher and students: baby

Students clap twice: ba- by

Teacher and students: fry

Students clap once: fry

Activity #6

Teacher: I will say five sounds. Put them together and tell me the word. /s/–/t/–/a/–/n/–/d/

Students all together say the word: stand

What about Phonics?

We have talked about phonemes, graphemes, and morphemes, but have not been specific about the detailed relationships among them. To teach reading, you must understand how our language is structured and how graphemes and morphemes relate to phonemes. What are the basic rules that govern these relationships? What are the "real rules" of English? What about phonics? We will talk about these in the next chapter.

What to Teach

Preschool	Kindergarten	Grade 1	Grades 2 to 3	Remedial Readers
Basic alphabet	Basic alphabet	Review alphabet	Usually know alphabet	Usually know alphabet
	Common additional graphemes	All graphemes	Review all graphemes	Learn all graphemes
	Some prefixes and suffixes	Common prefixes and suffixes	Most prefixes and suffixes	All prefixes and suffixes
Categorization of sounds	Categorization of sounds	Review categorization of sounds		
Phonemic awareness Levels 1, 2, 3	Phonemic awareness connected to graphemes; all levels	Phonemic awareness connected to graphemes; all levels	Phonemic awareness connected to graphemes; all levels	Phonemic awareness connected to graphemes and not connected to graphemes; all levels
Rhymes	Rhymes	Rhymes	Rhymes	
	Syllables	Syllables	Syllables	Ability to chunk words in decoding big words

Summary

To become a good reader, one must. . .
1. Be able to hear the individual sounds in speech.
2. Know the letters that represent those sounds.
3. Understand how to spell and add prefixes and suffixes.
4. Be able to spell and use Latin and Greek roots.
5. Engage in extensive reading.
What you need to know about phonemic awareness
• There are six levels of phonemic awareness.
• Phonemic awareness needs to be taught.
• All types of students benefit from phonemic awareness instruction.
• Phonemic awareness is most effective when taught in conjunction with letters and letter sound.
• Phonemic awareness taught in conjunction with graphemes develops understanding of the alphabetic principle.
• Phonemic awareness needs to be taught using kinesthetic activities.

What phonemic awareness is NOT
• It is not the ability to break a word apart into syllables.
• It is not the ability to hear and identify rhyming words.
• It is not the ability to represent sounds with the correct letter.

Six levels of phonemic awareness
Level 1: Hear beginning sounds in words.
Level 2: Hear end sounds in words.
Level 3: Hear middle vowel in words.
Level 4: Hear all the sounds in words with four or more phonemes.
Level 5: Manipulate phonemes (adding and deleting sounds).
Level 6: Blend phonemes.

Characteristics of a good phonemic awareness activity
• Words are given orally.
• Students must segment the sound.
• Students are asked to listen for individual sounds in words, not groups of words.
• Students respond individually in a tangible way.
• Students use all four sensory modalities.
• Students identify the grapheme that is represented by the sound.

Answers to Activity 5.1

Activity #1	Activity #4
1. Yes	1. Yes
2. N/A	2. N/A
3. Level 2, end sounds	3. Levels 4 and 6 (Students will usually blend under their breath doing this task.)
4. Visual, auditory, tactile, kinesthetic	4. Auditory, tactile, kinesthetic
Activity #2	**Activity #5**
1. No	1. No
2. Rhyming	2. Segmenting syllables
3. N/A	3. N/A
4. Auditory, tactile, kinesthetic	4. Auditory, kinesthetic
Activity #3	**Activity #6**
1. No	1. Yes
2. Categorization	2. N/A
3. N/A	3. Level 6
4. Auditory, tactile, kinesthetic	4. Auditory

Chapter 6

The "Real Rules" of English

Most early elementary teachers would say they teach phonics. However, if you would go into several classrooms in different schools, you would quickly realize that the term is used broadly to encompass a variety of approaches to teaching reading, approaches that differ considerably. How do we know which method to use? How do we teach phonics? We want to use an approach to teaching phonics that supports the way the brain reads. It must be based on the 44 phonemes and the graphemes that represent them. We call it *phoneme-based phonics*. As you will see, there are characteristics of this approach to phonics that differs from traditional phonics.

Using this method to teaching phonics is one of the secrets to obtaining unprecedented results in reading achievement. Every aspect is tied to the way the brain processes words. In order to teach it, you must understand how it differs from other phonics and begin to learn the way our language is structured. You will be returning again and again to the contents of this chapter as you start to teach reading using phoneme-based phonics. The essence of the language is found here.

Characteristics of Phoneme-based Phonics

- **The phoneme and how it is spelled is introduced first. "How do you spell the sound . . . ?"**
  A speech sound is introduced followed by one or more ways the sound can be spelled. The starting point is the phoneme followed by the grapheme, which reflects the process the brain uses in analyzing words in the Speech Sound Center and the Sound Symbol Center.

  phoneme $\implies$ grapheme

  In contrast, traditional phonics programs start with the introduction of a single letter or combination of letters, which make one or more sounds. The focus is not on the phonemes, but on letters and letter combinations, which may or may not be single phonemes.

letters ⟹ sounds they make

The difference between phoneme-based phonics and other types of phonics is significant. One reflects the process the brain uses in reading words and the other does not. This is one of the reasons some children cannot learn to read well even if they are taught traditional phonics.

- **All of the spellings of the individual phonemes are taught.**
All of the spellings of the 44 phonemes are taught to beginning readers, whether first grade children or remedial readers. All beginning readers must quickly have access to all the graphemes.

   In contrast, traditional phonics programs usually do not teach all of the grapheme representations. This leaves holes in student knowledge.

- **Only the spellings of the phonemes are taught.**
Students learn only the spellings of the individual phonemes. When they encounter *st,* they see two graphemes, which represent two phonemes rather than a blend. This simplifies the learning process.

   Most traditional phonics programs teach both the spelling of individual phonemes *and* consonant blends but do not help students distinguish between the two. St, str, gr, dr, nk are taught in the same way as m, th, and ph. This can be confusing to children, especially those who are at risk. However, introducing the concept of consonant blends become unnecessary if a student is at a Level 4 in phonemic awareness and can hear all of the sounds of words.

   In addition to the consonant blends, traditional phonics often teaches "r-controlled" vowels. *Er, ir, ur, or*, and *ar* are introduced without reference to the phonemes represented. However, the spellings *er, ir,* and *ur* are the graphemes for /r/, *ar* is the grapheme for /ar/ and *or* has two graphemes that represent two phonemes /o/ and /r/.

- **A handful of principles govern the language: the "Real Rules" of English.**
Basic structural principles govern the behavior of graphemes. Expressed as rules in the "Real Rules" of English, these regulate our language, affecting thousands of words. These rules are particularly appealing to kinesthetic learners who like to see the *big picture.* You will be learning these principles in this chapter.

   In contrast, the rules of traditional phonics attempt to describe the relationships of one *letter* and its place in a syllable. Notice in these examples, there is no reference to the graphemes, but everything is described in terms of vowels and consonants. "If a vowel comes between two consonants, the vowel sound is short." What about *wild, told, cold?* Or, "When words of one syllable end in one consonant and have only one vowel before the last consonant, double the last consonant before adding an ending that begins with a vowel." Did you understand that? It is confusing to students, too. In addition to being confusing, there are many exceptions as well as limitations to these rules.

- **The language is regular with few exceptions when taught at the level of phonemes.**
Using a phoneme-based phonics, you will find that only about 15 words of the 300 words on the Dolch or Frye Sight Word Lists are truly sight words. The rest are structurally predictable when the rules that govern phonemes are understood.

In contrast, since traditional phonics describes the language with letters and syllables rather than phonemes and graphemes, there are many exceptions to the rules.

- **Morphemes are introduced almost immediately.**

Students learn to add prefixes and suffixes to words at the outset, even if they are in kindergarten and first grade. Once they can write and read the word *hat,* they are taught how to add the suffix *_s.* Once they can write and read the word *jump,* they are taught how to add the suffixes, *_s, _ed,* and *_ing.* Table 6.3 will give suggested grades to introduce each prefix and suffix.

In contrast, most traditional phonics programs introduce morphemes in separate lessons after children can read many words. For example, a separate lesson on the prefix *re* or a *lesson* on the suffix *_ly* will be taught, usually late in the school year.

- **Graphemes give only the approximations of sounds.**

Letters and letter combinations only give an approximation of sounds. This is true of all phonics. A linguist understands the complexity of our language and is able to differentiate between the /d/ at the end of a word and the /d/ at the beginning of a word. In teaching reading, however, we do not need to be that specific. Our brains are able to associate the sounds of the language with the graphemes that represent them.

Almost all correspondences are direct such as m representing /m/ and th representing /th/. However, even when the correspondence is more remote, as students become more confident in their ability to translate the sounds into words they know, they are able to read words that are in their vocabulary. For example, *said* is an irregular word, but even young students who say *sade* can determine from the context that it is *said* and feel confident to make the adjustment. They approach words like *there, where,* and other irregular words in the same manner. This gives them power to decode and read almost all words without having to memorize a list of "sight" words.

The "Real Rules" of English

The "Real Rules" of English unlock the mystery of reading to students who must see the big picture and who need to know why. Understanding these principles will enable you to teach the language in a way that brings exceptional results. These principles are taught over a period of several months so students are introduced to only one rule at a time and engage in accumulative practice over all they have learned. How to teach phonics will be introduced in Chapter 11.

The following is the content knowledge you will need to teach phonics. You, as a teacher, will need to be able to:

- Hear the phonemes in a spoken word.
- Write the grapheme representations of those phonemes.
- Understand the fundamental principles that govern the language.

If you are a proficient reader, you already have this knowledge because this is the way your brain has stored information. When teachers are asked to write all the graphemes of the language, they can do it. When teachers are asked to read nonsense words such as lancingful, or defidge, they can do it because they know the phonemes, the graphemes, and the fundamental rules of the language. However, when it comes to teaching all of this, this knowledge must be articulated.

Table 6.1 outlines the fundamental rules that govern how graphemes are used in our language and will be your invaluable guide to teaching reading. The English language is so predictable using these rules that any exception will be a surprise. However, words borrowed from other languages such as Latin, Greek, and French are sometimes the exceptions, as well as proper names. I tell students that names often do not follow the rules.

Table 6.1   The Real Rules of English

The markers: e, i, y	The letters e, i, and are markers in our language that make
	• a vowel say its own name (e.g., *side, shady, making*).
	• the c say /s/, (e.g., *ice, icy, icing*). <u>The marker must immediately follow the letter.</u>
	• the g say /j/. (e.g., *age, gym, gem, giant*). <u>The marker must immediately follow the letter.</u>
	• You only need one marker, so when adding an ending (suffix), throw the extra marker one away. (e.g., shade + ing = shading)
	• You can stop a marker by doubling the consonant or adding another consonant. (e.g., *hopping, picnicking, little, badge*)
	• An l is so skinny that it does not stop the marker from working (e.g., *table, idle*). You need another consonant.
	• A *v* can stop a marker all by itself (e.g.,, *have, live*).
The letter y	• y says /i/ at the end of one syllable words such as in *my, fly*.
	• y says /ee/ at the end of multisyllable words such as *baby, extraordinary*.
	• y is the most common way to spell the sound /ee/ at the end of a word.
	• Change these ys to i before adding all endings except _ing.
	• The suffix _ly uses the y that says /ee/.
Rule of v	• v never comes at the end of an English word. There is usually an e after it.
	• v is never doubled.
	• v can stop a marker even though it is never doubled.
The sound /uh/	• The short u says /uh/, and so does e as in th<u>e</u>, o as in <u>o</u>ther, and a as in <u>a</u>way.
	• The unclear sound of any vowel is an unstressed syllable resembles /uh/, as in dent<u>i</u>st.
Middle and end spellings of vowels	• All vowels, except short vowels, have middle and end spellings that are usually only used in those positions.
ou/ow au/aw	• Use ou in the middle of a word and ow at the end, except if the word *ends* in l or n such as in *owl, scowl, frown, town*.
	• Use au in the middle of a word and aw at the end. Aw is also a middle spelling found in words including those that end in l or n such as in *crawl, sprawl, dawn, fawn*.
The spellings that come only after a short vowel	• _tch, _dge, _x, and _ck come only after a short vowel.
	• Sometimes ch is used after a short vowel instead of tch as in *such, much, rich, which, attach, and sandwich*. The less common exceptions where ch is used after a short vowel instead of tch are *bachelor, ostrich*. By the time young or remedial readers have to read and spell these words, they will not be a problem.
/l/ at the end	• The most common way to spell the sound /l/ at the end of a word is _le.
	• The way to spell the suffix /l/ is ___al (departmental)

Table 6.1 continued

/k/	• c is used at the beginning of a word, k at the end of a word, ck after a short vowel. • k is used at the beginning if followed by a marker e, i, or y.
/sh/	• The most common spelling of /sh/ is ti.
Compound words	• Compound words are two words put together without any changes to either word.
Adding suffixes	• Usually, just add the suffix to the base word *without doing anything else* except throw away the extra marker. • Change the y to an i before adding the suffix. • When adding a *suffix* that begins with a or o, *drop the e.* However, sometimes the marker is necessary, such as in knowledgeable. You must keep the e so the g will say /j/.
Adding prefixes	• Almost all prefixes are added directly to the word. • The exceptions are some Latin prefixes such as in_ and ad_. The second letter is often changed to match the beginning letter of the word. For example, in + mature = immature, ad + prove = approve
_able or _ible	• Usually use _able. If the word ends in e, throw it away before adding _able unless the e is necessary as a marker • Use _ible after /s/ or/j/ (e.g., *responsible*).
_ant/_ance _ent/_ence	• Usually use _ant instead of _ent. • Use _ent after the sounds /s/, /d/, and /j/ (e.g., *descent, evident, regent*). • Change ant to ance or ent to ence by "throwing away the t and adding ce."

Voiced and unvoiced pairs	**Unvoiced** **Voiced**
	  p b
	  s z
	  f (wife) v (wives)
	  th (thin) th (these)
	  t d
	  ch j
	  k g
	  sh zh (vision)
	  wh w

_ed	• When _ed is added to the end of a word, it can say /t/, /d/, or /ud/.

Reprinted from Sporleder, "Word Workshop C," 2007.

The Remarkable Markers: e, i, y

• **The letters e, i, and y are markers in our language that perform three functions.** They make a vowel say its name, the c say /s/, and the g say /j/. Markers affect thousands and thousands of words. The concept is fairly simple and straightforward and will give students a broad understanding of words. This is the very first principle taught to students in grades 2 and up. By the third lesson, they should be able to read about 8,000 words they could not read before.

- **Markers make the c say /s/.**
  A marker right after the letter c will make it say /s/ as in *bicycle, receive,* and *nice.* The one exception is *Celtic* but it can also be pronounced with the c saying /s/.

- **Markers make the g say /j/.**
  A marker right after the letter g will usually make the g say /j/ as in *giant, garage, age,* and *gym.* A few common words are the exception: give, gift, and get.

- **Markers make vowels long.**
  The vowel has a long sound when you have a <u>vowel</u>–<u>consonant</u>–<u>marker</u> arrangement. It does not matter if it is at the end of a word such as in ***li<u>ke</u>*** and *explo<u>ding</u>,* or if it is in the middle of a word such as in *repr<u>es</u>ent* and *bi<u>cyc</u>le.* It is everywhere in our language. There are exceptions, but they are few (Venezky 1970).

  One "exception" is the <u>vowel</u> – <u>consonant</u> – <u>l</u> – <u>marker</u>, as in *title.* The letter l is so skinny it does not stop the marker from working, so in the words such as *table, staple,* and *title,* the marker is still making the vowel long.

- **Throw away the extra marker.**
  You need only one marker in a word, so when adding suffixes that have markers, we throw away the extra marker as in *make* and *making* or *shade* and *shady.*

- **Stopping the marker—We don't want all long vowel sounds!**
  We do not always want a long vowel sound, so we can stop the marker from working by doubling the consonant or making sure there are two consonants between the vowel and the marker. Examples of doubling the consonant are found in *ho<u>pp</u>ing* and *li<u>ttl</u>e.* We write *commi<u>tt</u>ed* and double the *t* to stop the marker *e* from working. However, when we write *commi<u>tm</u>ent,* the *t* and *m* are sufficient to stop the marker from working. Some examples of stopping the marker are found in these words: *hopping, happy, supper,* and *hammer.* Notice they all have the double consonant between the vowel and the marker.

  The graphemes g and c present a potential problem because they can be affected by markers. If I want to spell the word /b/ - /a/ -/j/, (badge), I run into difficulty. I need the marker e to make the g say /j/, but I want the vowel short so I must stop the marker from working. Usually I would double the g and write bagge (bag – gee). But I don't have the word I want because the first *g* says /g/ and the marker is making that last *g* say /j/. The spelling *dge* is the solution for the problem and I write the word *badge.* The function of the *d* in the word is to stop the marker.

  We face the same problem when adding _ing or _ed to words ending in the letter c, such as *picnic* and *traffic.* If I try to double the consonant c, I have *picniccing (picinic –king).* By using the ck, I stop the marker from working and write *picnicking.* The dge and ck come only after short vowels, and the purpose of the spelling is to stop the marker from working, so I can write words *tricking* and *budges.*

Kinesthetic Learners and Markers

Kinesthetic learners love the concept of the markers because it gives them the "big picture" and makes sense to them. Traditional phonics uses the "magic e" or the "silent e" to touch on this concept, but it is misleading. The letter e is not the only letter that makes the vowel long; letters i and y do the same thing. In addition, the letter e is not always silent and it can come in the middle of a word, not just at the end. Rather than address only one marker and one task of the marker, it is best to give the full story of all three tasks of all three markers.

The Letter y

- **y says /i/ at the end of one syllable words and /ee/ at the end of multisyllable words.**
  Examples of the long i sound at the end of words are *my, try,* and *fly.* Examples of the long e sound at the end of words are *baby, happy,* and *extraordinary.* Although we do not have many one-syllable words that end in the grapheme *y,* there are some two-syllable words that appear to have the y that says /i/: *reply, supply, apply.* However, these words come from a one-syllable Latin root *ply,* with Latin prefixes added.

- **y is the most common way to spell the sound /ee/ at the end of a word.**
  This is an important concept to know. Beginner readers will try to use the letter e at the end of a word to say /ee/, but if they know it is usually y, they get in the habit of writing it correctly. The common suffix _ly uses the y that says /ee/.

- **Change y to i before adding all endings except _ing.**
  Changing the y to i before adding all endings except _ing is applied to both one syllable and multisyllable words. Examples are *happiness, merriment, emergencies,* and *hurriedly.*

  This simple rule of English is misunderstood by individuals just learning to read. Words such as try, tried, tries; cry, cries, cried, and dry, dried, dries are often difficult for them to spell because they do not understand that the y is changed to i before adding suffixes.

  Some may ask what happens if a word ends in ay or oy or ey? These are graphemes for other sounds. As students approach the language thinking of representations of phonemes, they do not "see" the y in these graphemes but look at them as a whole just as you see th as /th/ or sh as /sh/. We are only concerned with the grapheme y that says /e/ or /i/.

The Rule of v

The letter v is never doubled so the vowel can be either long or short. It can stop a marker all by itself. One exception is the word *savvy,* which is a slang word derived from French. The letter v also never comes at the end of an English word. If the phoneme /v/ comes at the end of a word, there is usually followed by its friend the e as in *leave* or *sieve.*

The Sound /uh/

The phoneme /uh/ can be represented by any vowel including y in an unstressed syllable. The following chart shows examples of the ways the sound /uh/ is used.

u	a	e	o	Unstressed Syllable
undo	away	the	other	dentist
unfold	along	oven	wonder	exhibition
hug	was	token	brother	analyst
run	a	open	of	
lung				
under				

Middle and End Spellings of Vowels

It is almost frightening to think that we have over 15 vowel sounds with 54 ways to spell those sounds. However, the pattern is so predictable that first-grade students understand most of them before they are even introduced. Some spellings come only at the beginning and middle of words; some spellings only come at the end. There is also a pattern in the spellings from one vowel sound to another. Because you know how to read, you know what those patterns are even though you may have never articulated them.

Although short vowel spellings are the easiest to spell, they are the most difficult to hear and distinguish from one another. Students often have difficulty differentiating between the short /e/ and the short /i/ sound. By contrast, long vowels sounds are easy to hear, but are difficult to spell because there are so many options.

All vowels, except short vowels, have beginning, middle, and end spellings that are usually only used in those positions. When you look at the common end spellings of all the vowels, they have similarities. Notice they all have y or a w in their spellings. All of the long vowels have the vowel–consonant–marker that is represented by a _e.

Common End Spellings

The Sound	a	e	i	o	u	oo	au	oi	ou
The Spelling	ay	y	y	ow	ew	ew	aw	oy	ow

How do we usually spell the sound /ee/ at the end of a word? y

Common/Beginning Middle Spellings

The Sound	a	e	i	o	u	oo	au	oi	ou
The Spellings	a_e	e_e	i_e	o_e	u_e	u_e	au	oi	ou
	ai	ea	igh	oa		ui			

ou/ow and au/aw

The diphthongs *au* and *ou* also have an additional rule. Use *au* and *ou* in the middle of a word and *aw* and ow at the end, except if the word *ends* in *l* or *n* such as in *owl, scowl, frown, town, crawl, sprawl, dawn,* and *fawn.*

Special Consonants

The Spellings That Come Only after a Short Vowel

tch, _dge, _x, and *_ck* are spellings that come only after a short vowel. They never come after a long vowel. Sometimes *ch* is used after a short vowel instead of *tch* as in *such, much, rich, which, attach,* and *sandwich.* The less common exceptions are *bachelor, ostrich.* By the time young or remedial readers have to read and spell these words, they will not be a problem. As explained above, the *_dge* and *_ck* are necessary to stop the markers from working.

The Spelling of /l/ at the End of a Word

Although we usually think of l as the most common way to spell /l/, it is not. We use the grapheme _l at the end of one-syllable words, *_le* at the end of multisyllable words, and _al when it is added as a suffix as in *departmental*. How do we usually spell /l/ at the end of a word? *_le*

Spellings of /k/

There are three common spellings of /k/ with predictable positions in words:

- c is usually used at the beginning of a word.
- k is usually used at the end of a word. Although we usually spell /k/ with a c at the beginning of words, if the /k/ is followed by a marker, we are forced to use a k, as in the words kitchen, kilt, and kind. If we used the grapheme c, we have a problem because the marker would cause us to pronounce the words sitchen, silt, and sind.
- ck after a short vowel. The exception is yak.

ch is a spelling that comes from Greek and is used in only a few words such as school, character, scholar.

Spellings of /sh/

We have spellings of /sh/ from Anglo-Saxon, from French, from Latin, and from Greek. sh is Anglo-Saxon, ti, and si as in nation and mission are Latin, ci as in musician is Greek, and ch as in chauffeur is French. The most common way to spell /sh/ in our language is _ti as in *nation, station,* and *institution.*

Making Compound Words

Compound words are two words put together without any changes to either word.

Adding Suffixes and Prefixes

Suffixes

Usually, just add the suffix to the word without doing anything else except throw away the extra marker. Once students understand how to add a suffix, they become confident in changing *hope* to *hopeful* to *hopefully* by tacking on the suffixes. It is really quite easy.

If a word ends in the grapheme y, then change the y to an i before adding the suffix.

When adding a suffix that begin with a or o, such as _able and _ous, also throw away the marker even though you don't have two markers. However, sometimes the marker is necessary, such as in *knowledgeable*. You must keep the e so the g will say /j/.

Prefixes

Almost all prefixes are added directly to the word. The exceptions are some Latin prefixes such as in_ and ad_. The second letter is often changed to match the beginning letter of the word. For example, *in + mature = immature, ad + prove = approve.*

Do We Use _able or _ible?

Usually use _able. This is a suffix that we add to words. If the word ends in e, usually throw it away before adding _able unless the e is necessary as a marker such as in *knowledgeable* or *noticeable.* The Latin _ible is part of the word such as *admissible* and usually not added to a root word. You will need to use the dictionary to check for sure.

Do We Use _ant or /_ent?

Usually use _ant. Usually use _ent after the sounds /s/ and /j/ because these words will need the marker e to make the c say /s/ and the g say /j/ such as *adjacent* and *urgent.* You will need to use the dictionary to check for sure. These words can be turned to nouns by adding ce or cy. Change ant to ance or ent to ence by "throwing away the t and adding ce or cy." Examples are *assistant* to *assistance* and *intelligent* to *intelligence.*

Voiced and Unvoiced Pairs

Unvoiced	Voiced
p	b
s	z
f (wife)	v (wives)
th (thin)	th (these)
t	d
ch	j
k	g
sh	zh (vision)
wh	w

What Are Voiced and Unvoiced Pairs?

These consonant pairs are formed in the same way with the mouth, but a "voiced" grapheme uses the voice box and the other "unvoiced" grapheme is whispered without the voice. Students who do not have phonemic awareness or are just learning English often confuse the voice and the unvoiced sounds. They may pronounce one sound instead of the sound intended, or they may choose the grapheme that represents the opposite sound. When you see a p written instead of a b, an f instead of a v or a j instead of a ch, or vice versa, you know it is a problem with hearing the sound and not a problem of letter recognition. Take time to talk about how the sounds are formed in the mouth and throat and help students distinguish how the two sounds are produced.

The Difficulty with Voiced and Unvoiced Pairs

It is interesting that in our language we often interchange the voice and unvoiced pairs even in the grapheme representations. Here are some examples:

- The letter s that comes at the end of words can be pronounced /s/ or /z/ such as in *was, marches, hats.* When we pronounce it with the /z/, we are using the voiced pair of s. (Note: The word *was* follows all the rules. The *a* says /uh/ just as it does in many other words such as *away* and *adjust* and the *s* says /z/ just as it does in many words that end with the letter *s.*)
- The grapheme *f* is changed to a *v* when forming the plural in several words, such as *wife/wives, leaf/leaves, knife/knives.* The word *of* is not as irregular as it would first

appear. The *o* says /uh/ just as it does in many other words such *as mother, brother, other* and we use the voiced sound /v/ rather than the /f/. Try saying the word *of* using the /f/ sound at the end. It is almost impossible.

- We interchanged /d/ and /t/ in many words. For example, it is often difficult to differentiate those sounds in *letter, ladder, little*. This interchange also explains why the suffix _ed can say /d/, /t/, or /uhd/. When that suffix is introduced, I say, "When we add the ending _ed to a word, it can say /d/, /t/, or /uhd/."

- The phoneme /wh/ is disappearing from our language and the voiced pair /w/ is used instead. When saying a word like *whale* or *when,* do you feel a puff of air when you hold your hand in front of your mouth? Some individuals do and some don't. The younger you are, the more likely you don't. In time, the *wh* might be just another grapheme to represent the phoneme /w/.

Historical Layers of English

Understanding the historical influencers on written English will help demystify the reasons for the diversity of graphemes and morphemes. The basic structure of our language is Anglo-Saxon, yet 80 percent of the words in the English dictionary have Greek or Latin roots or affixes. Each of these languages has unique graphemes, prefixes and suffixes, and different ways to combine words. Our basic words come from Anglo-Saxon while our complex words come from French, Latin, and Greek. To complicate our language even more, we attach Latin affixes to Anglo-Saxon words and Anglo-Saxon affixes to Latin and Greek words.

Anglo-Saxon

When the Anglo-Saxons encountered the Romans, they adopted their alphabet despite the fact the Romans had only 5 vowel sounds while they had 20. The mismatch between the number of phonemes of our language and the Roman alphabet remains to this day, although we have only 15 or 16 vowel sounds now instead of 20.

Anglo-Saxon is the foundation of our language. Both the common, everyday words and the grammatical structure are Anglo-Saxon:

> English remains preeminently Anglo-Saxon at its core: . . . no matter whether a man is American, Britain, Canadian, Australian, New Zealander, or South African, he still loves his mother, father, brother, sister, wife, son, and daughter, lifts his hand to his head, his cup to his mouth, his eye to heaven and his heart to God, hates his foes, likes his friends, kisses his kin and buries his dead; draws his breath, eats his bread, drinks his water, stands his watch, wipes his sweat, feels his sorrow, weeps his tears and sheds his blood, and all these he thinks about and calls both good and bad" (Nist 1966, p. 9, cited in Henry 2005).

Compound words, contractions, and common prefixes and suffixes are all contributions of the Anglo-Saxon. Some of the graphemes include *ough, eigh, igh, kn, wr, gn, er, ir, ur, sh* and the spelling of /l/ spelled _le at the end of two syllable words such as in *little*.

Latin (and French)

The Romance languages contribute longer words and a new set of prefixes, including inter_, intra_, pro_, ad_, in_, and co_. Suffixes include _ic, _al, _ous, _age, _able, and _tion. However, in Latin, the way affixes are added to roots differs from Anglo-Saxon. The root may not be a standalone word. For example, *dict* is a root in Latin that does not stand by itself. However, Latin adds prefixes and suffixes to form words such as *diction, contradiction,* and *dictionary.*

In teaching these affixes, we use the Anglo-Saxon method. If the root is a word by itself, we refer to these as affixes. If the root is not a word by itself, then we spell the word, listening for the phonemes and representing them with the appropriate grapheme without reference to the affix. For example, we refer to words like *nation* and *plantation* as whole words and not as roots with affixes. All of the rules are explained in the "Real Rules" of English.

Besides words, Latin also contributes graphemes:

- /l/ spelled *al* when added to words, such as in *departmental, temperamental*
- /r/ spelled *or* when added as a suffix, such as in *actor* and *doctor*
- /sh/ spelled *ti,* the most common way to spell /sh/ in our language

French also contributes graphemes:

- /sh/ spelled ch, as in *chauffeur* and *Charlemagne*
- /e/ spelled i, as in *machine*

Greek

The Greeks have yet another way to form words. They take roots and place them together to form words. For example, *photo,* which means *light,* and *graph,* which means *write,* are put together to make the word *photograph,* which literally means to write with light. We have a myriad of scientific and medical terms in our language that are formed from these Greek roots.

Greek also contributes graphemes:

- /f/ spelled ph, as in *phenomenon* and *elephant*
- /k/ spelled ch, as in *school* and *character*
- short /i/ spelled y, as in *symphony, sympathy*
- /sh/ spelled ci, as in *musician* and *physician*
- /s/ spelled ps, as in *psychology*
- /n/ spelled pn, as in *pneumonia*
- /m/ spelled mn, as in *mnemonic*
- /r/ spelled rh, as in *rhombus* and *rhythm*
- unstable diagraphs where each vowel is a phoneme, such as found in cre-ate, vi-olate

Despite the different language systems embedded in English, it is remarkably regular with few exceptions when taught at the level of phonemes with the graphemes that represent them.

Table 6.2 General Sequence of Introduction of Phonemes with Grapheme Representations

Timeline for Introduction of Graphemes			
Preschool	**Kindergarten**	**Grade 1**	**Grade 2 and Up**
After learning alphabet letters and sounds and after levels 1, 2, and 3 phonemic awareness, introduce phonemes with grapheme representations: • Single letter consonants • Short vowel sounds	After learning alphabet and after levels 1, 2, and 3 phonemic awareness, introduce phonemes with grapheme representations: • Single letter consonants • Short vowel sounds • Consonant digraphs • Vowel digraphs	After two week review of alphabet, introduce phonemes with grapheme representations: • Single letter consonants • Short vowel sounds • Easy consonant digraphs • Markers e, i, y • Stopping markers • ge, gi, gy, dge • vowel digraphs • y to i • Vowel diphthongs • Consonant digraphs	Introduction of phoneme with grapheme representations: • Markers e, i, y - vowels • ce, ci, cy • Stopping markers • ge, gi, gy, dge • y to i • ar/ ti • Vowel diphthongs • Consonant digraphs • Vowel digraphs • Latin affixes • Greek roots

Table 6.3 When to Teach Prefixes and Suffixes

Suggested Grades to Introduce Prefixes and Suffixes					
Grade Level	**Grade K to 1**	**Grade 1 to 2**	**Grade 2**	**Grade 3**	**Grade 4 to 6**
Suffixes	_s _es _ed _er _ing _y _ly	_en _et _est f to v _ful _less _ist _or	_able _ness _ment _ous _age	_ship _hood _ic _ist	_ance/ence _ee _eer _al
Prefixes	a_ un_	re_ be_	dis_ mis_	sub_ pre_ non_ anti_ over_ mid_	anti_ under_ trans_ inter_ intra_ semi_ counter_ super_ fore_ in_ ab_ co-

What about Word Families?

Teaching onset and rime, or what we also call word families, is an approach to teaching reading that is used extensively. The teacher introduces a rime such as _ate and then asks students to identify onsets, or beginning sounds to form a word.

Some examples are:

The -ate family	The –ike family	The -oke family	The -eet family
m - ate	l - ike	br- oke	b - eet
r - ate	b - ike	j - oke	f - eet
f - ate	sp- ike	sp - oke	str - eet
gr - ate	tri - ike	p - oke	m - eet

Although onset and rime require some level of phonological awareness, the concept considers neither the syllable nor the phoneme. It does not require phonemic awareness and does not construct words in the same way the brain is wired. In the research conducted in the nine first-grade classrooms that was reported in Chapter 1 (see Figure 1.3 on page 8), group A used word families to teach reading. However, teaching phoneme-based phonics was significantly more effective than both the group using word families and the group using traditional phonics.

Building a Balanced Approach to Reading

Starting with a research base, we can begin building a balanced approach to reading. We want to include those things that research has told us as well as bring in pieces from our current curriculum that supports this research. This is what we have so far.

Although we have identified some of the critical content that goes into a research-based reading program, we have not yet identified a framework for teaching reading. What are all the steps in learning to read? In what sequence should they be taught? How do they build on one another?

Something to Think About

There are considerable differences in the efficiency when teaching students to read using word families versus teaching phoneme-based phonics.

Word Families	Phoneme-based Phonics
• Does not identify phonemes or graphemes.	• Identifies the phoneme and the grapheme that represents it.
• 2,000 word families are needed to read everyday words.	• 76 graphemes give an individual access to thousands of words in our language.
• 67 of the most popular word families give an individual access to about 300 words.	• Five vowels and a handful of consonants along with the marker rule give an individual access to nearly 8,000 words.
• Does not teach multisyllable words.	• Teaches how to decode words of all lengths.

Figure 6.1   Building a Balanced Approach to Reading

Building a Balanced Approach	
Research-based Paradigm	Select Current Strategies
Teach and assess phonemic awareness.	Teach alphabet and sounds as precursor for all graphemes.
Teach 44 phonemes and graphemes that represent them.	Teach rhyming as a precursor to phonemic awareness.
Teach prefixes and suffixes immediately.	Teach categorization of initial sounds as a precursor to phonemic awareness.
Use kinesthetic methods.	Teach syllables to aid in decoding and reading.
Teach the "Real Rules" of English.	

Meet My Students

Two First-Grade Classrooms

In 2007 to 2008, two first grade classrooms adopted the research-based model, teaching phonemic awareness and a phoneme-based phonics. It was a failing Title 1 school with 77 percent of the students on free or reduced lunch with 55 percent white and 45 percent black, Hispanic, and multiracial. It was common for nearly all students to leave the classroom reading below grade level.

Students in first grade were placed in classrooms according to their ability. Classroom A received the lowest achieving students and Classroom B received the higher students. What were the results? The school population is transient with some students attending only a few weeks so only students who remained in the class for the full year are shown. The following charts show the beginning and final reading scores. All students scored significantly above the expected level.

Classroom A: The Low Ability Group

Because of their low abilities, the goal for Classroom A students was to achieve *three-fourths* grade level by the end of first grade. They did not expect students to reach grade level because they began the school year reading or just at beginning kindergarten level.

Only 8 out of 20 students attended the full year; 2 of these spoke little or no English (ELL). See Figure 6.2.

All achieved higher than was expected.

Three students achieved grade level or near grade level.

Five students achieved above grade level.

Figure 6.2 Low Ability Group

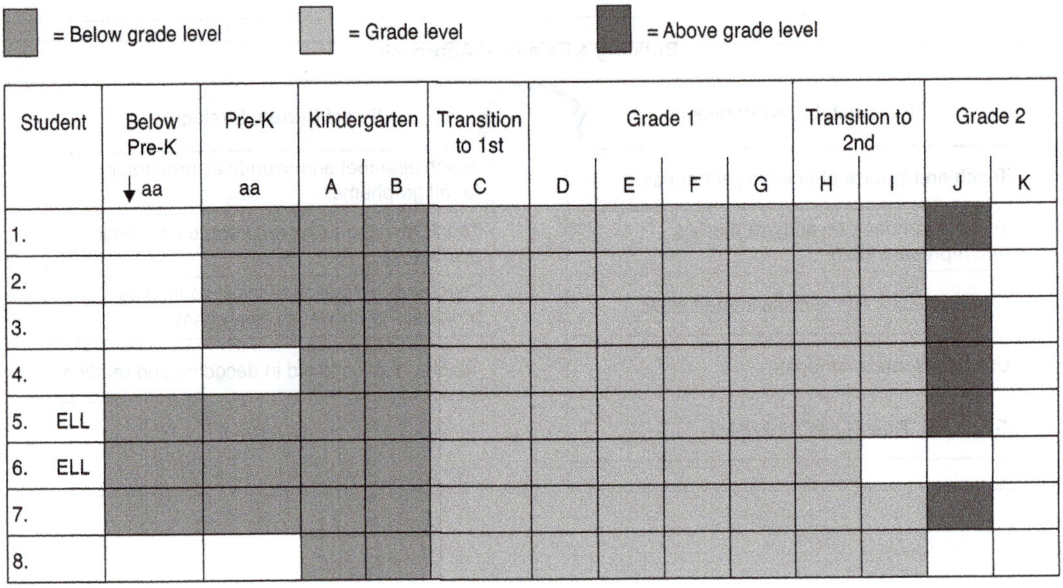

| ▓ = Below grade level | ░ = Grade level | ▓ = Above grade level |

Student	Below Pre-K ↓aa	Pre-K aa	Kindergarten		Transition to 1st	Grade 1				Transition to 2nd		Grade 2	
			A	B	C	D	E	F	G	H	I	J	K
1.													
2.													
3.													
4.													
5. ELL													
6. ELL													
7.													
8.													

Classroom B: The High Ability Group

Only 17 out of 25 students attended the full year. 16 of 17 students left reading at or above grade level. See Figure 6.3.

  1 student achieved beginning grade level

  3 students achieved grade level

  13 students achieved *above* grade level by 1, 2, and 3 grade levels

Figure 6.3 High Ability Group

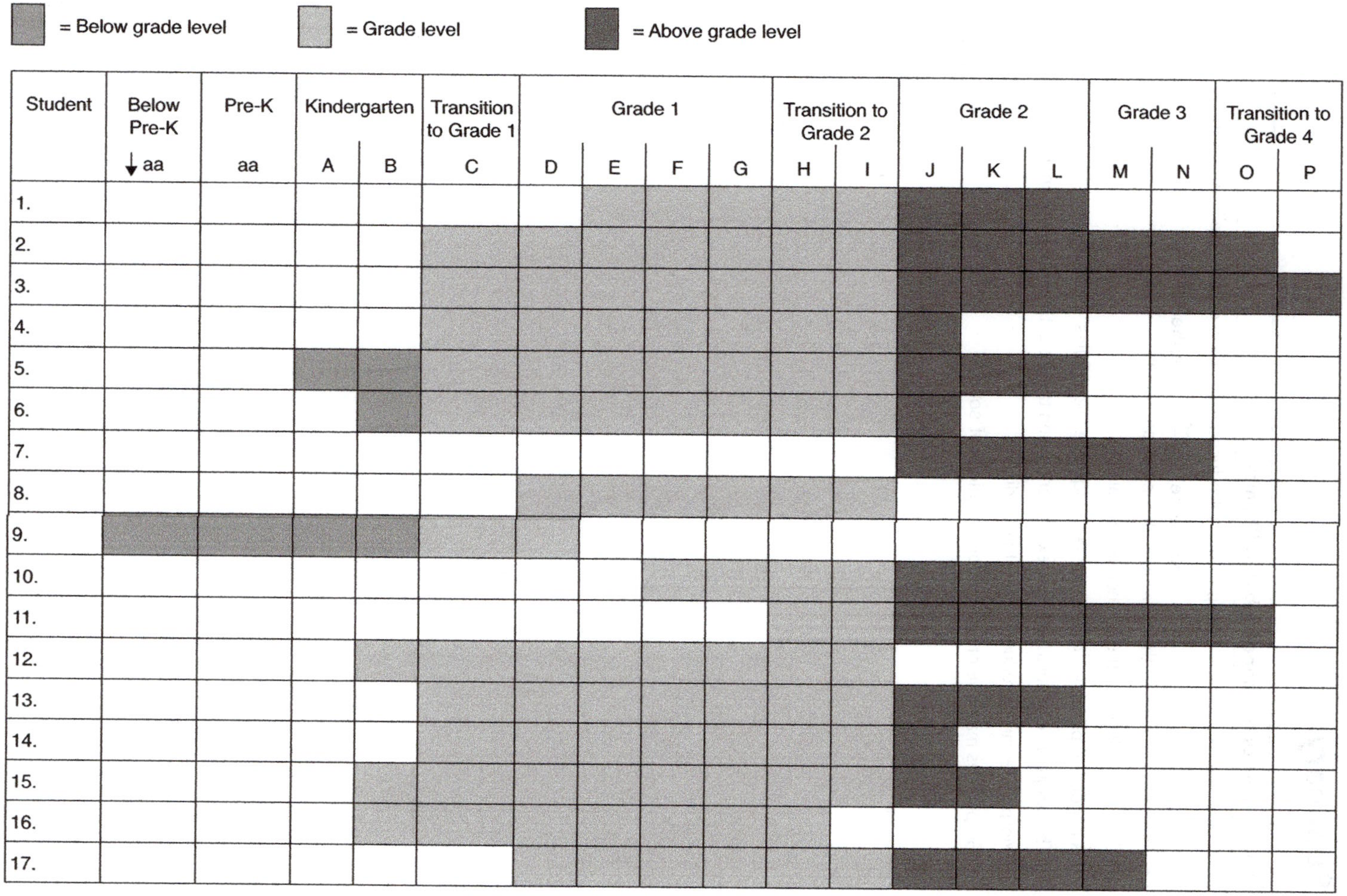

Legend:
- ▦ = Below grade level
- ▨ = Grade level
- ▪ = Above grade level

Student	Below Pre-K →aa	Pre-K aa	Kindergarten A	Kindergarten B	Transition to Grade 1 C	Grade 1 D	Grade 1 E	Grade 1 F	Grade 1 G	Transition to Grade 2 H	Transition to Grade 2 I	Grade 2 J	Grade 2 K	Grade 2 L	Grade 3 M	Grade 3 N	Transition to Grade 4 O	Transition to Grade 4 P
1.																		
2.																		
3.																		
4.																		
5.																		
6.																		
7.																		
8.																		
9.																		
10.																		
11.																		
12.																		
13.																		
14.																		
15.																		
16.																		
17.																		

Summary

Characteristics of Phoneme-based Phonics

- The phoneme and how it is spelled is introduced first. "How do you spell the sound . . . ?"

  phoneme $\Longrightarrow$ **grapheme**

- All of the spellings of the individual phonemes are taught.
- Only the spellings of the phonemes are taught.
- A handful of principles govern the language: the "Real Rules" of English.
- The language is regular with few exceptions when taught at the level of phonemes.
- Morphemes are introduced almost immediately.
- Graphemes may give only the approximations of sounds.

Chapter 7

A Framework for Teaching Reading

We are now ready to build a framework for teaching and monitoring reading skills that supports how the brain processes words. This framework will be a guide to determining what and when to teach as well as what to assess. It will direct what needs to be remediated with students who struggle. The two primary questions we need to answer are:

- What do individuals need to know in order to become proficient readers?
- Does it matter in what order this is taught?

Traditional Sequence for Teaching New Words

Traditional reading programs generally follow the same sequence of instruction although they may differ in the delivery of some of the elements. In kindergarten, children are engaged in reading and writing activities with conversations about print and the world. They also learn the letters and sound of the alphabet. Depending on the philosophy of teaching reading, the student either will be taught how to decode words using traditional phonics or will memorize words through repeated readings and sight word lists. These children may also be introduced to some kind of incidental phonics such as word families. The basic sequence is the same: start with the written word (graphemes) and help the child read the words through particular strategies.

After the research on phonemes, many classrooms have added phonemic awareness activities. Usually, these are taught using oral group activities that require students to listen to words and orally identify the beginning sound, break apart a word into individual sounds, or blend sounds together into words.

We are familiar with the sequence. It is most likely the way you learned to read. However, is it compatible with the way the brain reads? When I implemented phonemic awareness activities, used kinesthetic methods, and used a phoneme-based phonics, there were good results with *most* of the students. But what would help those bottom students? I had to align *all* of the elements of my teaching with research.

Figure 7.1 Traditional Approach to Teach New Words

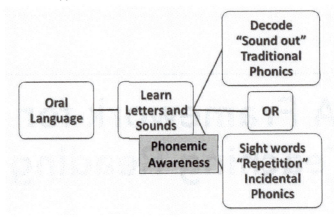

So what elements are important? What sequence do we use? To answer these two questions, we will look at different areas of research that in the end will point to the same powerful, but unexpected conclusion.

Early Spontaneous Readers

Young children who learn to read without any intentional instruction approach the process of learning to read quite differently than children sitting in a classroom. If we want reading to be a natural process, we can learn from them. As you read the stories below, note the important elements in learning to read and the sequence of those activities. What indication is there that the child is working on phonemic awareness? What do we usually leave out when we teach children to read?

These amazing stories of young children who learned to read without intentional instruction are samples lifted from three different research studies. It is noteworthy that intelligence, gender, and socioeconomic status are not determining factors in this ability to read early (Anbar 2004).

Jed

Jed learned to read although his mother never specifically tried to teach him. She only answered his reading-related questions. Jed progressed from an early awareness of print to collecting and stacking books. Then at 27 months, he recognized several letters, acquired a growing sight vocabulary, pretended to read, learned the sounds of letters, *made words with magnetic letters*, and finally, at the age of 2 years, 9 months, became a beginning reader, able to read unfamiliar easy picture books (Lass 1982, 1983).

Victor

Between 8 and 18 months, Victor gained knowledge of books and print, understanding that words on the paper communicated a message. At 18 months, he was able to identify letters and started learning some sight words found in the environment, such as the word STOP on a stop sign. By 26 months he knew the sounds of the letters. As soon as he knew his letters and sounds, he *began building words*. By 29 months, he could read a familiar book with his parents' help. At 32 months, he learned how to sound out unfamiliar words, and by 48 months he could read unfamiliar picture books (Anbar 1984, 1986).

Elizabeth

Between 15 to 18 months, Elizabeth showed great interest in books, turning the pages and looking at pictures. At 24 months, she played with the magnetic letters and learned the letters and sounds. Her parents read to her at least 30 minutes a day, pointing to the words and talking about the pictures. When she was just barely two years old, her favorite game was asking her father to *spell words for her*. They did this for 15 to 20 minutes every night. She would tell him a word to write and he would write it for her. At 36 months, she played with the magnetic letters on the refrigerator and *made words from them*. By 48 months she *began* reading books, and before turning 5 years old, she could independently read books and sound out words (Sporleder 1995).

Seven Steps to Reading Taken by Early Readers

All three researchers found early readers progressed through the same stages in learning to read.

Stage 1: Develop print awareness.

Stage 2: Learn letters and their sounds.

Stage 3: Build words out of letters, spelling them correctly.

Stage 4: Learn some words in the environment.

This step occurred just before, during, or after the word building stage

Stage 5: Read familiar picture books.

Stage 6: Learn to decode words, sounding out unfamiliar words.

Stage 7: Independent reading of unfamiliar books.

Stage 1: Develop Print Awareness

These early readers developed awareness of print at a young age. By the time these children were around a year old, they turned the pages of books and held a book correctly. They understood that print communicated a message. This early awareness of books seemed to come from parents reading to the children daily during the first year of life. Most of the parents read to their children at least 30 minutes during the day, pointing to the words and talking about the pictures.

Stage 2: Learn Letters and Their Sounds

Early readers learned the alphabet between 1½ and 2 years old. Most parents read a variety of alphabet books to their child. Manipulating magnetic letters seemed to be a favorite way these children associated the names of the letters with the letters. In addition, they sang the Alphabet Song and put the letters in order. These young children learned not only the names of the letters but also their sounds. Kinesthetic activities with the letters were important.

Stage 3: Build Words out of Letters

Once these young children were familiar with letters and sounds, they showed an interest in making words using the magnetic letters. Encoding was a natural "next step" for these young children. They were not just playing with inventive spelling, but wanted to know how to translate spoken words to print using *correct* spelling. They spelled these words before ever being able to read them.

Stage 4: Learn Some Sight Words

At the same time these young children were making words, they were also learning how to recognize a few sight words, particularly words from the environment. Stop signs, store signs, and words on cereal boxes were common sources of their new vocabulary words. This helped solidify the association between the written word and the spoken word, the idea that print represents speech.

    CAUTION: Studies have shown that this ability to recognize words in the environment is, in most cases, not true reading. When preschool children below age five were shown the same words in regular font outside of the logo and environment, many were not able to identify the word. However, children who knew their letters and sounds and had some phonological awareness could actually read these words (Share & Gur 1999).

Stage 5: Read Familiar Picture Books

Between ages 3 and 4, these young children began reading the simple picture books they loved. Whether they depended on recognizing the words because they had spelled them or because they had memorized much of the story or both is not clear. What we do know is that these children could not do this before they had spelled words. It appeared their familiarity with the text of the story supported their development from spelling words to reading them.

Stage 6: Learn to Decode Words

The ability to decode unfamiliar words did not come until the child was already reading some words and reading familiar picture books. They had already been engaged in the spelling process before learning to decode. In traditional programs, decoding comes immediately after learning the letters and sounds; in early readers, this step comes after spelling words and after applying that knowledge to books they know.

    IMPORTANT: Encoding, which is the translation of spoken words into written words, is an entirely different skill than decoding. It begins with hearing the phonemes in the language and representing them with the appropriate grapheme. In contrast, decoding begins with the grapheme, requiring the student to attach speech sounds to graphemes and blend the sounds together smoothly to create a word. It is a more difficult task. These early readers could encode but they could not decode until later.

---

decoding—attaching speech sounds to graphemes and blending the sounds together smoothly to create a word. **grapheme** $\Longrightarrow$ **phoneme**

encoding—translation of spoken words into written words **phoneme** $\Longrightarrow$ **grapheme**

Figure 7.2 How Early Readers Learned to Read

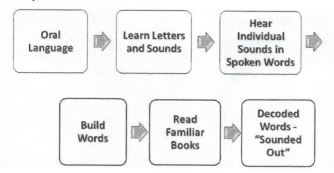

Stage 7: Read Unfamiliar Books

After some experience with reading familiar books and with decoding, these young children began reading unfamiliar books. Most could read chapter books by the time they were five years old. They were truly independent readers at this point

There are some notable differences and similarities between this sequence and the sequence of traditional programs. The similarities include the development of print awareness through listening to books and engagement in conversations about books. Almost all of the children studied listened to books about 30 minutes per day. Another similarity is learning the alphabet letters and sounds. From that point, though, the steps diverge from what we traditionally do in schools.

> Stage 3 is significant. Students built words out of letters.

All these early readers spelled words before ever being able to read them. They encoded words before decoding words. In fact, one child even wrote the family grocery list with correct spelling *before* knowing how to read (Sporleder 1995). What skills would be required in order to do this? How does this fit in with what we know about how the brain reads?

In order to spell, these children had fairly sophisticated phonemic awareness skills. For a simple three-letter word, they would need to be able to hear the beginning, end, and middle sounds (Phonemic Awareness Level 3). For longer words, they would need to be able to hear all of the sounds of a word (Phonemic Awareness Level 4). They would also need to know how to represent those sounds with the appropriate grapheme, knowledge they would have gained through learning letters and their sounds. As their repertoire of graphemes expanded, they could spell more and more words correctly.

Both of these skills focus on two main areas of the brain: the Speech Sound Center and the Sound Symbol Center. These children were using the language centers of the brain that are critical for proficient reading and *in the order the brain processes words,* from speech sound to sound symbol.

Those who have researched the brain are adamant about the necessity to change the sequence in which we teach new words:

One of the most fundamental flaws found in almost all phonics programs, including traditional ones, is that ***they teach the code backward.*** That is, they go from letter to sound

Figure 7.3 Speech Sound Center and Sound Symbol Center

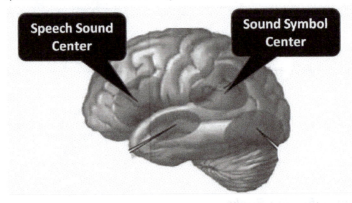

Adapted and reprinted with permission, Cambium Learning-Sopris.

instead of from sound to letter. . . The print-to-sound (conventional phonics) approach leaves gaps, invites confusion, and creates inefficiencies (Moats 1998, pp. 45–45).

"The process of learning to read should start with students constructing words—because this process requires them to pronounce words first" (Herron 2008, p. 78). Shaywitz (2003) explained that mapping speech sounds to letters is what takes reading out of the realm of pure memory and allows readers to decode words they don't yet know.

Although this sequence has now been verified by neuroscientists, many well-known reading researchers have also noted it over several decades. Spelling before reading was not the focus of their research but in the process of investigating other issues, they made the following observations about spelling.

> Research of the past two decades has once again placed spelling at the center of the reading/language arts curriculum. . . spelling and word study provide direct teaching of what to attend to in words.
>
> —Dr. Edmund Henderson
> 1992, p. 5

> Experience has taught me to distinguish clearly between writing and reading, and has shown me that the two acts are not absolutely contemporaneous. Contrary to the usually accepted idea, writing precedes reading.
>
> —Montessori
> 1964, pp. 296–297

> Spelling appears to precede reading by its very nature. It is primarily a creative endeavor. . .spellers compose words according to the way they sound, figuring out for themselves what comes first, next and so on. . . .[spelling has] a direct relationship to the way words are pronounced . . . translating from pronunciation to print.
>
> —Chomsky
> 1979, p. 46

> The ability to read seems almost like a by-product of the ability to print and spell.
>
> —Dolores Durkin
> 1966, p. 137

> Spelling may be a critical precursor to the ability to utilize phonics and many children may not need phonics instruction once they acquire and use the sound sequence analysis strategy.
>
> —Marie Clay
> 1979, p. 66

> A child does not need to know how to read before mapping speech to print. A child with good phonemic segmentation skills and good knowledge of letter-sounds can begin to construct an orthographic lexicon without necessarily having any formal experience of printed words. All the child would need is to have an understanding that spoken words can be written down—without ever having seen it in print.
>
> —Stuart and Colheart
> 1988, p. 172

Despite the confirmation from research that it is easier for children to learn to read by spelling before decoding, this has not been implemented in most classrooms. However, when the sequence of these early spontaneous readers has been applied to teaching beginning and struggling readers, the results have been phenomenal. With the nine classrooms discussed in Chapter 1, three classrooms implemented word families, three classrooms implemented traditional phonics, and three classrooms implemented spelling before reading with a phoneme-based phonics. Although there was no statistical difference in phonemic awareness scores or letter/sound knowledge among all three groups, Group C scored statistically higher in reading as shown in Figure 1.3 on page 8.

This same sequence can be applied to preschool children as well as struggling readers of all ages. When it has been intentionally used with preschool children, they have learned to read chapter books by the time they were five or six years old. Struggling readers of all ages, whether they have a disability or not, make extraordinary progress.

Figure 7.4 Comparison of Traditional and Research-Based Approaches

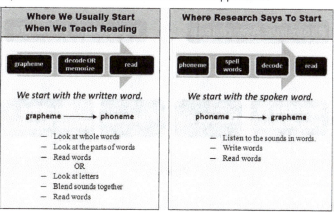

A Personal Note

I taught first grade for several years and then taught remedial readers, grades 1 to 12. I have found this approach is the key to unlocking the door quickly and easily for all students. After they know their letters and sounds, we begin phonemic awareness activities and *at the same time* introduce the spellings of the phonemes with the Real Rules of English. All of this is done using kinesthetic methods. After spelling the words, students read the words. I found it is much easier for students to spell the words first rather than start with the written word. We do not jump from learning the letters and sounds to decoding or memorizing words. We spell first. By using this process, almost all students in the bottom 20 percent become proficient readers. All of these poor students with whom I have worked have gained a minimum of two grade levels with 42 hours of instruction.

Framework for Teaching Reading

We now have the information we need to build a framework for teaching reading. Each skill is necessary to become a successful reader and is listed in order of acquisition. If a skill is weak, then each successive skill will be weak or nonexistent and the reading process breaks down. As soon as students are able to read connected text, even if it is only one sentence, they need to be introduced to the higher-level skills of decoding, fluency, and thinking while reading. These need to be added to the instruction while students continue to work on the lower-level skills.

Print Awareness

Children raised in literacy-rich environments develop print awareness early. It is a multi-faceted skill that includes understanding how to hold a book and turn pages to understanding that print has different functions such as a menu lists food choices, a book tells a story, and a sign announces a favorite restaurant. Children with print awareness:

Figure 7.5 Framework for Teaching Reading

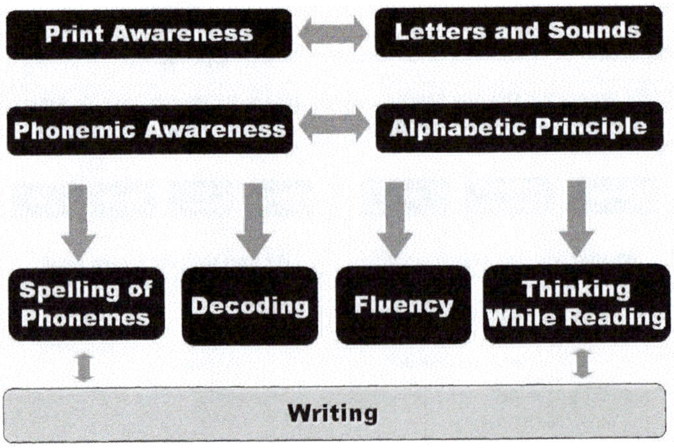

- Know that print communicates a message.
- Know print has different functions.
- Know print is read from left to right and top to bottom.
- Know print has words that consist of letters with spaces between words.

Letters and Sounds

It is important that children learn the names and the most common sounds of the alphabet since all graphemes are formed using these 26 letters. Strong alphabetic knowledge includes being able to identify a letter with its sound or when given the name of a letter or sound being able to produce a letter. It is also important that children can identify objects that begin with a particular letter sound. Keep in mind that this differs from phonemic awareness because someone other than the child has segmented the sound.

Phonemic Awareness

This is the critical predictor of reading success. Although older students usually have print awareness and alphabetic knowledge, they may not have phonemic awareness. This is a skill that must be assessed because even students who appear to be reading well might, in fact, only be memorizing words and consequently "crash" later on. At all times, every teacher needs to know the level of phonemic awareness each student has. Review the six levels of phonemic awareness until you know them well and can recognize them in students.

Alphabetic Principle

Understanding that individual speech sounds are represented on paper by specific graphemes is not automatic for many students, even older students. By spelling before reading, this connection between the phoneme and grapheme is firmly established and students understand that speech can be represented in print.

Spelling of Phonemes

As students learn how to represent the 44 sounds, they are able to create words by listening to the sounds in a spoken word and applying the principles of the Real Rules of English. From the very beginning of instruction, they also need to learn how to add prefixes and suffixes.

Decoding

This entirely new skill requires students to look at the code backwards. Amazingly, students can spell words but not necessarily be able to decode the words they have just spelled. This skill requires that the student break a word apart by graphemes and blend it back together to form the word. They need to be able to recognize the morphemes of words—the root, prefixes, and suffixes—and know how to break apart and blend both small and "big" words.

Fluency

Fluency is built on the ability to properly decode words. Words that are processed by the language centers of the brain and read repeatedly are stored in the Word Form Center for rapid retrieval. This provides the foundation for reading smoothly with expression. Students who do not have the previous skills will have difficulty with fluency.

Thinking While Reading

The goal of reading is understanding. Students who have the previous skills have the foundation upon which to build comprehension. These students:

- Can retell the story or recite the information.
- Can identify who, what, why, when, where, and how.
- Recognize repetition, comparison and contrast, cause and effect.
- Can make inferences based on facts.
- Use the facts and inferences to form an opinion.

Writing

Writing skills are tied directly to reading. Spelling, sentence structure, and text structure impact reading comprehension. The ability to write in response to reading refines logical thinking and higher level cognitive processing.

Using This Framework for Instruction and Assessment

The skills in this framework are sequential and equally important. Each one needs to be explicitly and systematically taught. At all times, you as a teacher need to know the proficiency level of each student on each skill. When you observe a breakdown in the reading process, you know that one or more of these skills are weak or even missing.

Older struggling readers usually have print awareness and knowledge of the letters and sounds but do not have phonemic awareness, an understanding of the alphabetic principle, or the ability to represent a speech sound with appropriate graphemes. These students might appear to be able to read, and the problem might appear to be with decoding, fluency, or comprehension, but it is a weakness in the previous skills. Always go back and assess phonemic awareness and the ability to represent those sounds with the appropriate grapheme whenever decoding, fluency, or comprehension problems surface. When these skills are addressed, decoding and fluency are easy to remediate.

We will be looking at ways to assess these skills for all ages. Before we do that in the next section, there is one more area of critical knowledge that needs to be addressed.

Building a Balanced Approach to Reading

We can add more strategies we currently use to the research-based paradigm to build our balanced approach.

Figure 7.6 Building a Balanced Approach to Reading

Building a Balanced Approach	
Research-based Paradigm	Select Current Strategies
Teach and assess phonemic awareness.	Teach alphabet and sounds as precursor for all graphemes.
Teach 44 phonemes and graphemes that represent them.	Teach rhyming as a precursor to phonemic awareness.
Teach prefixes and suffixes immediately.	Teach syllables to aid in decoding and reading.
Use kinesthetic methods.	Teach categorization of initial sounds as a precursor to phonemic awareness.
Teach the "Real Rules" of English.	Read aloud to students; talk about print and text.
Have students spell before reading. Start with the phoneme rather than grapheme.	Expose to different functions of print.

Meet My Students

My interest in early spontaneous readers was spawned by an experience with my own children. I was dictating sentences from a first-grade teacher's manual to give my six-year-old daughter practice in correct spelling and writing. When the phone rang, I left the room, and when I returned, I discovered my four-year-old had finished dictating the sentences to her sister. I didn't even know she could read. However, in the next 10 minutes, I discovered she could read anything, including the encyclopedia. I had no idea how this had happened. After reading the research, I knew exactly how it happened. She learned her alphabet and then spelled words before she could even read them. I had no idea that in the process of spelling words, she was processing words, and it was the door to reading.

Drew

When Drew was just a baby, I encouraged his mother to read to him and include books on the alphabet. She bought magnetic letters and in playful, short sessions talked with him about the alphabet letters and sounds. When he was three years old, I told her to call his attention to the beginning sounds of spoken words as they were riding in the car and hanging out around the house. She would point out an object, say the word, and then ask what sound he heard at the beginning of the word. When he could hear the beginning sound, I instructed her to call his attention to end sounds and then eventually middle sounds. I told her to let me know when he knew his letters and sounds and could hear the beginning, end, and middle sounds of words.

At four years old, Drew had all of these skills and was ready to learn to read. I dictated four or five simple three-letter words, and to his delight, he was able to spell them perfectly by listening to the sounds in words. I then taught him how to sound out the word. Just because students can spell a word does not mean they can read it, but because Drew had just spelled the word, the process was easy.

I dictated a few more words that would be a part of a sentence he would write. I then explained to him that a sentence was a complete thought and said the sentence with the words I had just dictated. I told him every sentence begins with a capital letter and ends with a period. He then wrote the sentence with perfect spelling and punctuation. He then read the sentence, and the look on his face was priceless. He was surprised because he had no idea he was capable of reading.

This whole session took no longer than 15 minutes, and yet he was on his way to spelling and reading. His mother continued to practice with him in the same way and provided little decodable books for him to read. By the time he was five years old, he could easily read small picture books. By the time he was in first grade, he could read chapter books. And the process was painless!

Manuel

When Manuel entered second grade, he was reading well below grade level. At the end of second grade, he still had not caught up even though many different interventions were in place. Nothing seemed to work. He had made progress, but not enough progress. The same pattern followed Manuel through third grade, and upon entering fourth grade, his reading level was still well below grade level. His teacher then began using a phoneme-based phonics, spelling before reading and kinesthetic methods. By the end of fourth grade, Manuel was reading *above* grade level. The only explanation the teachers could pinpoint for his progress was Word Workshop, the program used to teach the research-base approach to reading.

Summary

Framework for Teaching Reading

	The Student . . .
Print Awareness	• Knows that print communicates a message. • Knows print has different functions, such as a menu lists food choices, a book tells a story, a sign announces a favorite restaurant. • Knows print is read from left to right and top to bottom. • Knows print has words that consist of letters with spaces between words.
Letters and Sounds	• Can say the alphabet. • Knows the names of letters. • Know sounds of letters. • Can identify objects that begin with a particular letter sound.
Phonemic Awareness	• Can identify the first sound in a spoken word. • Then is able to identify the last sound in a spoken word. • Then is able to hear the middle and most of the sounds in a spoken word. • Then is able to segment all of the sounds in a word.
Alphabetic Principle	• Understands that letters are the building blocks that form words. • Understands that speech sounds are represented by letters or groups of letters. • Understands that speech can be mapped to print.

Spelling of Phonemes	• Can listen to the individual sounds in words and create the word from that knowledge. • Is learning the 120 ways to spell the 44 sounds in our language. • Is learning the structure of words, including prefixes and suffixes.
Decoding	• Can break a word apart by graphemes and blend it back together to form the word. • Knows how to break apart and blend both small and "big" words. • Recognizes prefixes and suffixes and can separate them from the word.
Fluency	• Reads smoothly and fluently, reading in phrases and paying attention to punctuation. • Reads with comprehension. • Reads with expression.
Critical Thinking	• Can retell the story or recite the information. • Can identify who, what, why, when, where, and how. • Recognizes repetition, comparison and contrast, cause and effect • Can make inferences based on facts. • Uses the facts and inferences to form an opinion.

Chapter 8

Don't Forget Reading!

You can't learn to drive without driving and you can't learn to read without reading.

We can't forget one of the most important aspects of learning to read, reading. In order to become proficient readers, students must read at least 30 minutes per day at their instructional level. There are no shortcuts. If they don't read, they won't be proficient.

We have looked at the importance of phonemic awareness and knowing the graphemes that represent them. Beginning readers show strong activity in the Speech Sound Center and Sound Symbol Center, but as they become more and more skilled in reading, the Word Form Center becomes the most active region (see Figure 8.1). After a word has been read several times and the reader has processed the word using the word analysis centers, it is stored in the Word Form Center for instantaneous retrieval. It usually takes at least 4 to 14 repetitions before this happens, but will vary with the ability of the student.

Students must read 30 minutes a day at their instructional level in order to become proficient readers. There are no shortcuts. If they don't read, they won't be proficient.

Figure 8.1 Language Areas of the Brain

Language Areas of the Brain

1. Speech Sound Center (word analysis)
2. Sound symbol Center (word analysis)
3. Word Form Center (storage of printed words)
4. Context and Meaning Center

How Students Become Automatic at Word Reading

Time to Read

Reading in school may seem like an obvious goal, but it is more difficult to achieve than one would suspect. A survey conducted several years ago showed the average amount of reading time during a school day was seven minutes. With the emphasis in reading, hopefully those numbers have changed some, but teachers still battle for time for students to read.

How is it possible that a student can go to school and read little or not at all? Read these scenarios and decide how the student avoided reading.

Scenario #1

Rather than have students read a new story silently to themselves first, the teacher reads the story aloud while students follow in their books. Good students may read and follow along, but most students don't.

Scenario #2

Rather than having students read a passage aloud together or read aloud with a partner, the teacher has students take turns reading a sentence or paragraph while other students follow along. The student reading is reading, but most of the other students are thinking about something else or trying to predict where they will be reading.

Scenario #3

Rather than have the students read the story themselves, the teacher reads the story and then has students respond to the story by drawing a picture, creating a bookmark, or other craft. Some refer to it as Language Arts and Crafts. In the average reading curriculum, there is 270 minutes of activities for every 20 minute story (Allington 2000). Many times the emphasis is on the extras rather than reading itself.

Scenario #4

The teacher reads the story line by line, having students orally repeat it together. The teacher asks questions or asks students to visualize what they see. When students are asked to read a section silently and then answer questions in a group discussion, some students don't read it at all.

Scenario #5

When students are to be reading a story silently, poor students do not. They find other things to do, like disrupt their neighbor.

Scenario #6

When working in groups that require reading instructions, some students never read any of the instructions. They let their friends read them and then tell them what to do.

Minutes of Reading per Day	Minutes per School Year	Hours per School Year	Add 15 Minutes of Reading per School Night
40 minutes	7,200 minutes	120 hours	120 + 45 hours = 175 hours
30 minutes	5,400 minutes	90 hours	90 + 45 hours = 135 hours
10 minutes	1,800 minutes	30 hours	30 + 45 hours = 75 hours
5 minutes	900 minutes	15 hours	15 + 45 hours = 60 hours

Between the opportunity to get away with not reading and the emphasis in the classroom on reading activities rather than reading, it is possible for a student to go through an entire school day and never read a single word. The impact on the student who reads little is exponential.

As a teacher, deliberately monitor the amount of time *each* student is reading each day. Keep a written record for three days. The goal is a minimum of 30 minutes of reading each day. For every 10 minutes you can add to that, students will benefit. If you have students who are not reaching that goal, design ways for them to engage in reading. In addition, plan incentives for students to read outside of school for 15 or 20 minutes per school day.

Students who read more:

- Become more fluent
- Learn more vocabulary
- Have a better knowledge base
- Are more proficient at comprehension

Rereading

In order to gain proficiency, students need to read and reread large amounts of texts:

- Rather than reading one story per week, students need to be reading four or five stories per week.
- Rather than the teacher reading a new story aloud first, students need to read the text silently first so they can decode any words they do not know. Reading silently also helps them increase their silent reading speed.
- Rather than having students wait for the teacher or another student to read aloud, have students read the text aloud together or aloud with a partner.
- Organize a classroom library so students have access to the same books over a long time. They will read and reread their favorite books.
- Encourage students to read series books such as Nancy Drew or Boxcar Children. Books in a series will have the same characters, similar settings, similar plots, and similar vocabulary. In many ways, it resembles rereading.

Decodable Texts

What is a decodable text? It is one that uses only grapheme representations students have learned. After they have learned most, if not all, the graphemes, they should be able to read any text that is appropriate for their age group and not depend on decodable texts.

Young beginning readers and remedial readers who can only read a few words need to start with decodable texts. However, *decodable* does not mean boring. The following is an example of a decodable story used in first grade. Students have been taught every grapheme used in this story.

> ## The Dove and The Ant
> An ant came to a river to drink. As she drank, she slid in and began to sink.
> "Save me!" she cried. "Save me!"
> A kind dove was nearby. The dove threw a twig into the river.
> The ant grabbed hold and floated to the bank.
> Later, the dove was sitting in a tree. A man was going to shoot her. The dove didn't see him aiming at her. The ant did. As the man fired, the ant bit his heel. The man missed, and the dove flew safely away.
>
> "The Dove and the Ant" from *The Gold Book,* 1985, p. 23.

Why is it important to use decodable text? When we remember how the brain processes words through analyzing both the individual sounds in the words and the grapheme representations of the sounds, what happens if a student does not have those sound symbols stored in the brain? They have few options. They can guess the word or ask someone. They may memorize the word, but retrieval will be slower than if they had properly processed the word through the language centers of the brain and stored it in the Word Form Center.

Some programs use predictable texts, texts with repetition of words and phrases that assist in memorization. This aids students in reading, but does not solve the problem of improper processing of words. Juel and Roper/Schneider (1985) found that beginning readers who were exposed to a mixture of noncodable and decodable words in their beginning readers were less apt to use letter-sound knowledge to read words than students who were exposed to mainly decodable words.

Beginning readers who are expected to read words that have graphemes they have not learned develop habits of guessing and may become discouraged with the reading process. They are being asked to read words without the proper tools to do so.

Choosing the Right Book for the Right Purpose

How do you determine a student's reading level? What texts would be too difficult, just right, or too easy? Three general descriptions can guide us to determine the difficulty of any given text for a particular student (Killgallon 1943). Through informal reading assessments, an appropriate text can be determined.

Independent Reading Level

Students can read these books and stories without any help. A student would say, *"This is easy."* Reading at this level will reflect these characteristics:

- There is no more than one unknown word per 100 words.
- The reader can read these words with excellent comprehension. If you ask questions about what was read, the student can tell you all the important facts with 90 percent accuracy.
- They read the text fluently with expression and accurate punctuation.

What is the value of reading at the independent reading level? Reading at this level will reflect these skills:

- Increases fluency, reading speed, and accuracy in reading words
- Develops the general knowledge base and vocabulary
- Increases enjoyment of reading because the task is easy

Because reading at this level has great benefits, students should be given free choice reading time during the day when they can choose books that are easy and enjoyable to read.

   CAUTION: if students only read at this level, their reading skills will not develop to the maximum potential. The primary reading instruction should not occur at this level.

Instructional Reading Level

This is the level where the most reading growth occurs. A student would say, *"I can understand what I am taught. When I have some help, it is easy."* Reading levels reflect these characteristics:

- The material is a challenge, but it is not overwhelming.
- The student is able to use decoding skills to read unknown words.
- There are only 2 to 5 unknown words out of 100.
- The reader not only can read these words but also understands what these words mean. If you ask questions about what was read, without instruction, the student can tell you the overall correct sense with 70 percent accuracy.

Students just beginning to read will have to decode many of the words in a text, but they will have the knowledge and skills to do so if they know the graphemes found in the words.

   What is the value of reading at the instructional reading level? This is where maximum reading growth occurs. Students are being "stretched" to understand new ideas and new vocabulary with the help of a teacher. All assigned reading should be at this level.

   Teachers also need to help students be aware of their own reading level. Students can be instructed in how to choose a "just right" book by counting how many words they have to stop and figure out. Have students turn to the middle of the text where there are no pictures and begin reading. Have them raise a finger for every word they have to stop and figure out. One or no fingers raised means the text is too easy, two to five fingers means the book is "just right," and more than five means the text is too difficult. There are times when a student is insistent on reading a text that is too difficult because it is of high interest to them. Under most circumstances, it is acceptable to allow them to read the text because their determination to read it will overshadow any frustration.

Frustration Reading Level

These texts are too difficult for a student to read. A student might say, "I don't understand what I read. I don't like to read. I can't read it. It's too hard." Reading levels reflect these characteristics:

- There are 6 or more unknown words per 100.
- By the time the student finishes the sentence or a paragraph, he or she does not know what has been read because of the effort spent on trying to read the words.
- If you ask questions about what was read, the student can only give a few details with less than 50 percent comprehension.
- A student may refuse to read, have difficulty pronouncing many words, use a finger to point at words, and/or engage in word-by-word reading.

Students should never read at this level. It is *harmful* for the student. It contributes to the following:

- A hatred for reading develops.
- Vocabulary development that is critical for continued reading progress is stalled. Each year, a student learns about 10,000 vocabulary words from context. If a student cannot read enough words to be able to understand the meaning or context, that vocabulary development is hindered.
- Reading fluency is interrupted and comprehension plummets.
- Students do not make progress in their reading skills when they read at this level.

One student said to me, "I can't read enough words in a sentence to figure out what the sentence is talking about."

Look at the following text. If I am a poor reader in fifth grade, what difficulties would I have in comprehending this text? How would it be impacting my reading growth? How would it influence my feelings about reading?

Treασυρε Ισλand

The εξχιτεμεντ of these last μανευσερσ had somewhat ιντερφερεδ with the watch I had kept ηιτηερτο, sharply enough, upon the χοξσωαιν. Even then I was still much ιντερεστεδ, waiting for the ship to touch, χρανινγ over the σταρβοαρδ βυλωαρκσ and watching the ριππλεσ spreading wide before the bows. I might have fallen without a στρυγγλε for my life, had not a sudden υνεασινεσσ σειζεδ upon me and made me turn my head.

Περηαπσ I had heard a χρεακ or seen his σηαδοω moving with the tail of my eye; περηαπσ it was an ινστινχτ like a cat's......

One of the problems classroom teachers face is the requirement to use grade level texts in reading, social studies, and science. Students who are reading below grade level are then forced to read texts at the frustration level. Students either do not read the material or accommodations are made that do not require them to read, such as provision of auditory materials. That means they have lost time reading. Since they need the content found in these texts, easier reading should be provided to make the content accessible. These are the types of students who can go through an entire school day reading little or not at all unless the teacher purposefully ensures they are reading at least 30 minutes a day at the instructional level.

Reading Levels

Independent Reading Level 99% accuracy	90% comprehension
Instructional Reading Level 95% accuracy	75% comprehension
Frustration Reading Level 90% accuracy	50% comprehension

Four Types of Reading in the Classroom

There are four types of reading that need to occur three to four times a week, if not daily. Each of these makes a unique contribution to reading proficiency (see Figure 8.2).

Teacher Reads Aloud to Students

This is a powerful way to model the value, enjoyment, and the fluency of reading. Students of all grade levels benefit. It is a nonnegotiable in the lower elementary grades and should occur daily no matter what. Read a picture book, poem, chapter book, riddle, joke, newspaper article or magazine article *every day*. Students benefit from hearing material that they themselves might not be able to read on their own:

- It motivates students to read and exposes them to a wide variety of genres.
- It expands their vocabulary and develops their general knowledge base.
- It develops their general language skills and develops cognitive abilities.

Figure 8.2 Reading and Rereading Sequence

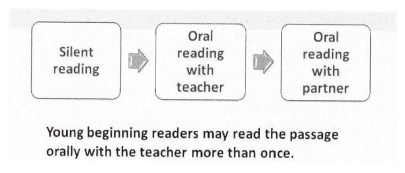

Young beginning readers may read the passage orally with the teacher more than once.

- It instills the value and enjoyment of reading.
- They hear what expressive, fluent reading sounds like.

For preschool and kindergarten, reading aloud with meaningful conversations about the text is essential for building print awareness, vocabulary, and building background knowledge. Students coming from literacy-rich environments often have had at least 30 minutes a day of reading aloud during their early years. That means they have had up to 900 hours of instruction that those coming from a literacy-deficient environment do not have.

Buddy reading is another form of reading aloud that benefits both the reader and the listener. Students in upper grades are paired with students in the lower grades. The older students choose or receive picture books or other texts to practice and then when ready, read to the younger students. The younger children enjoy working with an older student and the older student benefits by practicing reading aloud with expression.

Silent Reading

Students who can't read, don't read silently. If they have been given texts for which they have no tools, they give up. For this reason, the material should always be at the instructional level of the student and decodable if the student does not know most of the graphemes of the language. If there are words that may be difficult to read or understand, the teacher should call attention to those *before* silent reading begins.

CAUTION: If the teacher reads the text aloud *before* student reads it, it robs students of the privilege of using the tools of decoding and only encourages memorization of whole words. We want the words to be stored phonologically in the Word Form Center of the brain.

By grade 2, students should not be moving their lips during silent reading. We can only speak 150 to 180 words per minute maximum and by subvocalizing or moving our lips, we limit the reading speed to that level or below. In order to be a proficient reader, one needs to read between 300 to 400 words per minute. That can only occur with silent reading.

Reading Aloud

Reading aloud should occur *after* students have had time to read the text silently so they are familiar with the passage and have had time to decode any unknown words. For young children, this would occur the same day. For grades 2 and up, students can read the text silently one day and orally the next. This allows the teacher to rotate small groups of students where one group or more groups are reading silently on a particular day while other groups are reading aloud. The next day, the groups swap.

To be most effective, oral reading needs to occur in a small group where you can monitor whether each student is reading. Having individual texts is more effective than using a Big Book, because you can observe how well a student is following the text. Big Books should be reserved for reading aloud to students. Your goal is to have each student reading as much as possible during this time.

Why is it important for students to read aloud? It benefits both the student and the teacher:

- Students need to hear what the words sound like. Even middle school and high school students are sometimes surprised at what a particular word sounds like.
- Students learn to read new words and to read them accurately. It helps students learn unknown words that they may have skipped during silent reading.
- They need practice reading fluently with expression.
- Teachers can monitor how well students are applying decoding information.
- Teachers can monitor fluency.

Comprehension sometimes falters when we read aloud, no matter how well we can read. We may be concentrating so much on the flow of the words that we have not paid attention to the meaning. If a student has difficulty answering questions after reading aloud, this may be the case rather than poor comprehension skills.

Choose methods that allow each student to read aloud rather than taking turns reading.

Choral Reading

The entire group reads a sentence or a paragraph together with the teacher reading slightly behind the group, monitoring the participation of each student. If you are teaching fluency, particular sentences or paragraphs may be repeated so students can practice reading with expression.

Echo Reading

Sometimes beginning readers need help with fluency and expression. The teacher reads a sentence or section and the students read it back with expression. Students try to match the teacher's fluency and voice.

Reader's Theater

The passage or story is divided into characters or sections. It does not have to be a scripted play. You can be creative on the spot with expository text with individuals taking on the persona of information being described.

Partner Reading

This powerful strategy increases the time spent reading in the classroom, as well as providing immediate feedback for the readers. Partners help each other with unknown words and keep each other on track. In a 25-minute reading period, students can read 10 to 20 minutes, depending on the strategy chosen. This can be used for rereading, assigned reading, or for free choice reading. It is usually best to pair students who are same proficiency levels.

During partner reading many of the same strategies used in small group reading can be used:

- Partners take turns reading, alternating sentences, paragraphs, or pages.
- Partners read together simultaneously as in choral reading.
- One partner reads a line with expression and the other partner repeats the line.

- One partner reads the voices of the characters and the other partner reads the narrator's parts.
- Partners read silently, sitting near one another so that they can ask each other for help when they need it.
- Older students in upper elementary and middle school can take turns reading, but then discuss questions, draw a graphic organizer, or write a summary together.

Reading to Teacher or Other Adult

Individual students read to the teacher or aide during personal conference while the rest of the class is working independently. If there are volunteers that come into the classroom, students who need the most practice can read one-on-one with these adults.

Free-choice Reading

The ideal would be for students to read at home every night. However, we cannot depend on it. Teachers need to provide ample class time for reading so students reach the goal of 30 to 40 minutes or more of reading at the instruction level every day in school. Free choice reading is a proven way to provide some of this reading time. Here are some guidelines:

- Develop a classroom library. Make your classroom a literate environment. Students then have ready access to a wide variety of reading material—books, reference material, and magazines. It appears to be influential in helping students develop a love for reading.
- Let students choose what to read.
- Students should read 10 to 30 minutes every day, depending on the grade level.
- Sometimes, let students read with a partner.

Give students at least one time a week to share what they are reading. For example, one day a week after the students are ready to go home, quickly divide them into groups of four or five and send them to a predetermined corner of the room. Each one in the group has two minutes (timed by a timer) to read, show, act out, or share something from what they have been reading.

Meet My Student

When Kirby came into my second grade classroom, he could read only about ten words. He would not attend to his work but instead disrupted the class in countless ways. Through the manipulation of sound cards, he gained phonemic awareness, and by using the whiteboard to spell before reading, he learned the spellings of the phonemes and the Real Rules of English. I taught him how to decode both small and big words. He read and wrote in a meaningful way every day. By Christmas time, I had a different problem. "Kirby, it is time to go out for recess. "

"I know, teacher, but I want to finish this work. "

I would see him secrete a chapter book under his desk so he could carefully pull it out just enough to sneak read it during a class discussion. "Kirby, I know you love reading, but we want to hear what you have to say during our discussion. You will have time to read your book later."

His new-found ability to read totally changed his attitude toward school. Once he had the skills to complete the work, he *wanted* to do it. Reading becomes a joy to him rather than a burden.

Assessing and Implementing Instruction

We have discussed the critical knowledge needed to teach reading. We have looked at the following:

- How the brain processes words
- The kinesthetic learner
- Phonemes and phonemic awareness
- Phoneme-based phonics
- The Real Rules of English
- The framework for teaching reading
- Reading levels and strategies

Now it is time to think about how we are going to use this knowledge to develop proficient readers. How do we assess these skills and teach them? How do we ensure that every student is developing into a proficient reader? In the next section, we will provide you with the tools.

Summary

How Students Become Automatic at Word Reading
• They must read a minimum of 30 minutes a day at their instructional level.
• They must read and reread large amounts of texts.
• Young beginning readers and remedial readers who can only read a few words need to start with decodable texts.
Three Reading Levels
Independent reading level: 99% accuracy; 90% comprehension
Instructional reading level: 95% accuracy; 75% comprehension
Frustration reading level: 90% accuracy; 50% comprehension
Four Types of Reading in the Classroom
• Teacher reads aloud to students
• Reading silently
• Reading aloud
• Free choice reading

Part II

Monitoring Skills and Implementing Instruction

Chapter 9

Assessing and Monitoring Skills

W hy do we need to assess? Kids can fool you. They can know it and you think they don't. Or, they don't know it and you think they do. A kindergarten student might not respond to alphabet flash cards or might have difficulty writing letters. However, when given letter tiles and instructed to find certain letters, surprisingly, this child can name them and give the sound. All that was needed was a kinesthetic way to express what was known. A third grader can read at grade level, but is reading in a choppy manner. It appears to be a fluency problem. In reality, this student has memorized all the words, has no phonemic awareness, and knows only about half of the spellings of the phonemes. Fluency is not the real issue.

> Know exactly which skills each student has and does not have.

Assessment is not just a single moment in time when students are given a particular test, although it does include that. Assessment occurs every day as you evaluate what students know and do not know as they play the phonemic awareness games, read aloud, and write words.

How Do We Know Which Skills Students Have?

The Framework for Teaching Reading (see Figure 9.1) outlines what skills students must have and the sequence of their development. These are the basic proficiencies that must be assessed. If we are to help students progress in reading, we must know *exactly* where students are in regards to each of these skills. When a student is not making progress, we need to provide the extra practice using kinesthetic and other methods to remediate the particular skill. This framework will help us know what they yet need to learn or what extra practice they may need to become skilled readers.

Figure 9.1 Framework for Teaching Reading

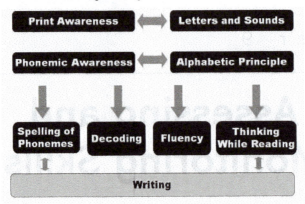

The sequence of the framework also provides a logical, systematic way to search for the source of a reading problem. In the example of the third-grade student, what appeared to be a deficiency in fluency was not the real problem. Instead, the student was lacking in several skills that preceded fluency. No matter what the presenting problem might be, we have to make sure all of the foundational skills are in place. When those are addressed, many times the original issue disappears.

Using the Framework for Teaching Reading as a guide, ask the following questions about each student.

	Question	Grade
Print awareness	1. Does the student have print awareness?	K–1
Letter and sounds	2. What letters and sounds does the student know?	K–1
	4. What letters and sounds does the student *not* know?	K–5
Phonemic awareness	5. Does the student hear the beginning sound in words?	K–12
	7. Does the student hear the end sound in words?	K–12
	9. Does the student hear the middle sound in words?	K–12
	11. Can the student hear each individual sound in a word?	K–12
Alphabetic principle	12. Can the student listen to a spoken word and map it to print?	K–12
Spelling of the phonemes	13. What spellings of the phonemes does the student *not* know?	K–12
	14. Does the student know how to add suffixes? prefixes? Which ones?	1–12
Decoding	15. Can the student decode a small word?	K–12
	16. Can the student decode a large word?	1–12
	17. Can the student read? At what level?	K–12
Fluency	18. Can the student read smoothly?	1–12

Critical Goals for Each Grade

Kindergarten

Critical Question	How to Teach	Goal
1. Is there print awareness?	• Read aloud. • Use Big Books. • Offer free choice "reading" for child.	
2. Do they know the letters and sounds?	• Use various activities to teach all letters and sounds. • Use alphabets games, songs, books. • Act out sounds. • Know how sound is produced in the mouth. • Response cards and tiles manipulated by child.	All children leave kindergarten able to identify and write letters and identify sounds.
3. Do they have phonemic awareness?	• Incorporate listening for the beginning sounds, then end sounds, and then middle sounds in words as you teach throughout the day. • Do phonemic awareness activities that involve manipulating tiles, cards, blocks.	All children leave kindergarten having phonemic awareness at levels 1, 2, 3, and 4.
4. Do they understand the alphabetic principle?	As soon as children have knowledge of some letters and sounds AND have some phonemic awareness, they will be able to start spelling words by listening to the sounds in words.	All children will know how to use knowledge of letters and sounds to build words.

Grade 1

Critical Question	How to Teach	Goal
1. Is there print awareness?	• Read aloud. • Use Big Books. • Offer free choice "reading" for child.	
2. Does the student know the letters and sounds	• Use various activities to teach all letters and sounds. • Use alphabets games, songs, books. • Act out sounds. • Response cards and tiles manipulated by child. • Provide extra practice using kinesthetic activities for students who do not know letters and sounds.	All children will be able to identify and write letters and identify sounds.
3. Do they have phonemic awareness?	• Incorporate listening for the beginning sounds, then end sounds, and then middle sounds in words as you teach throughout the day. • Do phonemic awareness activities that involve manipulating tiles, cards, blocks, response cards.	All children have full phonemic awareness at the end of four months.

continued

Critical Question	How to Teach	Goal
4. Does the student understand the alphabetic principle?	• Spell words by listing to the individual sounds in words.	All children can listen for the sounds in words and map them to print.
5. Does the student know the spellings of the 44 phonemes?	• Use all four modalities to teach the spellings of the phonemes. • Use response cards and spelling before reading. Keep track of exactly who knows and who does not know each of the spellings.	All children know the 76 common spellings of the 44 phonemes by seventh or eighth month.
6. Can the child add prefixes and suffixes to words?	• Teach students how to add prefixes and suffixes from the beginning.	All children leave first grade able to add common prefixes and suffixes to words.
7. Can the child decode both small and large words?	• Teach them how to decode both small and large words.	All children will read 30 minutes a day at their instructional level.
8. Can the child read smoothly?	• It takes about 15 minutes to teach fluency if the child can read the words.	Children are progressing toward fluent reading.
9. Can the child think while reading?	• Ask many questions. • Have children write daily.	Children can find facts and make inferences.

Grades 2 to 12

Critical Question	How to Teach	Goal
1. Does the student have phonemic awareness?	• Do phonemes awareness games and response cards. • Spelling before reading helps students make the connection between the spoken word and the written word.	All students in these grades gain phonemic awareness ASAP. It takes six to eight weeks to learn.
2. Does the student understand the alphabetic principles?	• Dictate words and have them write them on a white board.	Students are able to map speech to print using knowledge of graphemes.
3. Does the student know ALL the spellings of the 44 phonemes?	• Use all four modalities to teach the spellings of the phonemes. • Use response cards and spelling before reading. Keep track of exactly who knows and who does not know each of the spellings.	All students know the 120 spellings of the 44 phonemes. They need to know the most common ones ASAP.
4. Can the student add prefixes and suffixes to words?	• Teach students how to add prefixes and suffixes from the beginning.	Students know how to add affixes required for their grade level.
5. Can the student decode both small and large words?	• Teach students how to decode both small and large words. • Practice decoding multisyllable words.	All students read 30 minutes a day at their instructional level.
6. Can the student read smoothly?	• It takes about 15 minutes to teach fluency if the child can read the words.	All students read fluently.
7. Can the student think while reading?	• Ask many questions. • Have children write daily.	Students can find facts, make inferences, and see implications.

The Assessments

Five basic assessments are found in this chapter that will help you determine reading skills. Some of these can be incorporated into daily activities and provide ongoing information on the progress of students:

1. Letter Recognition Test for kindergarten and first grade
2. Phonemic Awareness Test for kindergarten and early first grade
3. Developmental Spelling Test for grades 1 to 12
4. Phonemic Awareness Tests for grades 1 to 12
5. Informal Reading Analysis for grades K to 12

The Letter Recognition Test

This is an individually administered test to determine what letters and sounds a student knows.

Materials: Set of lowercase alphabet cards arranged in the order of the letters in the chart.
   Procedure: *When I show you a letter, tell me the name of the letter and the sound of the letter.*
   If the child needs prompting:
      What is the name of the letter?
      What is the sound of the letter?
Mark + correct response.

	Name	Sound
h		
l		
s		
e		
m		
r		
d		
f		
k		
n		
t		
x		
q		

	Name	Sound
c		
g		
i		
y		
u		
b		
j		
p		
a		
w		
o		
z		
v		

Phonemic Awareness Test: Kindergarten to Early First Grade

Section 1

Ask the child to tell you the sound they hear at the beginning of the word.

After the child identifies the sound orally, ask if he or she can find the letter on the page.

Have the student do two practice words.

> What sound do you hear at the beginning of *hat*?
>
> Show me the letter that makes that sound.
>
> What sound do you hear at the beginning of *rock*?
>
> Show me the letter that makes that sound.

If students are not able to do the practice words after you show them how, **STOP. DO NOT GO FURTHER.**

> ### Assessment
> What sound do you hear at the beginning of *red*?
>
> Show me the letter that makes that sound.
>
> Continue with these words:
>
> *home*   *box*   *water*   *fist*

Section 2

Proceed with the next set of words, asking for the end sound.

Practice words: ***hat, sad***

If students are not able to do the practice words after you show them how, **STOP. DO NOT GO FURTHER.**

> Now we are going to listen for the sound at the end of the word.
>
> What sound do you hear at the end of *bat*?
>
> Show me the letter that makes that sound.
>
> Continue with these words:
>
> *fell*   *top*   *some*   *dress*

Section 3

Proceed with the next set of words, asking for the middle sounds.

Practice words: **hit pet**

If students are not able to do the practice words after you show them how, **STOP. DO NOT GO FURTHER.**

> Now we are going to listen for the sound in the middle of the word.
>
> What sound do you hear in the middle of *sit*?
>
> Show me the letter that makes that sound.
>
> Continue with these words:
>
> *bat*　　　　　　*pot*　　　　　　*bet*　　　　　　*hut*

Section 4

Proceed with the next set of words, asking for the middle sounds

　　Practice words: **take meat**

　　If the student is not able to do the practice words after you show them how, **STOP. DO NOT GO FURTHER.**

> What sound do you hear in the middle of *smile*?
>
> Show me the letter that makes that sound.
>
> Continue with these words:
>
> *feet*　　　　　　*cake*　　　　　　*soon*　　　　　　*mule*

Kindergarten and Early First Grade Record Sheet

Sound ü	Letter ü	Beginning Sounds
		red
		home
		box
		water
		fist

Sound ü	Letter ü	End Sounds
		bat
		fell
		top
		some
		dress

Sound ü	Letter ü	Middle Sounds (Short)
		sit
		bat
		pot
		bet
		hut

Sound ü	Letter ü	Middle Sounds (Long)
		smile
		feet
		cake
		soon
		mule

Developmental Spelling Test

Every teacher should administer this test at the beginning of the school year to identify reading skills.

The Developmental Spelling Test is a screening tool that identifies poor readers or those who are at risk for poor reading. It is administered as a regular spelling test to a group, but scored differently. It provides a wealth of information on several skills in our Framework for Teaching Reading, including letter knowledge, phonemic awareness, understanding of the alphabetic principle, knowledge of the spellings of phonemes, ability to add prefixes and suffixes, and understanding of the Real Rules of English. These skills are missing in poor readers no matter what the age. To address their needs, they must be distinguished from readers who only have weaknesses in fluency or comprehension. The approach to solving the reading problems of these two distinct groups is significantly different.

The basis for this test is rooted in decades of research. When the phenomena of writing before reading was researched by Read (1971, 1975), he observed that preschoolers apply phonological knowledge in a systematic manner in their spellings. The children's omission or substitution of certain letters in their spellings was not random or haphazard, but based on an underlying knowledge of how speech sounds are produced.

From Read's research, attention was drawn to early development of spelling ability and to the knowledge and strategies that children use in beginning reading/writing. When Henderson and his colleagues (1980) applied Read's analytical framework to hundreds of spelling samples of first and second graders, they found the same strategies consistently being used. From documentation in longitudinal studies, the stages of spelling development emerged (Morris & Perney 1984).

The stages of spelling development (see Table 9.1) reflect a progression in the awareness of the relationship between the speech sound and its representation in print. The student applies phonological knowledge and an understanding of the alphabetic principle to the print code. In the first stage, the prephonetic stage, children start to represent speech sounds with letters of the alphabet. Although they may write one letter for a whole word or write only the first and/or last consonant, there is a conscious connection between speech sounds and the letter. In the next stage, the phonetic stage, children employ a fairly reliable use of the letter-sound strategy to represent the phonological pattern of the word. First and last letters are usually present, along with a vowel, although the choice of the vowel or vowel spelling may be incorrect. In the third stage, the transitional stage, children use short vowels correctly, use markers for long vowels and are able to form groups of letters. Spelling is nearly correct. In the final stage, correct conventions of spelling are used.

The stages of spelling reveal the progression of understanding of the concepts that support the ability to both read and to spell (Henderson 1980). Because of this, spelling becomes an important diagnostic tool for determining how much progress the student has made in learning the sound/symbol system and what further instruction needs to occur (Morris and Perney 1984). The Developmental Spelling Test uses this research as a basis for scoring and evaluation.

Table 9.1 Developmental Stages of Spelling

Stage 1: Prephonetic Stage Speech sounds represented with letters of the alphabet. Use of one letter for a whole word or first and/or last consonant.	i lc t g hm h rd i cr
Stage 2: Phonetic Stage Fairly reliable use of letter-sound strategy to represent the phonological pattern of the word. First, last letters, and vowel are usually present, but the vowel might be incorrect.	i lik t go hom. he rod in a cro.
Stage 3: Transitional Stage Short vowels used correctly, long vowels are indicated, but might not be spelled correctly. Spelling is nearly correct.	I lick to go hoem. He rod in a car.
Stage 4: Conventional Stage Correct conventions of spelling.	I like to go home. He rode in a car.

Using the Developmental Spelling Test

1. Select the test that matches the grade level of the student and *not* the reading level. For example, if a student is in fourth grade and reading at a first-grade level, choose the test for fourth grade.

2. The test can be given in the same manner as a regular spelling test to a whole classroom for screening purposes or to an individual student.

3. The developmental spelling list and scoring can be used to assess growth in first grade and screen for remedial readers in grades 2 to 12. Rarely will you have a poor reader with a visual memory good enough to score well on the test. For example, out of a school of 300 students, there was one such student. For this reason, phonemic awareness tests should be used to follow up on all students.

Scoring the Developmental Spelling Test

Number of Points	Description
0	**No letters are correct.**
1	**1 letter is correct.** This can be at the beginning or at the end.
2	**2 letters are correct.** Only beginning and end letters are correct OR only beginning sound and vowel sound are correct
3	**3 letters are correct.** Spelled phonetically but some sounds are *left out*. Main vowel (vowel of the accented syllable) ***must be correct*** although the choice of the grapheme representation may be incorrect such as e to represent ee or ea.
4	*All* the sounds are represented, although the correct spelling of the sound may not be used (for example, sircl for circle). Spelled phonetically correct. No sounds have been left out and no sounds have been added. No reversal of letters such as d/b. This knocks the score back to a 3.
5	Correct spelling is used.

Developmental Spelling Lists

A: Grade 1	B: Grades 2, 3	C: Grades 4, 5	D: Grades 6–8
back	track	basket	packaging
sink	switched	pitcher	literature
mail	wrong	belonging	successful
dress	when	dentist	destination
picking	crunch	questions	cucumber
lake	place	publicly	replacement
rice	skating	placement	investigate
peeked	screams	inflated	argument
stamp	crawled	partner	awesome
sold	brook	awful	mistook
light	germ	bookkeepers	torment
seed	thirsty	ordered	permanently
dragon	choices	certainly	confirmation
stick	houses	confirm	poisonous
side	true	ointment	bountiful
feet	phone	proudly	avenue
bed	quiet	value	physician
gate	circle	elephant	equipment
test	gem	quail	participated
pen	morning	circus	gigantic

General Interpretation of Scores

Test scores 90 and over indicate that the student needs no intervention. We all make some mistakes in spelling.

Test scores between 80 and 89 indicate weak skills that need to be addressed either through individual help or whole class activities.

Test scores below 80 indicate a need for individual or small-group interventions. These students need phonemic awareness games and instruction in all of the graphemes.

Information Gained from the DST

Phonemic Awareness Skills

The Developmental Spelling Test reveals which sounds are difficult for students to hear and whether or not the student hears all of the sounds in words.

- Do they hear the beginning sounds? End sounds? Middle sounds?
- Do they hear all the sounds? Omit sounds? Add sounds?

- Can they hear the difference between voiced and unvoiced pairs?
- Do they use letters for sounds (q for cu or r for ar)?
- Are there letter reversals?
- Are they trying to visually remember the word? The word may have some of the correct letters but they are in scrambled order, such as otiment for ointment.
- Were some of the words previously learned? If a student is making gross errors on words, but suddenly spells one or two words correctly, it is noticeable that the correct spelling came from memory and not from understanding word structure.

Language Structure

The test also reveals the basic understanding of the spellings of the phonemes and the "Real Rules" of English.

- Do they know how to spell the sounds of speech?
- Do they know how to add prefixes and suffixes?
- Which graphemes do they know? Which ones don't they know?
- What fundamental rules do they not understand? (for example, how e, i, and y affect other letters; or how to change the y to i)

Interpreting DST Scores

The DST scores are interpreted by the range in which the fall and not by the exact score. This gives some flexibility in scoring when it is not clear how many points should be assigned to a word. Whatever is decided, the total score will usually fall within the same range. What is the real difference between a score of 74 and 68? There is no difference.

The following general explanations will guide you in identifying the needs of readers in grades 2 and up. Be aware that there are individual students who do not fit the description. That is why additional assessments help give the full picture.

Good Readers: DST Scores of 90 to 100

Good readers benefit from good instruction in the reading process, comprehension, and vocabulary. Ninety-nine percent of these students most likely read at grade level and above.

Fair Readers: DST Scores of 85 to 90

Fair readers have a few "holes" in their understanding of language structure, but mainly need good instruction in the reading process, comprehension, and vocabulary. Whole class instruction in the spellings of the phonemes and the "Real Rules" of English helps these students.

Most of the time they read at grade level, although some in this group fall behind if they do not have phonemic awareness, do not know the grapheme spellings, or do not have enough opportunity to read.

Poor Readers: DST Scores of 80 to 84

These students have some skill deficiencies and may or may not read at grade level. Some may read one or two grade levels below their grade. They benefit from instruction in phonemic awareness, spellings of the phonemes, language structure, and vocabulary, although they have more vocabulary development than those with lower scores. They may know how to decode and are fluent in reading, but benefit from instruction that increases reading speed because they are often slow readers. These students can progress almost immediately to spelling and decoding multi-syllable words

Poor Readers: DST Scores of 50 to 79

Most remedial readers fall into this group. These students usually read two or more grade levels *below* their grade, with most not reading above the fourth-grade level. They do not have phonemic awareness, often do not understand the alphabetic principle, do not know the spellings of the graphemes, and do not understand the structure of the language.

Their inability to decode may not be obvious because they have memorized so many words and have developed highly sophisticated compensation skills. Instead, this inability to decode may appear as "not liking to read," "word calling," or "the inability to comprehend much of what is read."

Vocabulary development has been impaired unless they have received stimulation from listening to books on tape and/or from being engaged in meaningful discussions in the home. Once they can decode, they need to be taught fluency and how to increase their reading speed. When taught the missing skills, these students usually make significant progress (four to nine grade levels in a year).

Very Poor Readers: DST Scores of 49 and Below

These students usually read at a low level, often at the first-grade level. Although they know all of their letters and sounds, they may confuse a few of the consonants, such as w or y. They do not have phonemic awareness, do not understand the alphabetic principle, do not know the spellings of the graphemes, and do not understand the structure of the language. They often have difficulty with voiced and unvoiced pairs (/b/p/, /d/t/, /ch/j/). Many have difficulty with letter reversals. Their vocabulary development has been grossly impaired through lack of reading.

Some of these students may have some type of cognitive delay or impairment and often (but not always) receive some kind of special services from the school. They also could be English language learners.

Most of these students can make significant progress (two to three grade levels in a year) when their weaknesses are targeted and taught. Usually, this requires extra practice one-on-one or in a small group with plenty of repetition in the skills being taught. Once they learn to read, they will need help in gaining fluency.

Scoring a DST

The percentage of students in your school who pass state-mandated test will most likely be near the percentage of students who pass the Developmental Spelling Test at 80 and above. In a local middle school, we administered the Developmental Spelling Test to sixth and eighth grade students. These were the results (Sporleder 2009).

	6th Grade	8th Grade
Scored below 80 on DST	59.6%	31.7%
Failed state mandated test in literacy	48%	38.3%

After reading through the scoring and the analysis, try your hand at scoring a test. This is a tool you will want to use in your classroom.

Sample DST: Real Test from a Real Fifth-Grade Student

Correct Word	5th Grade Student	Score	Reason for Score
basket	dascit	3	Reversal is an automatic 3 or lower. Does not understand the marker makes the c say /s/.
pitcher	piche	2	Only 2 sounds, beginning and middle.
belonging	deeloing	2 or 3	Reversal is an automatic 3 or lower. The main vowel /o/ is meshed with the ing. If it is counted, it makes the score a 3. Understands _ing.
dentist	bentest	3	Reversal is an automatic 3 or lower. All sounds represented.
questions	cwetns	2 or 3	Depends on whether the cw should be counted as qu. Used _s correctly.
publicly	pudlik	2	Only beginning and middle sound correct. Does not know the suffix _ly.
placement	plaesmnt	3	Beginning, middle, and end correct. Trying to use the marker to make the a long. Does not know suffix ment.
inflated	infated	3	Beginning, middle, and end correct. Used _ed correctly. Missing sounds.
partner	partner	5	☺ Incongruent with all the word knowledge. Did the student just memorize this?
awful	oful	4	Phonetically correct. Understands suffix _ful.
bookkeeper	dukcepers	3	Reversal is an automatic 3 or lower. Does not understand that markers make c say /s/. Does not understand compound words. u does say /oo/ as in put.
ordered	orberb	3	Reversal, so still counts b as /d/ in the middle and end. Does not use _ed correctly.
certainly	sertele	3	Beginning, middle, and end correct. Does not know the suffix _ly
confirm	cunferm	4	Phonetically correct.
ointment	itmit	1	End sound correct. Does not understand suffix _ment or the spelling oi.
proudly	prodle	1 or 2	Beginning sound correct. Does not know /ou/ or suffix _ly.
value	valu	4	Phonetically correct.
elephant	elufet	2 or 3	Beginning and end correct; middle e does say /u/.
quail	cwael	3 or 4	Phonetically correct. 4 if count cw as /qu/.
circus	secus	2 or 3	Beginning and end correct. /r/ not represented.
TOTAL		55–61	

Sample DST: Analysis

Although this student scores right on the line between a poor reader and a very poor reader, he, in fact, could only read a handful of words and was not able to even read a first-grade primer.

He did not hear all the sounds in words, although he could usually hear the beginning and end sounds. He definitely did not know the spellings of the graphemes, how to spell them, or how to add suffixes, and he did not understand the impact of the markers on the letter c. Letter reversals were also a problem.

After 45 hours of instruction that included phonemic awareness games, phoneme-based phonics that used spelling before reading, and some extra practice in between, he was able to read at grade level.

Sample DST: Now try it yourself. This, too, is a test of a real student.

Correct Word	Third Grade Student	Score
track	trak	
switched	wich	
wrong	wrag	
when	when	
crunch	cruch	
place	places	
skating	skating	
screams	skeams	
crawled	cared	
brook	brooker	
germ	gram	
thirsty	creet	
choice	chess	
houses	housse	
true	chel	
phone	phone	
quiet	qiet	
circle	sodl	
gem	gym	
morning	moning	

Answers are found at the end of the chapter.

Phonemic Awareness Assessments

Phoneme Segmentation

Materials: colored counting chips, two colors, ten each.

Give kindergarten students only ten of one color. They will not be distinguishing between consonants and vowels.

Today we're going to play some games with words.

I will say a word and I want you to break it apart. You are going to tell me each sound in the word in order.

Let's try these together. Listen to the sounds in *dog*. /d/ - /o/ - /g/

Now listen to the sounds in the word *tell*. /t/ - /e/ - /l/

Now you try one. What are the sounds in *ride*? /r/ - /i/ - /d/

Give the student the chips.

Now instead of telling me the sounds right away, put a chip down for every sound you hear in the word. I will say a word and you will put down a chip for every sound you hear in the word. You will not be spelling the word—only putting a chip for every sound.

*The _____ (name the color) **will be consonants.***

The _____ (name the color) will be vowels.

What are vowels? If the child has no idea, then tell the child to use any color he or she wants.

If the sound is a consonant, put down _____ (color).

If the sound is a vowel, put down _____ (color).

NOTE: Kindergarten students will NOT be making this distinction.

Do TWO practice words before you start recording:.

- Say the word.
- Have the student put down the chips.
- Then have the student say each sound as he/she points to the appropriate chip.
- If the chips are incorrect, help the student correct it.
- On the record sheet, put a slash through every incorrect chip. Ø

Students will lay down one chip for every sound in a word. The black and white circles provide the answers for the correct arrangement of chips.

This is an example for the word *destitute*.

d | e | s | t | i | t | u | t

Phonemic Segmentation Record Sheet

Level K   Use for kindergarten and early first grade
Level 1   Use for grades 1 and early second grade
Level 2   Use for grade 2 through about grade 4
Level 3   Use for grades 5 and up

	Words	Chips	Question to Ask Student about a Word*
Practice	mat	● ● ●	
K	go	● ●	
1–2	little	● ○ ● ●	
3 and up	computer	● ○ ● ● ○ ● ●	
Level K	me	● ●	*What sound do you hear at the end of the word? /e/ How do you usually spell /e/ at the end of a word? y.
Level 1	bent	● ○ ● ●	
Level 2	nicely*	● ○ ● ● ○	
Level 3	perspective	● ● ● ● ○ ● ● ○ ●	
Level K	pet	● ● ●	*What sound do you hear at the end of the word? /t/ How is spelled? ed / ed/ can say /ud/, /d/, or /t/. What does it say here? /t/
Level 1	funny	● ○ ● ○	
Level 2	mismatched*	● ○ ● ● ○ ● ●	
Level 3	motivation	● ○ ● ○ ● ○ ● ○ ●	
Level K	home	● ● ●	*What sound do you hear at the end of the word? /e/ How do you usually spell /e/ at the end of a word? y.
Level 1	wiser	● ○ ● ●	
Level 2	unwisely*	○ ● ● ○ ● ● ○	
Level 3	sophisticated	● ○ ● ○ ● ● ○ ● ○ ● ○ ●	
Level K	plant	● ● ● ● ●	*What sound do you hear at the end of the word? /l/ Except for really short words like ball and tall, how do you usually spell /l/ at the end of the word? le.
Level 1	platter	● ● ○ ● ●	
Level 2	flexible*	● ● ○ ● ○ ● ●	
Level 3	proclamation	● ● ○ ● ● ○ ● ○ ● ○ ●	

Phonemic Manipulation Record Sheet

You will use the chips again, but it does not matter what color you use. When I say a word, you will put down a chip for each word.

○ = indicates the changed or inserted chip

Manipulating Beginning Sounds

Words	Chips	Question
sat	○ ● ●	Which chip will you change if I change the word from *sat* to *hat*?
bat	○ ● ●	Which chip will you change if I change the word from *bat* to *hat*?
hat	○ ● ●	

Manipulating End Sounds

pat	●● ○	Which chip will you change if I change the word from *pat* to *pass*?
pass	●● ○	What chip will you change if I change the word from *pass* to *pal*?
pal	●● ○	

Adding and Deleting Sounds

bet		How would you change *bet* to *bent*?
bent	●● ○●	How would you change *bent* to *best*?
best	●● ○●	How would you change *best* to *test*?
test	○● ●●	How would you change *test* to *tent*?
tent	●● ○●	How would you change *tent* to *ten*?
ten	●● ●	

Phonemic Awareness Assessment Summary

Student Name _____   Date _____

Student Age _____   Grade _____

Birthdate _____

Phoneme Segmentation Summary

Each number represents one of the words given, Put an X through the number to indicate an incorrect response.

1 2 3 4	Distinguished whether beginning sound was a consonant or vowel.
1 2 3 4	Correctly identified the first three sounds of the word.
1 2 3 4	Correctly identified the number of sounds (correct number of chips).
1 2 3 4	Correctly identified all sounds *and* whether they were vowels or consonants.

General Summary

Put an X before all the appropriate descriptions.

_____ Student has difficulty distinguishing beginning sounds.

_____ Student has difficulty distinguishing end sounds.

_____ Student has difficulty distinguishing every sound in a word.

_____ Student has difficulty distinguishing whether a sound is a vowel or a consonant.

_____ Student has difficulty hearing the middle sounds of words.

_____ Student has difficulty manipulating beginning sounds.

_____ Student has difficulty manipulating end sounds.

_____ Student has difficulty deleting and/or adding sounds to a word to make a new word.

Indicate Level of Phonemic Awareness

Put an X on the level.

_____ Level 1: Hear beginning sounds in words.

_____ Level 2: Hear end sounds in words.

_____ Level 3: Hear middle vowel in words.

_____ Level 4: Hear all the sounds in words with four or more phonemes.

_____ Level 5: Manipulate phonemes (adding and deleting sounds).

_____ Level 6: Blend Phonemes.

Short and Long Vowel Sounds: Grade 1 and Up

Materials: 1 set sound cards with short vowel spellings (a, e, i, o, u,)
               1 set sound cards with all long vowel spellings (a, e, i, o, u, oo)

Here is an example of the short vowel sound cards. Use the spellings for the cards that are found in Table 4.2 on page 37.

<table>
<tr><td>a</td><td>e
ea</td><td>i</td></tr>
<tr><td>o</td><td>u
a
e
o</td><td></td></tr>
</table>

Word Levels: Choose the correct level for your student.
                 Level 1 for grades 1 to 4
                 Level 2 for grades 5 and up

Short and Long Vowel Sounds Record Sheet

Instructions to student:

> Lay the sound cards out in a row on the table in front of you. These are the long vowel sounds.
>
> I will say a word. Find the card that shows the sound you hear in the middle of the word. Show it to me and say the sound you hear in the middle.
>
> *What sound to you hear in the middle of the _____ ?*

Say the word twice.

Let the student find the card with the middle sound and say the sound.

Put a slash through any word missed. Circle the vowel that goes with the word. Tally errors.

Level 1	rage	hiked	soaked	mules	rule	meter
Level 2	enabled	assigned	explode	amused	duty	pier
	a	i	o	u	oo	e
Level 1	spooned	stream	thrown	traded	smile	fumes
Level 2	wounds	siege	enrolled	weighty	exile	bugle
	oo	e	o	s	i	u

Lay the sound cards out in a row on the table in front of you. These are the short vowel sounds.

I will say a word. Find the card that shows the sound you hear in the middle of the word. Show it to me and say the sound you hear in the middle.

Level 1	little	fetch	drink	sank	wished
Level 2	fiddle	wreck	shrink	shrank	persist
	i	e	i	a	i
Level 1	breath	strong	pen	plant	hung
Level 2	breadth	along	wrestle	platter	cluster
	e	o	e	a	u

Caution on Choosing Phonemic Awareness Assessments

When choosing your own phonemic awareness assessments ask two questions:

1. Is it truly a test of phonemic awareness?
2. Does it provide a tangible way to respond?

Phonemic awareness is a relatively new term to education, and for that reason there are both activities and assessments that do not require phonemic awareness skills. Use the same guidelines for an assessment as you do for an activity:

- Words are given orally. It starts with the spoken word and *not* the written word.
- Students, not the teacher, must isolate the individual sounds in a spoken word. If the teacher isolates a sound such as saying, *"Which picture begins with /t/?"* it is a categorization activity and not phonemic awareness.
- Students listen for individual sounds in words, not groups of words. They are not listening for rhymes or syllables.
- Students respond individually in a tangible way as well as orally. Some kindergarten and first-grade assessments require children to orally segment the sounds in words. For example, *"What sounds do you hear in the word cat?"* The student should reply

/c/ - /a/ - /t/ with a distinct break between each sound. However, in using this type of response, students can *stretch out* the word so it is impossible to know if they segmented or not. In order to determine if they can hear the individual sounds in the word, a kinesthetic component must be added. Students need either to clap as they say each individual sound or to put down a chip for each individual sound.

Informal Reading Analysis

The Informal Reading Analysis assesses the independent, instructional, and frustration levels of a student by determining the number of errors made when reading a selected text. Any text can be used to conduct an Informal Reading Analysis. However, in making a formal assessment, a published Informal Reading Inventory is a helpful tool because it provides texts at predetermined reading levels.

In addition to determining the reading levels of the student, specific information on missing skills can be gathered:

- Ability to recognition graphemes and sounds they represent (ee, ea, ie, ck, dge, etc.)
- Understanding of basic rules of English (e, i, y, changing y to i, affixes, etc.)
- Ability to decode small words
- Ability to decode multisyllable words
- Fluency (ability to read smoothly in phrases and with expression)

This assessment enables the teacher to find appropriate reading material for the student, develop flexible groups for instruction, monitor progress in reading, and design instruction to meet student needs. When students are taught phonemic awareness and phoneme-based phonics using kinesthetic methods, they will progress rapidly. The teacher must be informed so instruction is always meeting current needs.

Differences between a Running Record and Informal Reading Analysis

Most teachers are familiar with the Running Record and the data collected through that process. It is similar to the Informal Reading Analysis in that the reading and comprehension levels of the student are determined by the number of errors made by the student. However, the type of data gathered on reading behaviors differs. A *miscue,* a term initiated by Goodman (1969), is "an observed response in the reading process that does not match the expected response" (p. 123). The philosophical foundation of the miscue is rooted in the whole word method of reading so behaviors are based on the ability to recognize a whole word. These miscues include:

- Insertion—inserting a word that is not in the text
- Omission—leaving out words
- Repetition—repeating a word or portion of the text
- Reversal—reversing the order of the print or the word
- Substitution—using another word instead of the word in the text such as *away* for *around*

In contrast, an informal reading analysis looks for the ability of students to use the skills found on the Framework for Teaching Reading. It is noted whether the student is just guessing words or is using knowledge of graphemes and language structure to tackle difficult words. The following types of errors are recorded:

- Lack of knowledge of specific graphemes
- Lack of knowledge of basic rules of English
- Inability to decode small words
- Inability to decode multisyllable words

Table 9.2 outlines the similarities and differences between the Running Record and the Informal Reading Analysis.

Table 9.2 Comparison of Running Record and Informal Reading Analysis

Running Record	Informal Reading Analysis
Similarities	
Counts number of errors in reading to determine independent, instructional, and frustration level. Is the student fluent? Comprehension level is determined.	
Differences in Data Recorded and Analysis	
1. Substitution	1. Are students guessing or decoding?
2. Insertion	*Identify missing skills:*
3. Omission	2. Spellings of specific sounds
4. Reversal	3. Basic rules of English
5. Repetition	4. Decoding small words
6. Meaning change	5. Decoding multisyllable words
• Did the errors made by the child make sense or sound right? • Did the child use the meaning, structure, and visual cues to identify words and get meaning from the text? Did he or she use them in an integrated way, or did he or she rely heavily on one particular source of information?	• If student guessed, what strategy was used? (Looked at first and last letter, recognized a letter or little word, arbitrary?) This gives a clue as to what they know and don't know. • Do they know the sounds of the spelling in the word? (For example, in "beagle" do they know that ea says /ee/? "What does ea say?) Is guessing a habit? • Do they know how to use the strategy of decoding small words? multisyllable words? • Do they know all the words and sounds but still read word by word?
"It must be remembered that accurate recognition is *not* the major objective in reading. The goal is always meaning." —Goodman 1971, p. 14	The goal is accurate decoding that will increase reading speed and fluency, which, in turn, will increase reading comprehension.

How to Code an Informal Reading Analysis

Target Skills	How to Code
1. Are students guessing or decoding?	1. Use a G or D.
Identify missing skills:	2. Underline spellings they do not know.
2. Spellings of specific sounds	3. Note which rules they don't know.
3. Basic rules of English	4. Yes/no (circle words they can't decode).
4. Decoding small words	5. Yes/no (circle words they can't decode).
5. Decoding multisyllable words	

Relationship of Informal Reading Analysis to Developmental Spelling Test Scores

Developmental Spelling Test Scores are usually consistent with the reading levels identified using the Informal Reading Analysis. The lower the DST score, the further below grade level a student is reading. However, sometimes student scores will not be consistent with the expected results. What can each of these mean?

Anomalies

- *Students with low Developmental Spelling Test scores read at grade level or above.* The low DST shows that the student does not understand the structure of words so most likely has memorized the words. This puts the student at risk for reaching a limit in word knowledge and crashing.

- *Students with high Developmental Spelling Test scores read below grade level.* The student may have memorized the spelling of the words in the DST, but the low reading score reveals that the student does not understand the structure of the language. Or, the student may understand the structure of words, but has not spent adequate time reading to gain proficiency.

Student Reading Log for Remedial Readers

A student reading log provides some of the same information as an Informal Reading Analysis. This is a helpful tool to monitor student progress when working with students individually or in a small tutoring group. After choosing a book at the instructional reading level, the student records the following information each day.

Date	Minutes Spent Reading	Pages Read	Words I Stopped to Figure Out

Over time, the teacher can see the progress of the student. The student is reading more pages during the same amount of time and the number of words he or she must stop and figure out is decreasing. There will also be a change in the type of words the student has to decode. That means the reading level has become too easy and the student needs to choose a text that is at a higher instructional level.

Essential Assessments and the Relationship to the Reading Framework

The five assessments we just reviewed were selected to provide a way to monitor and assess the skills in our Framework for Teaching Reading. Skills can also be monitored on a daily basis through instructional methods that will be presented in the next chapters. We need to know where each student is at all times with each of these skills. We will explore how to teach and assess them on a daily basis.

Summary

Relationship of Assessments to Framework for Teaching Reading	
Framework for Teaching Reading	**Assessment Used to Assess**
Print awareness	• Informal Reading Analysis
Letter and sounds	• Letter Recognition Test for kindergarten and first grade • Developmental Spelling Test for grades 1 to 12
Phonemic awareness	• Phonemic Awareness Test for kindergarten and early first grade • Phonemic Awareness Tests for grades 1 to 12 • Developmental Spelling Test for grades 1 to 12
Alphabetic principle	• Developmental Spelling Test for grades 1 to 12
Spellings of phonemes	• Developmental Spelling Test for grades 1 to 12
Decoding	• Informal Reading Analysis for grades K to 12
Fluency	• Informal Reading Analysis for grades K to 12
Thinking while reading	• Informal Reading Analysis for grades K to 12

Answers for Developmental Spelling Test

This student has memorized words, but does not hear individual sounds in words, know spellings of many graphemes, or know how to add suffixes. Without instruction in the basic skills, this student will not be able to read proficiently.

Correct Word	3rd Grade Student	Score	Reason for Score
track	trak	4	Phonetically correct. Does not know when to use ck.
switched	wich	1	Only middle sound. Did not hear beginning or end sound.
wrong	wrag	1	Did not hear middle sound. Does not know the /ng/ sound or spelling.
when	when	5	☺ Incongruent with all the word knowledge. Did the student just memorize this?
crunch	cruch	3	Beginning, middle, and end correct. Did not hear all sounds.
place	place	5	☺ Incongruent with all the word knowledge. Did the student just memorize this?
skating	skating	3	☺ Incongruent with all the word knowledge. Did the student just memorize this?
screams	skeams	3	Beginning, middle, and end correct. Missing sound.

Correct Word	3rd Grade Student	Score	Reason for Score
crawled	cared	2	Beginning and end correct. Does not hear all sounds. Does not know /au/.
brook	brooker	3	Why the er ending?????
germ	gram	2	Beginning and end correct. Tried to substitute ar for er.
thirsty	creet	0	For some reason there is no relationship between the letters and the sounds in the word.
choice	chess	2	Beginning and end sound. Does not know the /oi/ sound or that marker can make the c say /s/.
houses	housse	3	Did not add the _es ending. Was the double s for that?
true	chet	0	For some reason, there is no relationship between the letters and the sounds in the word
phone	phone	5	☺ Incongruent with all the word knowledge. Did the student just memorize this?
quiet	qiet	2 or 3	Does not know qu must have a u.
circle	sodl	2	Beginning and end correct; middle vowel wrong; added/d/.
gem	gym	2	Beginning and end correct; Could not differentiate between /e/ and /i/.
morning	moning	3	Beginning, middle, and end correct. Did not hear /r/.
TOTAL		**51–52**	

The Many Facets of the Alphabet

H ow important is it to teach the alphabet? What needs to be taught and what can be skipped? Letters and combination of letters that form graphemes are stored in the Sound Symbol center of our brain as a part of the word reading process (see Figure 10.1). In order to read proficiently, the brain processes the symbol along with the sound in order to produce the word. This tells us that letter knowledge is necessary in order to learn to read. "Skillful readers visually process virtually every individual letter of every word as they read, and this is true whether they are reading isolated words or meaningful connected text" (Adams 1990, p. 18). In order to be a proficient reader, one must readily recognize individual letters and the combination of letters that form the graphemes.

Figure 10.1 Framework for Teaching Reading: Letters and Sounds

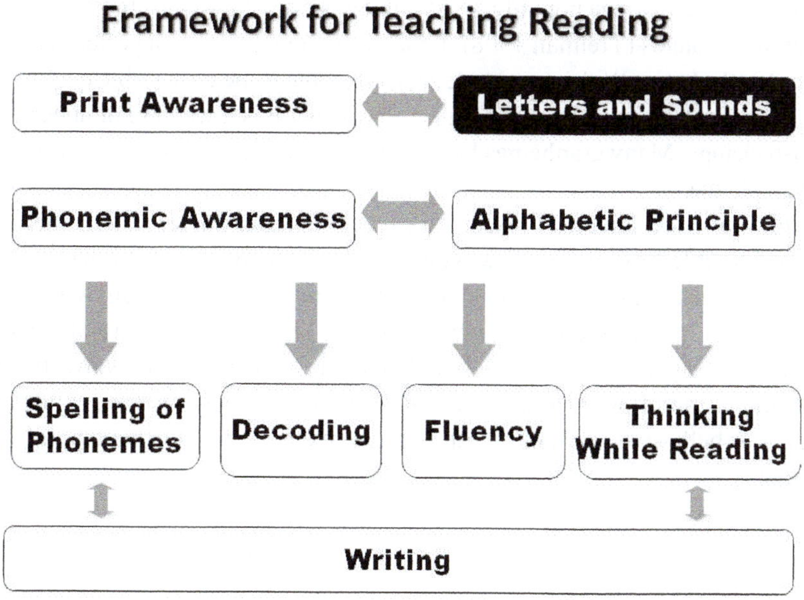

Framework for Teaching Reading

| Print Awareness | ⬌ | Letters and Sounds |

| Phonemic Awareness | ⬌ | Alphabetic Principle |

⬇ ⬇ ⬇ ⬇

| Spelling of Phonemes | Decoding | Fluency | Thinking While Reading |

| Writing |

Should We Teach Letter Names?

One of the debates is whether it is necessary to teach the names of letters or if just teaching the shape and the sounds are sufficient. Just how important are letter names? Surprisingly, there is a large body of research that demonstrates that letter-name knowledge has a significant impact on letter-sound acquisition. Children learn the sounds more readily when they know letter names than when they do not (Ehri 1983; Treiman Tincoff, Rodriguez, Mouzaki, & Francis 1998; Allen, Newhaus, & Beckwith 2005).

Most letter names contain the sound that the letter represents. For example, the sound /t/ comes at the beginning of *tee,* the name of the letter t. Letters that provide letter-sound cues in the initial position of their names are more readily acquired than letters that have the clue at the end or not at all (Cardoso-Martins et al. 2011; Kim, Petscher, Foorman 2010). This is consistent with the levels of phonemic awareness, where the initial sound is easier to hear than the end sound. In teaching letter sounds, this relationship can be brought to the attention of children having difficulty associating the name with the sound.

b, c, d, g, j, k, p, t, v, and z	Letter names spelled with the consonant + vowel, such as bee, cee, kay, tee, vee	Sound cue at beginning
f, l, m, n, s, and x	Letter names spelled with a short e + consonant such as ef, el, em, ex	Sound cue at end
q, h, x, y, and, w	Letter names have no sound clue	No sound cue
a, e, i, o, u	Letter names are the same as the long vowel sound	Short vowel sounds unrelated to name of letter

Letter name knowledge not only assists students infer the sounds but also helps them remember those sounds (Treiman 1998). Labeling an item provides an effective way for it to be stored in the brain. With regard to letters, the name is the only stable quality. The appearance changes with fonts, type of script, and whether it is lowercase or uppercase. The sounds also change. Many graphemes have multiple sounds, and many sounds have more than one grapheme.

In addition to the scientific reasons for teaching letter names, it also makes communication about letters easier. How would you refer to an object if it had no label? The idea that a letter has a name, makes a sound, and comes in various sizes is not confusing to children. In the world in which they live, they are used to objects and living things having not only a name but also making a sound. They know that dogs bark, cats meow, and lions roar (see Figure 10.2). They recognize the sounds made by a truck, a door bell, or an airplane. Letters are no exception. They have both a name and a sound.

Figure 10.2 The Similarities Between Cows and Letters

How are cows and letters alike?

- They both have a name.
- They both make a sound.
- They both come in large and small.

Forming the Letters

Writing is the best way to help children remember letters and their shapes (Honig 2001). Teach even young children how to form the letters of the alphabet correctly. Here is the caveat. The fine muscles needed to write well do not develop in some children until as late as eight or nine years old. We can teach them correct letter formation, but they may not perform well. However, children *will* write, and it is best that they attempt to write correctly than to form bad habits of writing letters incorrectly.

In order to reach all learners, we must use all four sensory modalities in teaching letter forms. When students only see the letter, we have limited instruction to the visual sensory modality. If we provide verbal instructions on how to form the letter, we add the auditory. If students write the letters on paper, we have added the tactile. Writing in the air, on a whiteboard, or with crayons on newsprint adds the kinesthetic component.

Introduce the name and sound of the letter along with the lower and upper case at the same time. This helps children associate all the information with a particular letter. Show students how to form the letters. Whether or not you have a required system of penmanship, the following guidelines may help you teach students how to form letters using reference to line letters and clock letters (Spalding & North 2003). Older students with poor letter formation and letter reversals also benefit from this approach.

Line letters

When teaching a line letter, show students how to begin at the top and draw a straight line down. The following are line letters.

Bb D E F Hh Ii Jj Kk Ll Mm Nn Pp Rr Tt Uu

Clock Letters

Clock letters start at 2:00 and go in a curve counterclockwise around the clock. This prevents starting the circle at the bottom or starting at the top but not enclosing the circle. When teaching a clock letter, young children need to see a clock with numbers and hands and identify the position to start the clock letters. They need to practice starting at 2:00 by writing in the air.

a Cc d f Gg Oo Qq Ss

Letters with Slant Lines

There are a few letters that start with a slant line. These still start at the top, but rather than coming straight down, there is a slant to the right or the left.

A Vv Ww Xx Yy

Horizontal Line Letters

There are three letters that start with a horizontal rather than a vertical line.

e Zz

Almost all letters are either clock letters or line letters.

Exercises in Forming Letters

If students are to learn how to form the letters properly, they need to have lined whiteboards and lined penmanship paper so they practice making their letters correctly. For any given letter, they should write three or four upper and lowercase letters and then choose the one that is formed best by placing an x above the letter. This self-evaluation helps students develop awareness of letter formation. Handwriting is practiced in conjunction with the introduction of new letters as well as integrated into any writing activities related to the words and sentences being introduced. It need not be a separate "subject."

Kinesthetic learners usually have difficulty with fine motor skills, and the inability to write well can continue as late as middle school. It is important for these learners to engage in writing activities that use the large muscles, such as writing in sand for preschool children, writing in the air and with crayons for kindergarten and grade 1, and on whiteboards for all ages. They also need clues on how to place letters they see three dimensionally on a two-dimensional surface. "The capital B and the lowercase b face the same way. One has two bumps and the other has just one." Or, "Your *s* is looking the wrong way."

They might need many reminders. The letters b, p, d, and q are particularly troublesome for them, although they can reverse other letters as well. The clues used for these learners will help all students, since the issue of reversals is not limited to kinesthetic learners.

For students who are having great difficulty remembering the name of letters, tracing five- or six-inch-high letters while standing at a chalkboard or whiteboard may help them. They need to say the name of the letters as they trace them.

Travis was a special education student who was mainstreamed into my classroom. He was seven years old but placed in the kindergarten class. Although teachers had been working with him since he was three years old, he still could not recognize or write a single letter or write his name. After he had been in my classroom about three months and I had tried all the traditional methods of instruction and encountered the same problem, I began implementing kinesthetic methods for him. I wrote his name on the chalkboard in letters about six inches high and had him trace the letters. In about three weeks, he could write his name independently.

How Do We Teach Letter Names and Sounds?

In the traditional classroom, we have focused mainly on the letter names and sounds of the 26 letters of the alphabet. This is appropriate for preschool children and kindergarteners, but as students advance to higher grades, the focus must be on all the graphemes that represent the 44 phonemes. First-grade students need access to all of them in order to gain proficiency in reading. A two-week review of the alphabet should be sufficient for most first-grade students before launching into a full phoneme-based phonics program.

NOTE: Remedial readers usually know most of the letters and sounds, even if they can only read a handful of words. What they need is instruction in all of the graphemes of the language embedded in phoneme-based phonics. Most of the activities describe here will *not* be necessary for them.

Preschool	Kindergarten	Grade 1
Single letters of alphabet	Single letters of alphabet	Review the alphabet
	Additional common graphemes	All the graphemes

The Distinction Between Letters and Graphemes

It is important to make the distinction between the terms *letter* and *grapheme*. Because graphemes are composed of letters, many of the activities that teach letters and sounds can also be used to teach graphemes. In these cases, the terms *grapheme* and *letter* may be used interchangeably.

Letter	A single letter of the alphabet such as the letter f.
	There are 26 letters in the alphabet.
Grapheme	A representation of a sound (phoneme) that contains one or more letters such as the graphemes f, ph, and gh that represent the sound /f/
	There are 120 graphemes in our language.

General Guidelines for Teaching Letters and Graphemes

- Use all four modalities. Be sure to include the kinesthetic.
- When working individually or in groups with students who need extra practice, use only the letters or graphemes that children have learned previously, plus one new one. Do not have children work with several letters or graphemes they do not know. For example, if a child only knows three letters, use those three letters plus a new letter.
- Teach letters that have similar shapes or easily confused sounds two weeks or more apart from each other. This gives students time to place the information on the first in long-term memory before the other is introduced. These are the confusing letters: m and n, d and b, p and q, and the short /e/ and short /i/ sounds.
- Keep an appropriate pace. Do not introduce letters or graphemes too quickly.

Grade Level	Pacing
Preschool	1 letter per week
Kindergarten	2 letters per week
First grade	4 to 5 graphemes per week

- Place children close to you who have more difficulty with these tasks so you can immediately show them the correct answer. Always give immediate feedback.

Difference between Introducing a Letter and Introducing a Sound

How we introduce letters of the alphabet will differ from the way we introduce the sounds of our language. The difference may seem trivial, but it will impact whether or not all students have the opportunity to become proficient readers. After the introduction, many of the same activities can be used with both a letter of the alphabet or a grapheme that represents a sound.

Introducing a Letter	Introducing a Sound
• Second skill on Framework for Teaching Reading	• Fifth skill on Framework for Teaching Reading
• Comes before phonemic awareness	• Comes after or at the same time as phonemic awareness
• Starts with the letter shape	• Starts with the sound (phoneme)
• For example, introduce the letter m.	• For example, introduce the sound /m/.
• Provides the letter name and sound	• Provides the way to spell the sound (grapheme): "This is the way we spell /m/."

In preschool and initially in kindergarten, we introduce the letter shape and then supply the name and sound, the second step in our Framework for Teaching Reading. This provides an essential foundation for all subsequent skills. "Today, we are going to learn the letter f."

By first grade, we introduce a phoneme and then provide one or more graphemes that represent it, along with the principles found in "Real Rules" of English. This sequence focuses on the phoneme and the relationship to the grapheme, preparing students to immediately spell. Students then engage in phonemic awareness activities and spelling to solidify their understanding. "Today, we are going to learn another way to spell the sound /f/."

Writing the Letter of the Alphabet or a Grapheme

After introducing the letter or grapheme, demonstrate specifically how to form both uppercase and lowercase of the letter using verbal descriptions and penmanship lines. If it is a new grapheme that contains previously introduced letters, only show them how to form the lowercase. Have students write the letters in the air. Slightly turn your back to the students so you are writing in the air facing the same direction as they are.

Discover How the Sound Is Produced

Talk about how the sound is formed in the mouth. Have students observe the position of the lips and tongue and where the sound is produced. This is the time to compare voiced and unvoiced pairs and sounds that are easily confused, such as the short /e/ and short /i/ if both of the sounds have been introduced. This is not meant to be a scientific description of the formation of a sound. The purpose is to increase student awareness of the physical differences in producing each sound and to add the kinesthetic component.

Acting Out the Sound

Acting out the sound is one of the most powerful strategies you can use.

This is one of the most powerful strategies you can use. For some children, this activity alone makes the difference between reading failure and reading proficiency. Some students are not able to make the letter/sound connection without this kinesthetic activity. Others learn it more easily this way. And all enjoy it.

What is it, and why does it work? Students act out the *sound* that an object or action makes. For example, for the sound /ch/, students move their arms in a circular motion at their sides like the wheels on a train and say /ch/ as they do it. This is a kinesthetic motion that also creates a mental picture of a train in motion. By associating the sound with the picture while using the kinesthetic, the sound is stored in the brain. If students are also shown the grapheme ch as they do the motion, the connections between the grapheme and the phoneme is established. This strategy has helped students who were unable to learn letters and sounds in any other way, including those with cognitive impairments. Once students have learned a sound, review all of the sounds learned so far by showing flash cards and having students act out the appropriate sound. A list of suggested motions are found in Appendix A.

BE CAREFUL! The above strategy differs significantly from other strategies that incorporate kinesthetic motions. Let's see why.

Almost all pictures that represent sounds are objects that *begin* with the sound rather than *make* the sound. Some curriculums provide actions for these objects. This is helpful if the student can segment the initial sound from the word and hear that *cat* begins with /k/, but that requires phonemic awareness. The students who need the actions most usually lack phonemic awareness and are unable to segment that initial sound. That means any action would not be connected with sound but with the object, which has no benefit in the language centers of the brain.

There are also visual phonics strategies that have students use hand motions to indicate the letter and sound. Students learn a letter and then associate that letter with a sound and perform a hand motion. There is no mental picture associated with the sound. In my experience, remedial readers can do all of the hand motions perfectly and yet cannot read because they have compartmentalized that knowledge. The kinesthetic motion did not help them establish the connection between the grapheme representation and the phoneme. Although this strategy may be helpful for many students, for some it is not productive.

Categorization Activities

Activities that require students to find objects that begin with a particular sound help them establish the link between grapheme and phoneme. The teacher identifies the sound and asks students to find objects, identify pictures, or suggest motions that begin with the sound. Always include the names of students and places with which students are familiar. These activities can be done in a small group, in an activity center, or individually on paper. Most students enjoy cutting, pasting, and coloring in the matching process. Students also need practice in writing the correct letter under an object that begins with the sound. Keep in mind that this is *not* a phonemic awareness activity, although it is beneficial in helping students learn letters and sounds.

Reinforcement of Letter Name, Sound, and Shape through Activities

Preschool, kindergarten, and early first-grade students need games to provide a kinesthetic component to learn letter names, sounds, and shapes. For example, students can be given two to six letter cards or tiles. "Show me the letter d." Students identify the correct card or tile and hold it up or move it. The teacher can also say, "Show me the sound /d/." Students would respond the same way.

Use a variety of activities to reinforce the letter and sound. Literature, pictures, poems, games, songs, art projects, as well as learning center activities can reinforce the association between letter and sound as well as develop categorization, rhyming, and phonemic awareness skills. Choose a variety of activities that address all facets of learning letters and sounds.

What Students Need To Be Able To Do *Each of these is a different skill.*	
Say the alphabet.	• Have a sense of where a letter falls in the alphabet—near beginning, middle, or end.
Write both lower and uppercase capital letters.	• In kindergarten and up, use lined penmanship paper or whiteboards.
When given a name of a letter:	• Write it. • Find it. • Say the sound.
When given a sound of a letter:	• Write it. • Find it. • Name the letter. • Identify objects beginning with the sound.
When shown a letter:	• Give the name. • Give the sound.

CAUTION: When planning your games, worksheets, and centers, be aware that many times an object will be shown that begins with the correct letter, but not the correct sound. For example, a picture of an owl will be used to represent the letter o. However, the grapheme is *ow* for the sound /ou/, not the letter *o*. When you are thinking of only letters and not letters as graphemes that represent sound, this error can be made. *Watch* for this in materials. We want to use only the correct grapheme.

Meet My Student

Kevin

When I came into the resource room in November, Kevin was a six-year- old who did not know any of his letters and sounds. When I tested him, sure enough, he didn't know a single letter. I gave him a letter card to hold and manipulate and introduced the letter name and sound. I then gave him a second letter card. We played games with the two cards where he had to show me either the letter that represented a particular sound or name. As he gained skill with the two letters, I introduced one more letter. I continued in the same manner and within three days, he knew eight letters. The kinesthetic component was what he needed to learn the letters and sounds.

Connecting Phonemic Awareness with Letter Knowledge

Phonemic awareness is best learned when associated with letters. As a new letter or grapheme is introduced, incorporate that sound into the sound card games and other games you have selected. The Phonemic Awareness Assessments of Chapter 9 can be used on a daily basis as instructional tools. Just change the words used.

Choose activities that help students progress through the levels of phonemic awareness, making sure most students can respond correctly at one level before moving on to the next. Even preschool students can develop at least the first levels of phonemic awareness.

Teaching the Alphabet Holistically

The alphabet needs to be taught holistically as well as individually. Students not only need to know the individual letters and sounds but also need an understanding of the alphabet as a whole. The sequence of the alphabet provides an organizational structure in our culture that helps us find information in dictionaries, telephone books, catalogs, encyclopedias, and other lists of information. Everywhere we turn, we must understand the alphabet, whether it choosing a movie to watch or setting up file folders on the computer. All are alphabetized. There must be an understanding of the position of a letter in the alphabet. Students not only need to get a sense of which letters are near the beginning, middle, and end, but where they are in relationship to each other. The order counts. All of this starts by learning to say the alphabet and recognizing the order.

Alphabet Activities

- Alphabet is posted in the classroom.
- Sing the alphabet song, pointing to the letters. This version uses the traditional melody but with a different rhythm, which avoids the *elemenopee* that confuses children. Each letter can be distinctly sung.

    a-b-c-d-e-f-g

    h-i-j-k-l-m-n

    o-p-q-

    r-s-t-

    u-v-w-

    x-y-z

    Now I never will forget

    how to say my alphabet.

- Sing the alphabet song and suddenly stop at a predetermined letter. "We'll sing to the letter m." Let students choose a letter.
- Read alphabet books.
- Have students put alphabet tiles in order.
- Use alphabet games at learning centers.
- Play "Show me." Students match letter tiles to letters on an individual game board (see Figure 10.3). You say the name of a letter and students hold up the correct letter tile. Because the entire alphabet is displayed on the board, students begin to understand where a letter falls in relationship to the other letters. It is an effective kinesthetic method for teaching the correspondence between the letter name or sound and the written symbol. Figure 10.4 shows how the games are used in a preschool classroom.

Figure 10.3 Game Board for "Show Me" Alphabet Game

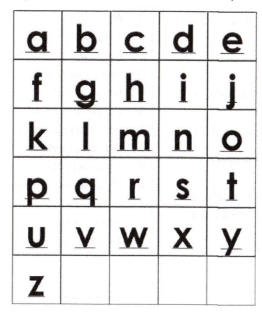

Figure 10.4 An Example of Preschool Activities

A Letter from Mrs. M. to the Parents of Her Preschool Class

First, we looked at the shape of the letter, and then used verbal cues to say how the letter was made. For example "A" would be drawn in the air while saying, "Slant down, slant down, go across." Small "a" would be, "Start at 2:00, go around the clock, come straight down." Each letter had its own verbal cues. We always drew the letter with our giant magic pencils (hands).

Next, the sound of the letter was introduced. We repeated it often, and described what it felt like in our mouths, where our lips and tongues were placed while saying the sound, and then looked at the wall cards that pictured things that made those sounds.

We then listened to various words that had the featured sound in it. We looked for things around the room, looked at things displayed that had the sounds, and we were especially excited to hear the sounds in our names!

We sang the alphabet song often. This version may be a bit different than the traditional groupings of letters. We sang it like this: AABCDEFG—HIJKLMN—OPQ—RST—UVWXYZ—Now I never will forget, how to say my alphabet. Singing this to the traditional tune, it has the advantage of doing away with the "elemenno peas." Instead, the name of each letter is distinct.

We sometimes even tasted things that began with the letters of the day. This multisensory approach allowed your child to fully experience the alphabet by seeing, hearing, feeling, and tasting the letters. The alphabet should be an experience!

We then got down to the business of writing. The children were watched and helped as they traced or wrote the letters. In some cases, the children's hands were guided (I tried to indicate when I helped by placing a star beside the letter). When needed, lots of individual encouragement and coaching was given, and they were allowed accomplishment with success.

We read stories, played games, and did art projects that corresponded to each letter. Rather than do many sit-down art projects, we got up and did "stuff!"

Activities			
A	Sang "The Ants Go Marching In"	N	Ate mixed nuts
B	Played with balloons	O	Sang "Oats, Peas, Beans and Barley Grow"
C	Decorated cupcakes	P	Played with the parachute
D	Played "Drop the Hanky"	Q	Had a quiet time
E	Played "Egg, egg, who's got the egg"	R	Rolled on the mats
F	Played "Farmer in the Dell"	S	Did somersaults on the mats
G	Made reversible, stick puppets "Glad Grins, and Gloomy Grumps"	T	Did tumbling tricks on the mats
		U	Did up and under activities
H	Did the Hokey Pokey, putting in "H" body parts	V	Ate vanilla wafers and delivered valentines
		W	Played wheelbarrows on the mats
I	Ice painted and added an Iris silhouette	X	Did exercises
J	Played with a mixture in a jar (oil and colored water); jumped	Y	Yelling contest
		Z	Took a zigzag walk
K	Practiced kicking a ball		
L	Licked a lollipop		
M	Played "Mother, May I?"		

Literature			
The following is a list of books we read in class.			
A	Abiyoyo	L	Lazy Jack
B	Baby Bears	M	Millions of Cats
C	Cookie's Day	N	Noisy Nora
D	There's No Such Thing as a Dragon	O	Oh, Say Can You Say?
E	Everything in the Whole Wide World Museum	P	Puss in Boots
F	Froggie Went A-Courtin'	R	Runaway Teddy Bear
G	The Gorilla Did It	S	Sleepy Story
H	Happy Lion	T	The Talking Turnip
I	Imogene's Antlers	V	How Spider Saved Valentine's Day
J	Jesse Bear, What Will You Wear?	W	Wet Cat
K	What Do You Do with a Kangaroo?	Z	Zoo Song

Alphabetizing for All Grades

Most of the previous activities are designed for children in preschool through first grade. However, alphabetizing will need to be taught to all students, first grade and up. Since information in our society is built around alphabetization, it is necessary for all students to be skilled. In order to complete the activities, students need to be able to read the words with which they are working.

Step 1: Teach How to Alphabetize

Demonstrate with a spelling dictionary how words are arranged on a page. How will you find the word you need? Over time, sequentially demonstrate and practice the skills represented on the following five different types of word cards. After the introduction to the particular skill, have students practice with sets of word cards. This provides kinesthetic practice.

Sets of Word Cards
1. Words that begin with a different letter
2. Words that begin with same letter but different second letter
3. Words that begin with the same two letters but different third letter
4. Words that are a mixture of the above, some different beginning, some same beginning, some same beginning two letters
5. Guide words from a dictionary and a list of target words that might or might not appear on the page with the guide words

Step 2: Play Dictionary Scavenger Hunts

Materials: Each student must have a dictionary. It is best if the game is played in a small group no larger than 12 students.

Procedure: Each student is holding the dictionary with hands placed on the front and back covers of the dictionary. No thumbs or fingers of either hand can extend over the edge to touch the pages.

Write the word that is to be located in the dictionary.

Say, "Go."

Students quietly stand when the word is found.

After all have found the word (some with the teacher's help), a student standing announces the page number where the word is found.

Types of Dictionary Activities
1. Find word. Tell page number.
2. Find the guide words. Tell page number.
3. Find word. Tell guide words. Tell page number.
4. Find word that is a noun, verb, etc. (specified part of speech, such as *light* that is a verb). Tell guide words. Tell page number. Read first definition.

Step 3: Show How to Use the Dictionary for Daily Use

Provide spelling dictionaries and/or dictionaries for each student or have them accessible in the classroom. Show students how to look up words to verify spelling when editing and revising their writing. Even first-grade students in the second semester are capable of doing this with a small spelling dictionary.

Which Activity Is Better?

Compare these activities. Which one is better? Why?

Activity 10.1   Comparison of Alphabet Activities

Activity #1 versus Activity #2	
The class as a whole recites the alphabet. The teacher shows children flash cards of the alphabet and the whole class orally identifies each letter as the teacher holds it up, They will either say the name of the letter or the sound of the letter.	Each individual child has an 8 × 11 sheet with the letters of the alphabet. Each child is also given alphabet squares (the same size and kind as the sheet) for the letters already learned. Child matches letter to letter on the game board by placing the small letter over the appropriate space on the game board. • Ask children to show you a particular letter/sound. (They lift the letter from the game board and show you the letter.) • OR Ask children to show you a particular sound.
Activity #3 versus Activity 4	
Each child receives four to six cards with a different letter on each card. As the teacher holds up the picture of an object or says a word, each child says the word after the teacher. Then each child must find and hold up the card that shows the sound at the beginning of the object and say the sound. Monitor and give immediate help to any child who needs individual help finding the correct letter.	The teacher holds up pictures of objects and the class orally tells the beginning sound of each picture.

Summary

Guidelines for Teaching Letters and Graphemes
• Teach both letter names and sounds, upper and lower case.
• Teach how to form letters properly.
• Use all four sensory modalities. Be sure to include the kinesthetic.
• Teach similar letters and confusing sounds two weeks or more apart from each other, such as m and n.
• Keep an appropriate pace. Do not introduce letters too quickly.
• Discover how the sound is formed in the mouth.
• Act out the sound.
• Teach the alphabet holistically.
• Teach dictionary skills.

A Constructivist Approach to Phonics

We have identified the spellings of the phonemes and the "Real Rules" of English. This is *what* we teach in phoneme-based phonics (see Figure 11.1). We have even identified at what grade levels these are to be taught. Now we have to think about *how* we are going to teach this content in such a way that students become proficient readers. How do we teach phonics without using skill and drill and rote repetition that ends up being unrelated to actual reading? We want our students to have an understanding that is demonstrated by transfer to reading and writing. That means we must rethink the way we teach.

Figure 11.1   Framework for Teaching Reading

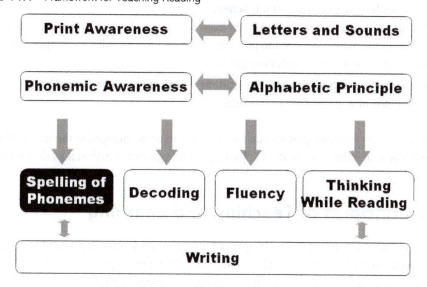

Transfer of Learning

In the traditional approach to teaching, the teacher explains and demonstrates while students watch and listen. A few questions or group responses may be a part of this instruction. It is largely, "I tell. You learn." After instruction, students engage in various activities that demonstrate they understand and can use the material with a fair amount of proficiency. Mastery is expected within a short period of time. Even if students do well in these activities, the information may not be transferred to reading if the activities focus only on separate skills. Students might memorize phonics rules such as "When two vowels go walking, the first does the talking," and ignore them altogether when actually reading (Ehri 1991). They might be able to identify and circle all the short *a* sounds in words on a worksheet, but not be able to read or spell words with a short *a* sound. The problem of transfer is real.

Fostering understanding and transfer of knowledge requires a different approach to teaching. To be able to transfer information to new situations, several components must be present (Niedelman, 1991):

1. **Students need to be taught concepts and principles rather than discrete facts. Facts usually do not help one solve a new problem.**
   In teaching phonics, the spellings of the phonemes and the "Real Rules" of English are the concepts and principles to be taught. These differ from the facts taught in many phonics rules because they can be applied broadly to thousands of words.

2. **Students must learn how to monitor themselves, being in charge of their learning.**
   How can we help students take ownership of their learning? We want to introduce a way for students to monitor their own understanding of the spellings of the phonemes and the "Real Rules."

3. **Students need to know how to apply those concepts to new situations. At first, this is under the guidance of a teacher.**
   How do we teach students to apply the concepts to words of all kinds? How will the teacher guide them? We need to provide activities where students can apply these principles to new words under our guidance.

4. **Questions are imperative to help students think through the situation.**
   What kinds of questions assist students?

From the very beginning of instruction, students must be engaged in the real world use of knowledge rather than the recall of knowledge. The question remains, how do we teach it?

Four Principles of Teaching and Learning

Researchers have identified four principles of teaching and learning that produce extraordinary results in student learning. These coupled with the principles of transfer will give us a framework for using a constructivist approach to teaching phonics:

1. Principle #1: Students construct their own understanding of concepts.

2. Principle #2: Questions are used as cues to prevent errors *before* they are made.

3. Principle #3: Learning is not a point on a scale but a continuum of behaviors.

4. Principle #4: Mastery comes with time and practice.

Principle #1: Students Construct Their Own Understanding of Concepts

"In order for a child to understand something, he must construct it himself, he must re-invent it" (Piaget 1972, cited in Chomsky 1979, p. 49). The key word is *construct*. Students are not listening to the teacher give a detailed explanation nor following instructions on how to complete an activity. Instead, they are producing a product using the concepts and principles that have been introduced (see Figure 11.2). The teacher does very little "explaining" and students have not memorized facts or rules. Instead, they are learning the concepts *while they construct the product*. It is in the process of producing that the concepts are understood at deeper and deeper levels. It is a personal endeavor that results in internalized concepts, rules, and general principles that can be applied in a practical real-world context. The student is active in acquiring knowledge.

A vital part of the construction of knowledge is dialogue. Vygotsky (1978) proposed that explaining the meaning to another supports reflective thought, or metacognition. In order to construct anything, one must be reflect, evaluate, and monitor the results. Verbalizing the justification for choices helps solidify concepts and expedites transfer to new situations. This type of learning "comes about not from isolated study but from social exchange" (Moran & Calfee 1993, p. 208).

How This Applies to Teaching Phonics

This is exactly how early spontaneous readers learned the code and applied it to reading. They reconstructed the code, learning the concepts as they talked about them and applied them. When we understand that we learn concepts by constructing, we know why it is easier to encode a word than to decode a word. Early spontaneous readers found spelling to be the natural next step after understanding letters and sounds. In a traditional approach, spelling comes *after* reading. Students are asked to look at new words and decode them, a skill that comes much later in a natural sequence of learning to read (see Table 11.1).

Figure 11.2   The Foundation of Instruction

Traditional Teaching	**Constructivist Approach**

The teacher explains. Students learn by watching and listening.

Students learn by doing it themselves.

The teacher guides them through questioning.

Table 11.1 Comparison of Traditional Approach to Phonics versus a Research-based Approach

Traditional Approach	Research-based Approach
Copy a word.	Spell a word.
Recite rules.	Dialogue about concepts.
Decode this word.	Build this word.
Repeat rules but not apply them.	Apply concepts to spelling and reading.

So how do these principles apply to teaching phonics? The teacher provides a one- to two-minute introduction of the spelling of the sound and concept and then guides students in building words before reading them. In fact, students will spell words they have never read before. How is this possible, and why is it necessary?

By spelling before reading, students must rely on their ability to hear the individual sounds in spoken words and on their understanding of the representation of those sounds in print. By constructing the code, the Speech Sound Center and the Sound Symbol Center of the brain, the two areas that analyze words, are activated. The student is compelled to process words in these areas of the brain, something that is critical for proficient reading. By spelling a word based on sounds and understanding of concepts, the schemata for the spellings of the sounds in the brain built. It also prevents the storage of the word as a picture without information on graphemes and sounds. As the teacher engages students in dialogue over the choices made in spelling, students reflect and monitor their own understanding.

To meet the needs of those who learn best kinesthetically, the large muscles must be used. If students spell words by writing on a whiteboard or manipulating letter tiles and not by writing on paper, all four sensory modalities are used—listening to the sounds, writing the sounds, and seeing the word after it has been spelled.

Principle #2: Questions Are Used as Cues to Prevent Errors *Before* They Are Made

In this approach to teaching and learning, emphasis is on dialogue, understanding, explanations, and building words rather than on recitations, worksheets, and copying (Calfee 1993). In teaching phonics, the teacher freely asks questions, gives answers, and provides support for the correct spellings of words. It is not possible for you to explain a spelling of a grapheme and its use in two minutes and then expect students to use that information to spell words. A longer explanation with examples makes no difference. Most students will still not be able to apply the information to spell words. Instead, one to two minutes is all the longer the initial instruction needs to be. After introducing the spelling of the sound, you immediately have students begin spelling words using the new information. Dictate the word and then ask questions, not to quiz students on their understanding, but instead to model the way they should be thinking about words. For example:

Write the word like.

What sound do you hear at the beginning?

What sound do you hear at the end? How would you spell that sound? Why?

What will you need at the end of the word to make the i say its own name?

Notice how these kinds of questions guide students in processing the information needed to write the word. *It will require you to anticipate any errors students might make in spelling the word* and ask a question *before* the error is made. Sometimes you will even have to give the correct answer to your own question. The goal is to help students spell the word correctly, without errors. As students become more proficient in using linguistic knowledge, the questions you ask will change to reflect the new concepts.

The emphasis in this type of instruction is collaboration between teacher and learner. In Russian and Hebrew there is one word that describes both a learner's learning and a teacher's teaching. The Russian word *obuchenyie* and the Hebrew word *lâmad* are words that recognize the active contribution of both learner and teacher in one act. In Western culture, the two ideas are separated, leaving room to assume that the teacher is active while the student is passive, or that the student is active while the teacher stands back and allows the student to construct understanding without guidance. Even when both teacher and student are active, the focus may still remain on teaching. In this approach, the emphasis is on the student's learning and the teacher adjusts instruction as student learning is monitored.

If the teacher keeps in mind the past or potential mistakes of the student when planning, then the student can be helped to think through the concept, skill, or strategy *as they are performing it.* In addition, the teacher can devise ways to mediate the learning *before* the mistake is made by using objects, phrases, questions, or other concrete means to guide the student's thinking (Bodrova & Leong 1996). For example, *before* a student makes the mistake of adding a suffix before throwing away the extra marker, ask, "*What do we do with the extra marker before you add the _ing?*" rather than waiting until the error has already been made.

In the traditional approach to teaching phonics, the interaction between teacher and student does not focus on problems solving nor on the collaborative construction of words (see Table 11.2). Instead, students are given the information by the teacher and expected to use it to read words.

Principle #3: Learning Is Not a Point on a Scale but a Continuum of Behaviors

The zone of proximal development (ZPD) is a concept developed by Vygotsky (1978) that describes the difference between what a learner can do with help and what he or she can do without help (see Figure 11.3). It is a tool that helps the teacher judge what kind of support students need.

Table 11.2 Traditional versus Constructivist Approach to Teaching Phonics

Traditional Approach	Constructivist Approach
Questions test understanding.	Questions guide construction and prevent errors.
Initial encounter is explanation.	Initial encounter is reflection.
Knowledge is strengthened through reinforcement.	Knowledge is strengthened through application.
Trial and error learning; corrects student work. Feedback after error has been made.	Errorless learning prevent errors or incorrect responses.
No prompts; after instruction must try on own.	Prompts provide assistance.
Does not anticipate errors.	Anticipate errors and create teaching routines that guarantee success.

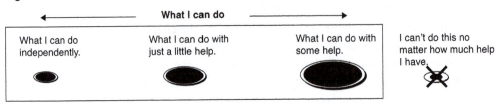

Figure 11.3 The Zone of Proximal Development

With only some help, I can do four times more than you think I can do.

At the lower level of the zone is what students know and can do alone. It is what the learner can perform independently without any help from the teacher. In traditional education, we instruct, and then this is what we expect and what we assess.

At the higher level of the zone is the maximum students can perform with some assistance from an adult or peer. With only some help, students can do exponentially more than you think they can do. This help may include hints, clues, rephrasing, demonstrating, or asking students to restate what they understand. What a student does with some assistance today may be done independently tomorrow. In traditional education, these higher levels in the zone of proximal development receive very little attention. Teaching and assessing is usually only focused on what the student can do independently.

Beyond the zone, the student cannot perform even with substantial help. The work is too difficult and causes frustration. It should not be attempted.

Realizing that there are different levels of performance and that these levels are natural and acceptable can help the teacher monitor the type of assistance needed. It also provides a broader perspective on assessment because the teacher is not just interested in what a student can do independently but what he or she can do with assistance. It is interesting that Vygotsky believed that what students can do with assistance is even more indicative of their mental development than what they can do alone (Vygotsky 1978).

We see the application of this concept in the workplace. In a new job, a person is shown the various tasks, but not expected to perform them independently right away. It is acceptable to provide assistance and cues to help the individual learn them. We know that eventually, those duties will be performed independently for the most part. However, there will always be parts of the job that require assistance, feedback, and consultation in order to produce the best product. It would be unthinkable to show the individual only one task at a time and expect independent performance on it before moving on to the next task. It would not be an efficient way to learn or to reach the goal of competency in the job. There would be considerable loss of time and talent if that approach were taken.

However, we traditionally do school this way. In teaching phonics, we teach one rule or letter at a time, expect mastery, and if that does not occur, we reteach. Often, what students can do with some help is not considered and yet the potential is there for students to be doing much more than anyone expected they could do. We limit what we teach students because we are only looking at what they can do independently. We know if we teach them certain concepts, they won't be able to perform independently so we don't teach them at all.

With Vygotsky's model, we have a way to successfully teach more difficult concepts. Assessment is ongoing with feedback given to the student. The teacher interacts with students to know what they are thinking, what they understand and what they do not understand. If students know how to perform the task, then adequate practice is given so they become fluent in the skill or concept. If students can perform the task with some help, then the teacher continues building on the concepts, knowing that eventually independence will come. If students cannot perform the task even with assistance, then the teacher knows the task is not developmentally appropriate at that time. Some students progress quickly while others students will need assistance longer than others.

This *scaffolding* provided within the zone of proximal development (ZPD) increases the performance level of the learner. The task is not changed nor made easier, but what the learner initially does is made easier with assistance. The teacher may perform the task with the learner, giving as much assistance as needed to make the student successful at the task. Within that framework, the amount of assistance is varied as the student progresses.

How This Applies to Teaching Phonics

In this approach to teaching phonics, the right level is one where you *must* ask questions to help the student perform. It is not too easy and it is not too difficult. It is too easy if students can spell the words with little or no guidance from you. It is too difficult if students need help with every grapheme in the word and cannot tell you why they use any of those letters. Just right is a level where students need some help from you to spell the words correctly. Just right means you must ask questions and/or give the correct answer in order for students to succeed. Always start just above the independent level and push as close to the top of the zone as you can. Constantly monitor how much and what kind of assistance students need (see Table 11.3).

A teacher asked me to come in and work with five fourth-grade special education students. I introduced the phoneme, the spelling of the grapheme, and the structural principle that accompanied it. As I began guiding them in spelling words, I discovered the teacher was working with them near the independent level. The students needed hardly any help at all. I kept increasing the difficulty of the words so they were near the top of the zone of proximal development. They could perform easily with that help. We then read the words but again, they were working near the independent level. I showed them how to decode

Table 11.3 Traditional versus Constructivist Approach to Student Assistance

Traditional Approach	Constructivist Approach
Learning is a point in time. Either students know it or they don't know it.	Learning is a continuum with various levels of assistance needed.
Pace is slow to make sure students master content.	Pace of instruction is as rapid as the student can process it.
What students can do independently is monitored.	What students can do with some help is monitored.
What is achieved by independent performance is assessed.	What is achieved by both independent and assisted learning is assessed.

"big" words, and with very little help they read multisyllable words with ease. The teacher almost fell off the chair. What these students could do with some help was exponentially more than they could do independently. However, with more practice working at that level, it would be no time before that would be the new independent level. What kind of impact do you think it made on student feelings of success? They could hardly believe they could do it, either!

The basic questions the teacher must ask are, "How much help does a student need to be successful? "What kind of support do learners need?" Besides guiding students in the introduction of a concept or skill, the teacher has a continued role by providing hints and clues, rephrasing, demonstrating, or asking the student to restate what she or he understands. The teacher must keep in mind that what a student does with some assistance today may be done alone tomorrow.

Most of the time, students can learn more and learn it faster than we think they can. If they can do it with your guiding questions, they are working at the correct level. Keep a good pace to the learning. You will be amazed how much they can learn. No, they will not be able to do it all independently at first, but with practice, they will. This is how my remedial students gained four to six grade levels in reading with 45 hours of instruction.

Principle #4: Mastery Comes with Time and Practice

Mastery comes with time and practice, not in one lesson. When we understand that learning is not a point in time, but a gradual understanding of concepts with various levels of assistance, we willingly provide that support. Don't expect mastery in one lesson. Also, don't stay on a concept until mastery is achieved to the neglect of all the other concepts to be learned. Instead, integrate the material into the next lessons by reviews in whiteboard spelling, word reading, dictation of words and sentences, and writing. Repetition of questions that focus concepts will eventually bring a student to independent mastery.

The way students deal with a particular misconception or error shifts over time. At first, students do not know what to do. Eventually, they will write as soon as you start to give the cue. Soon students will confidently write and self-correct without any assistance (see Table 11.4). Finally, students will perform correctly, independently. The amount of help needed for a particular concept has gone from much to none.

Table 11.4 Traditional versus Constructivist Approach to Transferring Learning

Traditional Approach	Constructivist Approach
Compartmentalized info; little transfer.	Transfer of learning; more rapid learning because applying concepts as constructing.
Significant anxiety can result in increased errors.	Successful.

Components of a Phonics Lesson, Kindergarten to Grade 1

These models for a phonics lesson will only be one segment of the reading and writing that students will do during a language block. A sample of an actual phonics lesson taken from Word Workshop B (Sporleder 2010) is found in Appendix B.

Introduce spelling of the sound.	• Give a one- or two-sentence introduction of spelling of sound. • Teach only one spelling of a phoneme at a time.
Show how to spell and write the letters.	• Write the spelling in the air. • This is handwriting instruction. Be careful not to model it "backward." • Students can sit or stand while writing the sound in the air three times. • Later, have them practice writing the letter/s and choose the best letter.
Discuss how the sound is produced.	• Talk about how the sound feels in the mouth with the tongue, teeth, lips, throat. • Helps children who confuse the voice and unvoiced pairs. (For example, ch and j, f and v, p and b.)
Act out the sound.	• Show students how to do the action (5–10 seconds). • Then do the action with them. • Students usually have to be standing to do this.
Review sounds.	• Students can act out the sound for the spellings they know. • They can play alphabet games like "Show Me."
Do categorization activities.	• Find objects, pictures, or names that begin with the sound.
Build words for kindergarten students who are ready and for first grade.	• Choose six to eight words that have only the spellings that students know. • Students build words with tiles or write on individual whiteboard. • Move at a fast pace: start at bottom of ZPD and move up. • Ask questions to guide thinking; tell the answer if necessary. • Anticipate and prevent errors—use errorless learning. • Have students who may have problems sit near you or someone who can give instant help. • Add suffixes and, for later first grade, prefixes.
Read words. **Read sentences.**	• Read words that were spelled and decodable sentences. • Teach how to decode both small and big words. • Talk about meanings of the words. • Bring attention to punctuation. • It takes reading a word 4 to 14 times to put it into long-term memory.
Play sound card game.	• Choose a set of sound cards to practice phonemic awareness.
Use dictation.	• Give the dictation as a spelling test. • Students write on paper without assistance. • They correct their own work. • If they find all their errors, they have a perfect paper.

Components of a Phonics Lesson, Grade 2 and up; Remedial

Play chip game.	• Phoneme segmentation of four multisyllable words.
Review spellings from previous lessons.	Students write answers on individual whiteboards (1–2 minutes). • Ask for the spellings. • Ask which spellings are usually used at the end, the middle. • Ask for any special rules associated with that spelling. • Always review words from previous lessons.
Always review words from previous lessons.	• Do power writes. Give students three words that have the same spelling, same pattern, or a base word that adds affixes. Students write on individual whiteboard (3 minutes).
Introduce spelling of sound.	• Introduce spelling of a sound (1 minute).
Spell words.	• Choose 10 to 20 words with spellings. Make sure they only have the spellings that students already know. • Dictate words while students write them on individual whiteboards. • Move at a fast pace; start at bottom of ZPD and move up. • Ask questions to guide thinking; tell the answer if necessary. • Anticipate and prevent errors—use errorless learning. • Have students add prefixes and suffixes.
Read words.	• Students read words they have spelled. • Talk about meanings of the words. • It takes reading a word 4 to 14 times to put it into long-term memory.
Read challenge words.	• Choose four to six multisyllable challenge words. • Students practice breaking apart and reading words they have not spelled.
Use dictation.	• Dictation requires students to write words both in the current lesson and previous lessons without teacher support. It is the bridge between learning how to spell the words and using the words independently. Because it is the bridge, it is an important component that should not be omitted. • Choose words and sentences that they will get mostly correct. • Dictate words and sentences to students; they write on paper without assistance. • The dictation level will be slightly below the level of words introduced. • Dictation can be done *almost* perfectly. Too easy is where there is none or one error; too difficult is where there are over six errors on dictation. • *Always* have students correct their own dictation papers immediately. If they find all their errors, they have a perfect paper.
Require independent reading at instructional level.	• In order to progress, students *must* read 30 minutes a day at their instructional level, which can include reading from other subject areas. Time it.

The Key to Working with Struggling Readers

Spelling before reading, providing assistance and cues, and working within the zone of proximal development are critical for these learners. Before any new concept, skill, or strategy is internalized, it exists for a period of time in an externally supported form. You can observe and hear how the student is processing information. However, by the time these students reach second grade, the processes have become internal and unobservable. As a teacher, you do not know how the student is processing words or what misconceptions they have. The concept is not easily accessible to correction. For example, some older students spell or read, but you don't know why they are doing what they are doing. You don't know why they are making the errors they are making.

The solution to working with these students is to have them spell words on a whiteboard so they are working kinesthetically and enter into dialogue with you on what spellings they are using and why they are using them. This quickly exposes the misconceptions and why they are making errors. Through assistance, they can work within the zone of proximal development and make rapid progress in learning to read.

How Do We Teaching Spelling?

Although it appears that this approach to phonics is teaching spelling, it is not. It is establishing the relationship between the phoneme and grapheme, solidifying understanding of the alphabetic principle. Students who are strong visual learners will become good spellers through this way of teaching phonics. However, other students will not. Students learn to read through spelling, but they learn to spell by writing.

> Students learn to read by spelling. They learn to spell by writing.

Traditionally, spelling has not been taught, only assigned. Students are given a list of words to study, exercises that use the words, and then a test at the end of the week. Rarely are the word meanings or word structures taught. Students are expected to memorize the words. As expected, the transfer to writing is poor. Even students who receive perfect scores on these spelling tests might not transfer that knowledge to writing. In fact, spelling has had so many problems, these are the kinds of things you hear:

"Some are naturally good spellers. . . ."

"I'm a poor speller—that's just the way I am."

"My dad is a poor speller, so I am, too. . ."

"Let's not teach spelling at all."

The rate of transfer from a spelling list to writing was so poor that spelling was dropped from the curriculum for a few decades. That didn't work. Educators found that you do have to teach spelling. So how *should* spelling be taught?

Spelling is like learning how to excel at a sport. You need some instruction, some corrective feedback, and lots of practice. How will you know your spelling program is working? Students will use correct spelling in their writing.

The Best Spelling Programs

These are the earmarks of a good spelling program. You will notice that we are accomplishing some of this through the phoneme-based phonics lessons.

- **The structure of words is taught. The list isn't just assigned.**
  Words are chosen on the basis of similar vowel spellings, suffixes, prefixes, special patterns, or word roots. Students are learning this through the phoneme-based phonics already. Choose words that students studied at least two weeks previously. You want to choose words that are near the independent level of the ZPD.

- **Words are in lists because it helps students to attend to the pattern.**
  If you use words from previously taught phonics lessons, you can group them by spelling pattern.

- **Words are used by students in writing and reading.**
  Assignments that require students to use the words in sentences, stories, or essays help them understand the real word use.

- **Attention is given to word meaning as well as spelling.**
  This should be done already in the phonics program, so only a review is needed. Also, if students are creating original writing with these words, meanings should become clearer.

- **Spelling tests include dictation of words and sentences.**
  Words and sentences are a part of dictation in the phonics lessons. In addition, short paragraphs can be dictated to older students. The sentences and paragraphs aid in the transfer of spelling knowledge. Students should be responsible for correcting their errors. This is the way they will learn how to spell.

- **Spelling is corrected by the student in all writing.**
  This is the best and fastest way to good spelling. Students correct spelling in their own work, learning how to use a dictionary to aid them. Once students have corrected the misspelling *tride* ten or more times, they remember how to spell it.

Reading Words

Learning the phonemes and spellings of our language is not an end in itself. If a student knows all of these concepts but still cannot read, we have failed in our purpose. So what is the next step in becoming a proficient reader? There are two additional skills needed to be able to read a text proficiently.

Meet My Student

Maria

Maria, a second-grade student, could only read a handful of words, hindering her ability to complete the normal tasks that were required at her grade level. None of the reading interventions made any difference in her skills. She was very intelligent but her lack of ability to read stumped everyone.

When I began teaching Maria, I observed that she was extremely bright and extremely kinesthetic. She caught on so quickly that two lessons per session were taught rather than the usual one. After 15 hours of research-based reading instruction that spanned over three months, she was reading at grade level. When she took standardized achievement tests near the end of second grade, she scored in the 99th percentile in almost every subject—science, social studies, reading, and math.

Summary

Four Principles of Transfer of Learning
1. Students need to be taught concepts and principles rather than discrete facts. Facts usually do not help one solve a new problem.
2. Students must learn how to monitor themselves, being in charge of their learning.
3. Students need to know how to apply those concepts to new situations. At first, this is under the guidance of a teacher.
4. Questions are imperative to help students think through the situation.
Four Principles of Teaching and Learning
Principle #1: Students construct their own understanding of concepts.
Principle #2: Questions are used as cues to prevent errors before they are made.
Principle #3: Learning is not a point on a scale but a continuum of behaviors.
Principle #4: Mastery comes with time and practice.
Characteristics of the Best Spelling Programs
• The structure of words is taught. The list isn't just assigned.
• Words are in lists because it helps students to attend to the pattern.
• Words are used by students in writing and reading.
• Attention is given to word meaning as well as spelling.
• Spelling tests include dictation of words and sentences.
• Spelling is corrected by the student in all writing.

Decoding: Taking Away the Fear of Words

O ur goal is reading. Students can have all the previous skills, but if they can't read, we have missed the mark. Fortunately, the skill of decoding is fairly easy for almost all students if they have spelled the words before ever reading them. They have already identified both the phonemes and the graphemes in the word, so all that is left is blending those sounds together to make the word.

When you have worked with students and observed how easily they can build words with their knowledge of phonemes and graphemes, you will have also observed how they can spell a word perfectly, but have no idea how to read it. It brings home the fact that decoding is a very different skill than spelling or phonemic awareness. We just have to help them take the next step (see Figure 12.1). Remember, it was one of the last skills early spontaneous readers acquired.

What is decoding? Decoding is the ability to look at a word, attach a sound to each grapheme, and then blend those sounds together. You decode in the exactly the same way the brain "reads." It involves breaking the word apart and then *blending* the sounds together smoothly to create a word in a process we call "sounding out a word." When students see the word *map* but do not know how to read the word, they can break the word apart into sounds and then blend those sounds together in sequence, /m/, /a/, /p/ to read the

Figure 12.1 Framework for Teaching Reading

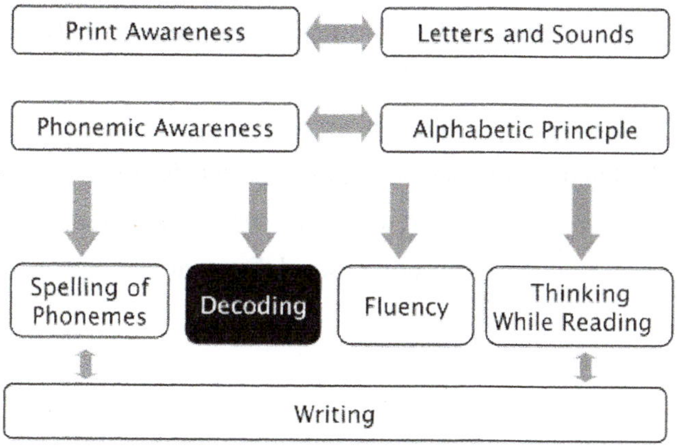

word. In contrast, students who have been taught a whole word approach to reading might look at the pictures, the context, and the beginning and/or ending sound, and then make a guess. There is not the sequential *sounding out* of each letter.

At first, decoding makes students slower readers. They must take the time to sound out the words. However, they will soon gain and surpass those who cannot decode. The more they read, the more quickly this will happen.

Decoding Simple Words

Young beginning readers need to be taught how to decode a word. Some will understand after just three or four tries and others need more practice. Most older remedial readers, even if they are reading at a first-grade level, usually understand the process of decoding simple words. They just need practice. Always check to make sure students understand the process of decoding.

To decode a word, say the first sound and then add the next sound. With those sounds together, add the next sound. Continue doing this until the word is completely blended.

map	
Blend the first two sounds together	/m/ + /a/ = /ma/
Say the first two sounds and add the last	/ma/ + /p/ = /map/
buckle	
Blend the first two sounds together	/b/ + /u/ = /bu/
Say the first two sounds and add the next one	/bu/ + /ck/ = /buck/
Say the first three sounds and add the last one	/buck/ + /le/

In decoding, notice how important it is to recognize that the <u>ck</u> and the <u>le</u> represent single sounds. If I did not know that, I could not decode the word. That is why it is important to know the graphemes for all of the sounds in our language.

How to Teach Decoding

On the first day after students spell the first words, teach them how to decode them:

Step #1:   Have students spell the word. For example, *at*.

Step #2:   *Let's read the word. What sound do you hear at the beginning? /a/*

Step #3:   *What is the next sound? /t/*

Let's put the two sounds together.

Stretch the pronunciation of the two sounds as you put them together /at/

Have students read the word together. Use it in a sentence.

Step #4:   Have students spell another word. For example, *hat*

Step #5:   *Let's read the word. What sound do you hear at the beginning?* /h/

Step #6:   *What is the next sound?* /a/ *Let's put the two sounds together.* /ha/

Step #7:   *What sound do you hear at the end?* /t/ *Let's add the sound.* /ha/ + /t/ = /hat/

At this point students need to practice reading words from a list. These are words students have already spelled. They also need to read stories using these words. It takes 4 to 14 times reading a word to put it into long-term memory in the Word Form Center of the brain. For some students, it may even take longer.

Problems Decoding Simple Words

Some students say each sound separately, but do not know how to put the sounds together in a fluent manner. You will need to show them how to group the sounds, It is very difficult to blend the sounds in a word if you try to blend each individual sound together all at once, such as /m/ + /a/ + /p/ = /map/. It is impossible with longer words. Instead, students must learn how to group sounds and then just add the next sound.

If /uh/ is added to consonant sounds such as /buh/ instead of /b/ or /kuh/ instead of /k/, you will not be able to blend the sounds together with that extra /uh/ sound. It is important to say these sounds correctly.

Some students are afraid they will make a mistake and so pull words apart that they already know. Reading the words with them at a reasonable pace helps them build confidence to read words that they know. I also tell them, "Your brain remembers the word, so you can just read it."

For example, Joel had just completed first grade, but was still sounding out every individual sound in a word. It was painful to listen to him read. After assessing him, I found he had all the skills necessary to read well. He was just afraid of making a mistake. He didn't want to read the word incorrectly. I explained to him that once he had sounded out a word his brain remembered it and he didn't have to keep on breaking the word apart. In order to help him gain confidence, I read a phrase in a sentence and he read it after me. I also read *with* him, reading just ahead of him so he was forced to keep on reading. I worked with him only twice because once he realized his brain retrieved those words quickly, he could read fluently.

Some students do not know that it is okay *not* to slowly say each sound in a word. They think sounding out the word each time is the proper way to read. Tell them that if they know the word, they can say it quickly the instant they see it. They just need to be told.

An extremely small percentage of students will have difficulty decoding. Students with mental retardation or other cognitive delays usually fall into this group. The following kinesthetic strategy used over time will sometimes help these students learn how to decode. If they cannot understand how to blend sounds together, they cannot become proficient at grade level reading. Practice must be done with words that have only two and three phonemes.

Blending the Word *map.*				
Holding arm straight or at a 45 degree angle, Place the opposite hand on shoulder as you say the first sound of a word.	Move the hand to the inside of the elbow as you say the next sound.	Start at the shoulder and slide the hand to the elbow as the two sounds are blended together.	Start at the shoulder and slide the hand to the elbow as the two sounds are blended together. Then touch the wrist and say the last sound.	Starting at the shoulder, slide the hand to the wrist as all the sounds are blended together. Then say the word.
/m/	/a/	/ma/	/ma/ + /p/	/map/

Decoding Multisyllable Words

Students may know how to decode and read simple words, but "big" words frighten them. They have no idea how to tackle them. In order to become proficient at reading, they need to know how to handle any word they encounter confidently.

The principle in decoding multisyllable words is the same as in decoding simple words except you are looking at chunks of the word rather than individual graphemes in the word. Once the word is divided into chunks, then you proceed as with simple words. You pronounce the first chunk and then add the next chunk. Saying the sounds of those two chunks together, you add the next one. You continue in this fashion to the end of the word.

So what is a *chunk?* Some suggest using the rules of syllabication to break apart the word. However, most of those rules depend on knowing whether the vowel is long or short. Since students don't know the word, they can't pronounce it and break it into syllables. If the teacher pronounces it and breaks it into syllables for the student, then they have been told the word and don't have to decode it.

There are easy tools *based* on syllabication that will accomplish the task. The word is divided by looking at the consonants. It is absolutely necessary that students "see" graphemes such ch, th, wh, sh, tch, and ng as a whole. For this reason, use only words with graphemes that have been introduced. If students recognize the prefixes and suffixes in the word, it expedites decoding. However, if students do not recognize them, it will not hinder their ability to decode the word.

Here are the guidelines for "chunking" words.

Divide *before* a single consonant.

Divide *between* two or three consonants in a way that makes sense.

Divide a prefix or suffix from the base word *if* you see one.

It is helpful if this information is posted in the classroom as easy reference for students while they are learning this process.

Observe the difference between the rules of syllabication and the rules to break apart a word you cannot read. You will notice the rules of syllabication require being able to read the word and knowing what sounds the vowels make.

Rules for Decoding Words	Rules of Syllabication
Divide *before* a single consonant.	1. Divide *before* a single consonant if the vowel is long.
Divide two or three consonants in a way that makes sense.	2. Divide *after* a single consonant if the vowel is long.
	3. Divide two consonants if the vowel is short.
Divide a prefix or suffix from the base word.	4. Divide a prefix or suffix from the base word.
	5. Divide two adjacent vowels when each has a separate sound.

Example of Chunking

The following example demonstrates how to divide a word in preparation for reading it.

The word is *unconstitutional* →	un / con / sti / tu / tion / al
1st break	Recognizable prefix OR between two consonants.
2nd break	Between three consonants. It does not matter whether the division occurs between the n and the s (con / sti) or between the s and the t.(cons / ti).
3rd break	Before one consonant.
4th break	Before one consonant.
5th break	Recognizable suffix (tion or al). If the suffixes are not recognized, it works to divide before the n (tio / nal).

The following example has anomalies that some words have. It might seem awkward to divide the word in such an unconventional way, but remember that it is only a temporary tool to handle the word.

The word is *autobiography* →	au / to / biog / raph / y
1st break	Before one consonant.
2nd break	Before one consonant.
3rd break	Between two consonants. The break can be before the g if students see the Greek root graph as a whole.
4th break	Between three consonants. The break must be between the ph and the y since the ph is one grapheme.

Once the word is divided into chunks, then start putting the word back together by saying the sounds of each chunk and adding them as you do with a simple word.

un / con / sti / tu / tion / al

/un/ + /con/ = /uncon/

/uncon/ + /sti/ = /unconsti/

/unconsti/ + /tu/ = /unconstitu/

/unconstitu/ + /tion/ =/unconstitution/

/unconstitution/ + al = unconstitutional

Students realize they can pronounce /un/ and /con/ and /sti/ and /tu/ and /tion/ and /al/. The task of reading the word has become manageable.

Pronunciation Issues with Multisyllable Words

Vowels are usually the problem in pronunciation. You don't know if the vowel is long or short. You can watch for markers and that will help many times. Tell students to try the vowels both ways. Tell them it is a real word. Many of these words are already in their listening vocabulary, so they will recognize the word.

- In multisyllable words, the u usually says /oo/ and almost always has a marker to indicate that it is the long /oo/. Examples include words such as constitution, exclude.
- Vowels can change from long to short or short to long as you add prefixes and endings.

apply ➔ *application*   (change in the sound *a* makes)

paralysis ➔ *paralyze*   (change in the sound *y* makes)

nation ➔ *national*   (change in the sound *a* makes)

Besides helping you figure out the pronunciation of a word, prefixes and suffixes sometimes help you know what the word means or where it is used in a sentence. The word *nation* names a thing. When we describe a nation, we add the suffix *al* and have *national* and it becomes an adjective. The prefix *inter* often means "between or among." Something that is *international* is between many nations. Teach the meanings of prefixes and suffixes along with decoding so the meaning is also stored with the word.

The placement of the stressed syllable can also change the pronunciation when prefixes and suffixes are added. Students need to be aware of this possibility.

prefer ➔ *preference*

expire ➔ *expiration*

Sometimes there are two vowels together that make separate sounds, as in *autobiography*. There is no grapheme in our language spelled io, so if students know their spellings, they will realize those two vowels must be pronounced separately. This is an anomaly that comes from Greek. There may be times where you must just tell the student to pronounce the vowels separately, as in the word *create*.

How to Teach Decoding of Big Words

Introduce multisyllable words late in first grade and then at the beginning of every grade thereafter. Two to four times a week, provide the students with four to eight challenge words to decode.

Step #1: At first, demonstrate on the board or overhead how to place slash marks in a word to divide it into chunks. Then show how to pull the chunks together one at a time to decode the word. Demonstrate how you may have to adjust the pronunciation because you know it is a real word.

Give this demonstration only once but provide help thereafter with any parts students may not understand.

Step #2: Give students a written copy of the words or have them copy the words onto paper or individual white boards. They must be able to mark up the words.

Step #3: Using slash marks, have students break the word apart using the guidelines for chunking. At first, they will break words apart using a pencil or marker to place the slash marks. It is not long, though, before they can break the word apart mentally.

Step #4: Have them silently and individually pull the chunks together to pronounce the word. As soon as they know the word, they can indicate that to you.

Step #5: Have an individual student pronounce the word. If the student has difficulty with the pronunciation, help him or her adjust it.

Step #6: Have the entire group read the word.

It will not be long before they are comfortable tackling any word, no matter how long and formidable it looks.

Problems Decoding Multisyllable Words

In order to decode multisyllable words, students *must* know the graphemes found in those words. That is the foundational skill for being able to read them. If there is a need for a particular grapheme before you planned to teach it, teach it when it is needed. Without this information, students can only resort to guessing.

Students who do not understand the process of decoding will try to "guess" the word by looking at the first two or three letters. Breaking this habit of guessing can only be accomplished by methodically taking students through the steps of decoding multisyllable words as soon as they begin to encounter them in their reading. Practice the process with them. And, continually reinforce the fact that it is faster to break a word apart than to guess. I love it when students say, "It IS faster to break the word apart than to guess!" Understanding this process builds confidence so students never again have to be afraid of running into words they don't know.

Summary

How to Teach Decoding of Simple Words
On the first day after students spell the first words, teach them how to decode them.
Step #1: Have students spell the word. For example, *at*.
Step #2: *Let's read the word. What sound do you hear at the beginning?* /a/
Step #3: *What is the next sound?* /t/ *Let's put the two sounds together.*   Slowly stretch the two sounds as you put them together. /at/   Have students read the word together. Use it in a sentence.
Step #4: Have students spell another word. For example, *hat*.
Step #5: *Let's read the word. What sound do you hear at the beginning?* /h/
Step #6: *What is the next sound?* /a/ *Let's put the two sounds together.* /ha/
Step #7: *What sound do you hear at the end?* /t/ *Let's add the sound.* /ha/ + /t/ = /hat/

Rules for Dividing Multisyllable Words
Divide *before* a single consonant.
Divide *between* two or three consonants in a way that makes sense.
Divide a prefix or suffix from the base word if you see one.

How to Teach Decoding of Multisyllable Words
Step #1: Demonstrate how to place slash marks in a word to divide it into chunks. Then show how to pull the chunks together one at a time to decode the word.
Step #2: Give students a written copy of the words.
Step #3: Have students break the word apart using slash marks.
Step #4: Have them silently and individually pull the chunks together to pronounce the word.
Step #5: Have an individual student pronounce the word.
Step #6: Have the entire group read the word.

Chapter 13

Detecting and Correcting Fluency Issues

W hat is reading fluency? It is the ability to read smoothly and accurately with appropriate pauses, tone of voice and expression. When fluent readers read aloud, they do so naturally and effortlessly as though they were speaking, Reading is automatic allowing them to focus attention on the ideas in the text and comprehend the meaning. It is no surprise then, that higher levels of fluency are associated with higher levels of proficiency (White 1995). The more proficient a reader is at decoding, the more likely they will be fluent in their reading (see Figure 13.1).

Good readers are fast readers. The association between reading fluency and oral reading rates has led to using oral reading speed as an indicator of fluency. However, reading fluency is *not* equivalent to reading fast. There is more to fluency than that. Focus on the

Figure 13.1 Framework for Teaching Reading

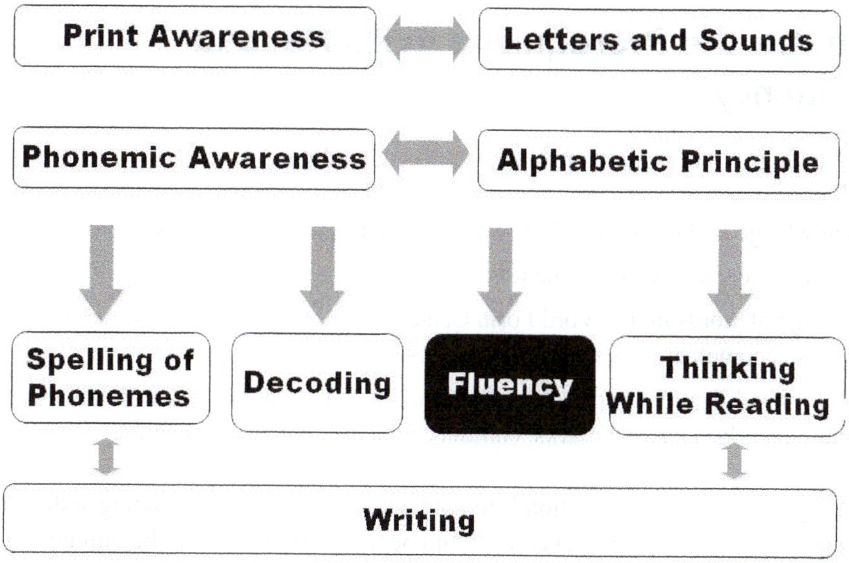

Print Awareness	⟷	Letters and Sounds

Phonemic Awareness	⟷	Alphabetic Principle

Spelling of Phonemes	Decoding	Fluency	Thinking While Reading

Writing

Table 13.1 NAEP Oral Reading Fluency Scale, Grade 4: 2002

Fluent	Level 4	Reads primarily in larger, meaningful phrase groups. Although some regressions, repetitions, and deviations from text may be present, these do not appear to detract from the overall structure of the story. Preservation of the author's syntax is consistent. Some or most of the story is read with expressive interpretation.
	Level 3	Reads primarily in three- or four-word phrase groups. Some small groupings may be present. However, the majority of phrasing seems appropriate and preserves the syntax of the author. Little or no expressive interpretation is present.
Nonfluent	Level 2	Reads primarily in two-word phrases with some three- or four-word groupings. Some word-by-word reading may be present. Word groupings may seem awkward and unrelated to larger context of sentence or passage.
	Level 1	Reads primarily word-by-word. Occasional two-word or three-word phrases may occur—but these are infrequent and/or they do not preserve meaningful syntax.

NAEP, *NAEP Oral Reading Fluency Scale, Grade 4: 2002* (U.S. Department of Education, Institute of Education Sciences, National Center for Education Statistics, 2002). Retrieved from http://nces.ed.gov/nationsreportcard/studies/ors/scale.asp.

speed of reading can misdirect the attention of the teacher away from the foundations of fluency to superficially focusing on ways to increase reading speed. Repeated readings of a selected text and memorization of sight words may take center stage in attempts to increase oral reading rate. Educators can become so anxious to improve reading rate that they may skip over the prerequisites for fluency. When a student has all the foundational skills, fluency can be taught, for the most part, in just a few minutes with follow up reminders (see Table 13.1).

What Are the Prerequisite Skills Needed for Fluency?

The following are the prerequisite skills for fluent reading:

- Knowledge of the sounds of all graphemes in the words to be read
- Ability to decode words in the text
- Storage of words in the Word Form Center of the brain for instantaneous retrieval that is accomplished by reading words about 4 to 14 times
- Understanding of basic punctuation found in the text: periods, question marks, exclamation marks, question marks, commas, hyphens, colons, semicolons

The goal of fluency instruction is to read with expression and meaning at the independent and instructional reading level. It should be taught from the very beginning. If a student can read one sentence, then both fluency instruction and comprehension instruction needs to begin.

How We Really Read

To understand fluency, we need to know how we read words on a page. We actually do not read word by word. Rather, we see groups of words at one time. The eye moves across a line of text and stops at intermittent points. These punctuated eye movements are called saccades (suh-**kahd**). For example in the sentence, "He went to the lake to fish," you will see the sentence in two or three groups of words. Your eye does not move smoothly from word to word, but stops at a group of words and then quickly moves on to the next group and stops.

You may see: <u>He went</u> • <u>to the lake</u> • <u>to fish.</u>
Or you may see: <u>He went to the lake</u> • <u>to fish.</u>

Your eye span can be two to six or seven words. These are the words that you see all at once as you glance at the page. Even the eye span of a first-grade student is two or three words. You can actually increase your eye span with practice. Rapid readers can see a whole line or even more in one saccade.

> How many words do you see in a saccade? Find a text and place a folded blank sheet of paper over it. Quickly pull the paper down and then up again to expose a line of text for an instant. How many words did you see?

Pointing at words, word by word, prevents the eye from doing what it wants to do—see groups of words. It will hinder the development of fluency. If a student needs help with staying on the correct line, have the student use a 3 × 5 card or a strip of paper placed under the line of text.

There is another unusual aspect to the way we see words. How do you know how to read something with the right expression before you have even read it? Remember, your brain can process words in the Word Form Center in nanoseconds. You not only see groups of words, but you also see five to six words *ahead* of what you are reading aloud. Fluent readers, who are reading easy materials, have an eye–voice span of five to six words. In other words, your brain has read the words before you read them aloud. In fact, you are doing two things at once—looking at a set of words while reading aloud another set of words!

Imagine how this could affect the accuracy of reading. We've all done it. We make minor changes to the text as we read aloud. We may reverse words, add words, or substitute words that have the same meaning. It is all part of reading with expression. Because you are reading aloud, virtually from memory, those kinds of errors will occur. These errors don't change the meaning. This is unlike the types of errors poor readers make. Instead of substituting *auto* for *automobile*, they will substitute *automatic* for *automobile*.

Identifying Fluency Problems

If a student does not read fluently, usually the first response is to implement strategies to remedy a fluency problem. But if the real difficulty is *not* fluency, hours of instruction will not result in overall improvement in reading. If a student is not fluent, the first step is to identify whether it is a true fluency problem or not, and if not, what the problem actually is.

The test of a true fluency problem is that the student can read all of the words without any hesitation. If the student cannot do that, then it is *not* a fluency issue. A student who merely has a fluency issue *can easily read all of the words,* but

Reads laboriously, word by word OR

Reads without expression OR

Reads right through punctuation as if it were not there.

This student can be taught fluency in a very short time using specific strategies that have been proven to correct the problem.

Fluency: Presenting Problem Is it a true fluency issue?	
YES Student easily reads all the words correctly.	NO Student stumbles on words.

If the problem is not truly a fluency problem, how do you know what the real issue is? Although it might look like a fluency problem, poor reading is rooted in a lack of other essential skills.

Step #1:   **Test for phonemic awareness using the segmentation assessment.**
This may be at the root of the problem. Inability to hear and segment the sounds in spoken words means this student has memorized many words that are most likely not stored in the Word Form Center of the brain for easy retrieval. This student would also have difficulty in word attack skills.

Remedy: Teach phonemic awareness, spellings of the phonemes, and how to decode.

Step #2:   **If the student has phonemic awareness, test knowledge of the spellings of the phonemes, using the sound card assessment.**
Choose several different card sets so all the graphemes can be assessed. A student who does not recognize the spellings of phonemes may stumble over words and read laboriously. Repeated readings of a text may bring a measure of fluency on that text but does not transfer to another text. If the essential skills are taught, then fluency can be taught in a very short time.

Remedy: Teach all of the spellings of the phonemes as well as how to decode words.

Step #3: **If a student has phonemic awareness and knows the spellings of the phonemes, test their ability to decode.**

For a young beginning reader, use a list of words that have the graphemes they know but require decoding. For older students, use a set of challenge words that require breaking the word into chunks and then blending those together.

Most students learn how to decode in a very short time.

Another Possible Issue

Brittany was in third grade when I started working with her. She did not have phonemic awareness and had no idea how the sounds were represented in speech. She was barely reading at a primer level. After just a few lessons, she gained phonemic awareness and understood the alphabetic principle. She could hardly wait to learn the next grapheme. However, even though she could decode, her reading was laborious, slow, and seemed to require her to stop and look at every letter in the word. Nothing seemed to correct the problem.

One day she walked into the room and said, "I know what we are going to do today! We are going to use the *ur* spelling." She spied the list of words on the table and while just glancing at them, she rattled them off: "nurse, purse, church.." We started the lesson and after spelling the words, she took the list and began reading. "/n/..../ur/...../se/" She could hardly read the words.

I knew then that there was some other issue. And there was. When a specialist tested her eyes, he found she had a severe tracking problem, a physical issue that prevented her from being able to track a line of text. Unfortunately, it was not until five years later that her parents found a doctor who was able to remedy the vision problem so she could read naturally.

This is uncommon, but as a teacher it is possible you will have students who have double vision or tracking issues. I have had more than one student who had to have the help of a physician.

How Do You Teach Fluency?

How you approach the teaching of fluency will be determined by your belief on how students learn to read new words. Oral fluency rate is an indication of fluency, but concentrating on increasing reading speeds does not teach fluency. It is the *result* of fluency.

Whole Word Method	Phoneme-based Phonics
Learn new words through memorization.	Learn new words through decoding.
Student reads memorized words.	Student decodes words and stores phonologically.
Repeated readings of a text.	Practice reading many different texts.
Timed oral reading rate on text used in repeated readings.	Ability to read smoothly and fluently any text at the independent and instructional level.

Fluency can be taught in a very short amount of time. Sometimes it only takes 10 to 15 minutes of instruction for a student to understand the concept of fluency and begin to implement it. Start using these strategies as soon as students can read one sentence. The following activities will help students learn to read fluently.

1. **Chunking**

   Show students how they actually read words in groups. Ask them to take a 3 × 5 card or a folded piece of paper and cover a line of text they have not read. Instruct them to quickly pull it down and up and tell you how many words they saw. They can usually tell you at least two words and often even more.

   Explain how the eye does not read word by word but actually jumps from one group of words to another. Practice seeing the groups of words in sentences that occur in their text and/or sentences you write or project for them to see.

   Show them how to read the "chunks" smoothly and all at once. For example, the sentence, "He likes to go fishing at the neighbor's pond." can be read as follows:

   "He likes"   "to go fishing"   "at the neighbor's pond."

   Students won't have to artificially chunk the words. The chunks are usually the group of words that they see in a saccade.

2. **Punctuation**

   Call attention to all punctuation and what it means. Demonstrate how the voice changes with different punctuation marks. This will include a discussion of periods, commas, exclamation marks, question marks, and quotation marks.

3. **Echo Reading**

   Demonstrate how to read fluently and with expression. Read a sentence or two with expression and have students read it back, practicing the fluency and the interpretation of punctuation.

   An example would be talking about the chunks and the punctuation in a sentence such as the following. Then demonstrate to students how to read it fluently and with expression:

   "Wait for me!" cried Anne.

   Have students practice it aloud together or individually.

4. **Choral Reading**

   Read a short passage fluently together. You read slightly behind the students. Let them take the lead.

5. **Reader's Theater**

   Take any passage and have students practice reading parts of it dramatically. It does not have to be a scripted play but any piece that lends itself to expression and/or natural divisions such as different people speaking or even different narrators as would be seen in a conversation on a talk show.

What Do You Do If a Student Reads a Word Incorrectly?

When a student reads a word incorrectly, the dilemma is whether to correct them and risk lowering their confidence or not correct them and allow the errors to continue. If students are constantly corrected every time they read a word incorrectly, they can lose confidence in their reading and go backwards in their fluency.

One solution is to wait until the student finishes reading the sentence or paragraph. It is possible the student will self-correct. We want students to learn how to think while they are reading and to quickly detect when something does not make sense. If we allow them to self-correct, they are more likely to learn how to pay attention to what they are reading and they become confident readers.

If the student does not self-correct by the end of the sentence or passage, give supportive feedback. Guide them in how to think about what they have read. "That didn't make sense. . ." Then ask a question about the passage that requires them to focus on the word. "What did the man say to the little boy?" If the student is unable to read the word, help them focus on the sounds of the graphemes and decoding. Give as much help as necessary, even if it includes telling the student the word. Then have the student reread the sentence with the correct word.

In planning instruction, keep in mind the ways to minimize students reading too many words incorrectly:

- Students need to be reading at their instructional level. That means they will only have to stop and figure out 2 to 5 words per every 100 words.

- Introduce difficult words to pronounce or unfamiliar vocabulary *before* students begin reading. That will provide upfront help with those 2 to 5 words they must stop and figure out.

- Have students read the story silently first before reading it aloud.

Silent Reading—How Important Is It?

The best of the best can only read about 180 words per minute orally (see Table 13.2). Why? That is all the faster we can talk. If that is all the faster we can read, we struggle to keep up with the large amount of materials we are expected to read on a daily basis. What used to be communicated by voice and phone is now communicated online in articles, emails, reports, blogs, and social media.

Students who read less than 150 wpm will find it almost impossible to keep up with the reading required in school. Rather than spending four or five hours a night completing homework, many opt to not do it at all. That is why silent reading and the silent reading rate must receive our attention. If the reading rate can be doubled, tripled, or even quadrupled, the amount of time it takes to read a text is substantially reduced.

Table 13.2 Oral Fluency Target Rates

Grade	Fall (WCPM)	Winter (WCPM)	Spring (WCPM)
1	----------	10–30	30–60
2	30–60	50–80	70–100
3	50–90	70–100	80–110
4	70–110	80–120	100–140
5	80–120	100–140	110–150
6	100–140	110–150	120–160
7	110–150	120–160	130–170
8	120–160	130–170	140–180

Three Ways to Silently Read Something

We have three different ways that we can read silently, and each one puts parameters on the speed with which we can read:

1. *Subvocalizing—max. 180 wpm.* Individuals who move their lips while reading cannot read faster than 150 words per minute because that is all the faster we can talk. Most poor readers use this method, articulating every word with their silent, but moving lips.

2. *Think–read—200 to 400 wpm.* Most individuals read using this method. Although the lips don't move during reading, every word is pronounced in the mind. Average readers read about 260 words per minute, which indicates they are using this method.

3. *Direct perception—over 400 wpm.* With this method, the individual sees groups of words but does not pronounce them in the mind. They trust that their brain knows what it sees. Most of these readers read between 600 and 800 wpm or more.

Age does not determine which method is used. There are adults who subvocalize and fourth graders who use direct perception.

Hindrances to Silent Reading Speed

Our goal is not to make speed readers of all our students, but to help them become proficient readers. By the time students reach fifth grade, they should read comfortably between 280 and 400 words per minute with good comprehension. We want them to move from subvocalizing to at least the think–read method of processing words. How can this be done? Here are some hindrances to faster reading. All of these can be removed with a small amount of practice.

Moving the Lips

Moving the lips while reading prevents reading faster than 150 wpm.

Reading Word by Word

This slows the rate because the reader is pronouncing each word, even though three to seven words are seen at a glance. Individuals with a narrow eye span of only three or four words can increase it to seven or more with some practice.

Rereading or Looking Back

Backtracking when reading is the mark of insecurity or can just be a bad habit. Eye movement photographs of 12,000 readers show that regression consumes one-sixth of reading time (Brown 1970).

Stopping at a Word or Phrase or at the End of the Line

Just pausing to decide where to go next slows reading speed. Many readers pause at the end of a text line before returning to the next line.

Increasing Reading Speeds of Students in Grades 2 to 4

Oral reading rates for those who can read in grades 2 to 4 may range from 50 to 120 words per minutes. Although, the demands of schoolwork have not increased yet, these readers need to form good habits to move into think–read and direct-perception reading, which will substantially increase their silent reading speeds.

By the time students reach second grade, they need to practice *not* moving their lips while reading. Otherwise, it can become a habit that hinders reading proficiency. Monitor your students and help them overcome this tendency. Some students have to literally hold their lips together with one hand while they read in order to break the habit. This alone will substantially increase their silent reading speed. If they are reading at 80 words per minute while moving their lips, they can immediately be reading 150 to 180 words per minute when they stop subvocalizing.

Increasing Reading Speeds of Students in Grades 5 and Up

After learning the structure of the language and being able to easily decode words, students are ready to increase their reading speed. Struggling readers who finally learn how to read well will still only read from 80 to 120 words per minute without direct instruction on how to increase reading speed. The following gamelike activities aid in removing the hindrances to reading speed. Do at least the first two in one session.

Materials Needed:

1. A book at the *independent reading* level for each student. This is an easy book with only one word per hundred that they do not know. It is not necessary that they have the same book.
2. 3 × 5 card for each student.
3. Stopwatch or watch with a second hand.
4. Record sheet for recording reading speed.

Timed Reading #1: Base Reading Speed

1. Have students read for two minutes in the book that is at their independent reading level. Time them.

> Now you are going to read in your book for two minutes. When I say "Go," begin reading and read until I say stop. Then mark where you stop.

2. Now have students count the number of words they have read. Usually, this is best by counting the number of words in a full line and multiplying that by the number lines. Then count the individual words in the partial lines. Once a total number of words is determined, have students divide by two. That will give the number of words per minutes. Have students record these numbers on the record sheet.

Timed Readings	Baseline	1	2	3	4	5	6
# of words in 2 minutes							
# of words per minute							

Timed Reading #2: Do Not Vocalize or Move Lips

1. Briefly explain the three types of reading students: subvocalizing, think–read, and direct perception.

> By vocalizing, you cannot read faster than you can talk. Consciously avoid moving your lips, even if you have to touch your fingers to your lips.

2. Time students again for two minutes as they continue reading in the book where they left off. Have them record the time on the record sheet. Many students find a significant increase in reading speed with this activity alone. Follow up with students to make sure they continue to avoid moving their lips.

Identify Number of Words in Eye Span

1. Explain how our eye sees a group of words at a glance. The more words we can read in a glance, the faster we can read. Have students discover how many words they see in a glance.

> Take a 3 × 5 card and place it over the line of words in the book. Now jerk the card down and back up, to make a split-second exposure of the words below the card (demonstrate). How many words did you see? What words were they?

2. Do this activity a few times and encourage them to try to increase the number of words they see at a glance.

Timed Reading #3: Keep a Good Pace and Indent

1. Sometimes we get in the habit of rereading words or sentences we have just read to make sure we have read them correctly. However, this not only reduces reading speed but also hinders comprehension because it disrupts the flow of the text.

2. We want to keep reading and not look back. Regressions can be prevented by using the 3 × 5 card on the line being read.

3. Because we read in chunks, if your eyes return to the beginning of a sentence, part of your sight is on a blank to the left of the beginning word. When we come to the end of the line, do not pause but rapidly return to the _second_ or _third_ word in the next line. That is, _indent_. Do not move your eyes to the edge of the line, but indent one or two words.

4. NOTE: I instruct students to not worry about comprehension but to force themselves to read as fast as they can. This is important to break the habit of regression. After practicing daily for about three weeks, they can reduce the speed to a comfortable level where comprehension is easy. This reading speed will be considerably higher than when they first started.

> Force yourself to read faster than is comfortable and resist the temptation to look back. Use the 3 × 5 card to help you to keep moving. Don't worry about comprehension.
> Do not pause at the end of a line, but rapidly return from the end of the line to the second word in the line (demonstrate)

5. Time students again for two minutes as they implement the strategies.

6. You may wish to do this activity two or three times in the session in which it is introduced.

Timed Reading #4: Read the Tops of Words

1. If we read the tops of words, we can read faster than if our eye rests on the bottom of the word.

> As you read, force yourself to read faster than comfortable and rapidly returning to the second word in the line. In addition, read only the tops of the words.

2. Time students again for two minutes as they implement all of the strategies. Some students will find no difference but others will see an improvement.

Practice for Three Weeks

1. For 15 minutes every day for three weeks, read at a faster-than-comfortable speed, not worrying about comprehension. As you drop back to a more comfortable speed, you will find you are reading faster with good comprehension. The reason you read a little faster than comfortable is to _prevent you from looking back_. Also, the added speed forces you to deal with word groups, and not single words.

   • Read groups words and do not read the individual words aloud or in your mind.

   • Use a 3 × 5 card or your hands to pace.

   • Do not allow yourself to look back at what you have read.

   • Indent when you read. Do not move your eyes to the edge of the line, but indent one or two words.

   • Read the _tops_ of words.

At the end of the 15 minutes, have someone time you for <u>exactly 2 minutes</u>. Count the number of words you read. Divide the number in half. Record that number.

Week 1	# of words in 2 minutes						
	# of words per minute						

Week 2	# of words in 2 minutes						
	# of words per minute						

Week 3	# of words in 2 minutes						
	# of words per minute						

2. Now, for 3 minutes, practice looking at words for only a split second. Take a 3 × 5 card and place it over the line of words in a book. Now jerk the card down and back up to make a split-second exposure of the words below the card. Your goal is to gain enough skills to get up to five or six words in a glance.

> Silent reading goal: To read comfortably with good comprehension at about 300 words per minute.

Understanding What Is Read

Unfortunately, being able to read well does not guarantee comprehension. Students can be proficient in reading the words of the text and not have any idea what it means. What is required for reading comprehension? How can we help students understand and enjoy reading? In the next section, we will explore ways to increase reading comprehension.

Meet My Student

Owen

Owen was a walking encyclopedia when it came to history, but he could not read well. He was a fifth grader who spent four to five hours every night trying to do his homework. He had hearing problems as a child and a speech impediment that would not improve in spite of three years of speech therapy. He finally concluded that he just had a cool "accent."

After 45 hours of research-based reading instruction that spanned over seven months, Owen was reading above grade level and enjoying reading about the history he loved so much. Toward the end of the instruction, he engaged in the activities to increase his reading speed. Although he could read well, he was only reading about 80 words per minute, too slow to function well in school. After three weeks of practicing to increase his reading speed, he was reading about 300 words per minute. His greatest delight was being able to finish his homework in less than an hour rather than the former four to five hours.

Summary

Prerequisite Skills for Fluency
• Knowledge of the sounds of all graphemes in the words to be read
• Ability to decode words in the text
• Storage of words in the Word Form Center of the brain for instantaneous retrieval
• Understanding of basic punctuation found in the text

Identifying True Fluency Problems
Step #1: Test for phonemic awareness using the phoneme segmentation assessment.
Step #2: If the student has phonemic awareness, test knowledge of the spellings of the phonemes, using the sound card assessment.
Step #3: If a student has phonemic awareness and knows the spellings of the phonemes, test ability to decode.
Step #4: If a student can decode, then the issue is fluency.

Strategies for Teaching Fluency
• Chunking—Show students how they actually read words in groups.
• Punctuation—Call attention to all punctuation and what it means.
• Echo Reading—Demonstrate how to read fluently with expression. Students echo what you read.
• Choral Reading—Read a short passage fluently together.
• Reader's Theater—Read parts of a text dramatically.

Hindrances to Silent Reading Speed
• Moving the lips while reading
• Reading word by word
• Rereading or looking back
• Stopping at a word or phrase or at the end of the line

Part III

Comprehending and Responding to Text

Chapter 14

What You Need to Know Before You Can Comprehend

The Real Truth about Reading Comprehension

What is reading comprehension? It is the ability to read a text and glean meaning from it. *What is the text about? What does it mean? What are the implications?* Understanding text is not as simple as ensuring that students can read all of the words. It is not as simple as asking a few comprehension questions after reading. It requires a repertoire of skills that are developed by reading, by listening to others read, and by engaging in deep conversations about the world.

Unlike learning how to read words, something that can be mastered relatively quickly, comprehension is an aggregation of knowledge and processes that takes many years to acquire. If we neglect this truth, we may assume that learning and practicing a small set of rules or strategies will dramatically increase understanding, grossly underestimating the complexity of reading comprehension (Catts 2009). Instead, if we embrace this

Figure 14. 1   Framework for Teaching Reading

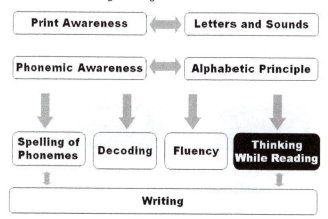

complexity and identify ways to provide students with the essential skills, our students can become proficient readers.

The Impact of Working Memory on Comprehension

What is working memory? It is a process central to getting meaning from text. Working memory refers to structures and processes in the brain used for *temporarily* storing and manipulating information *during active processing*. Only information that we are currently thinking about is in working memory. This ability to actively hold information in the mind enables us to accomplish complex tasks such as reasoning, comprehension, and learning.

How does working memory differ from short-term memory? Short-term memory generally refers to the short-term *storage* of information and it *does not* entail the manipulation of material. It is just stored for later retrieval. In contrast, working memory refers to the current *manipulation* of information. It is what I am thinking about right now (see Figure 14.2).

The Magic Seven

Working memory has a limited capacity. You can only think about so many things at one time. The number of elements an average human can hold in working memory is 7 ± 2. What an element is will vary, depending on the knowledge and experience of the person. It is the largest meaningful unit that a person recognizes. For a preschool child, a letter might be the largest meaningful unit recognized. For a second-grade student, a whole word might be the largest meaningful unit, and for a high school student, a whole phrase might be the largest unit. Thus, an element could be a single letter, a single word, or a single group of words, depending on the knowledge a person has of the language.

This understanding of the working memory explains why our telephone numbers are divided into groups, or elements. It would be difficult to remember 7655551829 because you are forced to look at and remember each individual number. However, it is quite easy to remember 765-555-1829 because it has been broken into three elements.

Figure 14.2 Working Memory vs. Short-term Memory

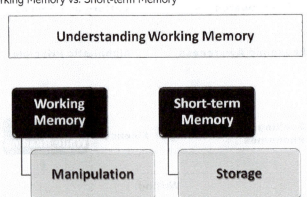

This idea of working memory impacts our ability to gain meaning from text. Since we can only process seven elements at once, if we are consumed with decoding we cannot retain all of the words in the sentence while we try to accomplish that. We just lost the meaning. Any time we must concentrate on elements other than thinking of meaning, we are distracted from comprehension. This is why developing skills to the point they are automatic is essential.

Two Aspects of the Reading Process

As shown in Figure 14.3, the reading process is often divided into two main categories, each with a specific set of competencies (Hoover & Gough 1990, 2010):

1. Reading the words of the text
2. Comprehending the text

Although both aspects occur from the beginning as students learn to read, the ability to read words in the text directly impact comprehension.

Reading the words of the text has been the emphasis of the previous chapters. We found that students must have phonemic awareness, be able to identify the spellings of the phonemes, know how to decode both small and big words, and be able to read fluently. Students who have poor phonological skills or who have not had enough practice in reading will not be able to read enough words to make sense of the passage or will have to pay so much attention to each individual word that the meaning of the whole is lost.

Students who have memorized a large number of words without proficiency in the essential skills necessary for reading the words of the text may also have difficulty with comprehension. It is less efficient and more time consuming to retrieve words memorized as whole words than those that have been phonologically recorded in the brain. For these types of students, most of working memory will be engaged in the process of reading the words, leaving little for comprehension. These students might be able to read lower-level texts easily, but at some point, they often become students who can't read well due to a lack of foundational skills.

Once students are able to read accurately and fluently, working memory can be engaged in comprehending the text. Even a beginning reader who can only read one sentence

Figure 14.3 Two Aspects of the Reading Process

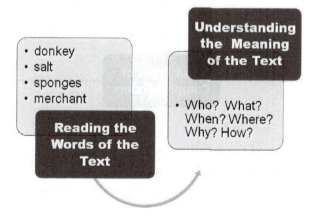

can focus on the meaning of the sentence as soon as the text can be read correctly and smoothly. It may take a couple of times reading the sentence until that point is reached, but when it is, the focus can be on comprehending the text.

Finding the Root of Comprehension Problems

Understanding the two aspects of reading will help in determining one of the root causes of reading comprehension problems. Like fluency, poor comprehension can be a presenting problem, but not the real problem. If you attempt to remedy poor reading comprehension issues when a student has little or no phonemic awareness, does not know the spellings of the graphemes, cannot decode, and is not fluent, it will fail. It is impossible to solve the problem using a myriad of comprehension strategies because the root cause has not been addressed. I hear many teachers say, "My students have difficulty comprehending text." But we must ask, "Why?" We must find the real cause before we can implement solutions. In many cases, these students are not able to read the words of the text. So much working memory is used in reading the words that there is none left for comprehension.

What is the solution? Focus on providing students with the basic skills so they can read accurately and fluently. In the meantime, choose texts at the instructional level rather than grade level. Then develop comprehension skills with those texts.

The Mystery of the Four Types of Comprehenders

What is necessary in order to both read and comprehend well? Researchers have studied four types of comprehenders as seen in Figure 14.4. By comparing what each group of students can do and can't do, they have identified the critical proficiencies for compression (Nation 2005; Catts & Weismer 2006; Rickets, Bishop, & Nation 2008). Individuals in Groups 1 and 2 identify those who can read and understand and those who can't read and can't understand perform exactly as expected. It is the other two groups that have been an enigma.

Figure 14.4   Four Types of Comprehenders

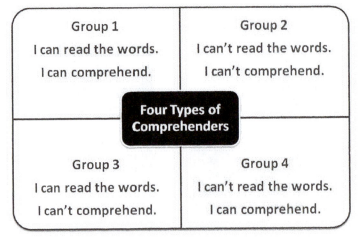

Group 1: I Can Read; I Can Comprehend

These students have strong phonological and decoding skills. They read fluently so working memory can be engaged in the comprehension process. They are proficient in all of the components necessary to understand the text. They are the shining examples of what we want all students to be able to do, possessing skills in both reading the text and comprehending the text.

Group 2: I Can't Read; I Can't Comprehend

These students have neither phonological and decoding proficiencies nor comprehension skills. Both aspects of reading need to be addressed. In the previous chapters, we investigated ways to help these students read the words of the next. In this chapter, we will address the comprehension issue they face.

Group 3: I Can Read; I Can't Comprehend

You would think that an individual who could read accurately and fluently would be able to gain meaning from text. But that is not always the case. This type of reader signaled to researchers that other competencies must be in place before comprehension can take place. We will investigate what these proficiencies are.

Group 4: I Can't Read; I Can Comprehend

These students are amazing. They stumble through a passage, reading only some of the words, but when they finish they can tell you exactly what they have read. How can they do this? By comparing the proficiencies of these readers with those who can read, but not comprehend, researchers were able to identify the critical competencies for comprehension. And they have them. Although they may get by for awhile, their lack of skills in reading the words of the text will eventually catch up to them and they will fall into the Group 2 category.

Three Indispensable Prerequisites for Comprehending the Text

One of the unexpected findings was that reading comprehension and listening comprehension require the same set of skills (Hoover & Gough 1990, 2010). As shown in Figure 14.5, whether reading or listening, students who understand bring the following competencies to bear on the text:

1. They possess a knowledge base.
2. They know meanings of words.
3. They understand structures of text.

Students who could not understand the meaning of text were deficient in most of these areas even if could read accurately and fluently.

Figure 14.5 Three Prerequisites for Reading Comprehension

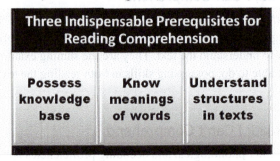

This chapter addresses the first prerequisite. Chapters 15 and 16 examine the second and third indispensable prerequisites.

Indispensable Prerequisite #1: Possess a Strong Knowledge Base

What do you know? We use what we know to figure what we don't know. Background knowledge is one of the major determinants of reading comprehension. In fact, the amount of prior knowledge a reader has about a topic indicates how much will be understood and remembered. In a study of 183 articles on reading comprehension, Dochy, Segers & Buehl (1999) found prior knowledge explained up to 81 percent of the variance in reading scores. The bottom line: We have to know something about what we are reading in order to comprehend it. In the groups of students studied, those who could comprehend what they were reading, whether they were good readers or poor readers, had background knowledge in the texts they were attempting to read. In contrast, those who could not comprehend what they were reading, even though they were good readers, lacked background knowledge (Catts 2009; Presseisen 1995).

Read the following selection. What is this paragraph talking about?

> **The scope calibrator is basically a simple solid-state stable multivibrator designed to close tolerances. Transistors Q2 and Q3 form the multivibrator, whose frequency is determined essentially by the values of the timing components C1, C2, R3, and R4. The nominal 1200-Hz frequency can be reduced to an exact 1000-Hz signal by merely shunting C1 and C2 with a 20-pf. capacitor.**

This paragraph may not be a problem for some individuals, but it will be for most. Why? You most likely can read all of the words accurately and fluently. In fact, you probably could answer questions on its contents. I've given tests over this text and almost all receive an "A," even though they didn't really know what the paragraph was about.

What is required to truly understand this text? Background knowledge of electronic circuits with an understanding of multivibrators, tolerances, transistors, frequencies, timing components, and capacitors provide the basis for comprehension of this text. This knowledge could not be built through reading a few pages, but would require reading, discussion, exploration, and application of these specific subtopics over a period of time.

What Background Knowledge Does for You

What is the impact of background knowledge on your reading? Write all the words and phrases that come to your mind when I say Abraham Lincoln. What floods your mind with just the name? If you are like most, you think, tall, beard, top hat, president, lawyer, Illinois, Kentucky, Civil War, slavery issues, honest, Gettysburg Address, and Emancipation Proclamation. You can easily write for one minute. Ideas and visual images inundate your mind. You might even think of personal experiences in visiting historical places connected to him or in memorizing the Gettysburg Address.

These ideas and images are not just about the man himself, what he looks like and acts like, but also what he did, the issues of the time period, big ideas connected to his life, your own personal experiences and attitudes, and general world knowledge.

For example, when you thought *president,* you also knew about the office of president of the United States and the duties that it entails or when you thought lawyer, you know what a lawyer does. Your background knowledge is a web of interrelated descriptions, concepts, emotions, and attitudes that comes from years of reading, listening, conversation, and experiences related to Abraham Lincoln. The more detailed and complex one's understanding of a topic, the easier it is to process new information and incorporate it into the existing knowledge base.

Now write all the words and phrases that come to your mind when I say Charles M. Russell. If you are like most, you will write nothing. Some may write western painter. Only a few could write one minute about him. For most, there will be no images, no attitudes, and no life experiences. For me, images, experiences, concepts, and ideas flood my mind. I can see what he looks like, I know his last painting sold for 5.6 million dollars, I see flashes of his paintings and sculptures I have seen through the years, I think of my experiences in the Montana capitol building where his massive mural spreads across the wall in the House of Representative. My mind trails off to the feelings and reasons I was there. I think of walking through the wing of the museum dedicated to his artwork and of the biannual auction that draws in potential buyers from over the world. I could easily write for one minute.

Let's assume you are going to read a story or an article about each of these men. How will your background knowledge impact your understanding and visualization of what you are reading? As one teacher described it, the story about Lincoln was rich, generating visual images and feelings, but the story about Charles M. Russell was interesting but "flat." The amount of "stuff" going on in the mind differs significantly. What you already know is dramatically impacting what you are trying to know.

Understanding the indispensable contribution of background knowledge causes us to turn our focus on how to get it. If it is a major determinate in reading comprehension and we can't read well without it, then what can be done to establish a strong and broad knowledge base?

One of the major contributions of psychology is the recognition [that]. . .much of the information needed to understand a text is not provided by the information expressed in the text itself but must be drawn from the language user's knowledge of the person, objects, states of affairs, or events the discourse is about.

—T. A. Van Dijk and W. Kinstsch
Strategies of Discourse Comprehension

What Builds a Strong Knowledge Base?

Most of our background knowledge comes through reading, experiences, and meaningful conversations. It does not matter if information is formally gained through required reading and assignments or informally through casual reading, events, and substantial conversations. As we interact with knowledge, we build mental frameworks that are complex networks of information, attitudes, and emotions (Geelan 1997). When we read, we use these conceptual constructs to understand the text. We do not simply look at the content of the text, but combine that content with past knowledge to achieve understanding (Catts 2009).

This process of building background knowledge begins early in life. Parents who read to their children and engage in discussions about texts and the environment are building a foundation for reading comprehension. In contrast, children who come to school without that experience usually lack a strong knowledge base for understanding text. This makes it imperative that once students enter school, an intentional focus must be on building broad content knowledge. This requires teaching units of knowledge with carefully selected books and activities to engage students in the acquisition of the detailed, systematic content of a domain. Proficiency in reading comprehension cannot be obtained without it.

Strategies That Build Knowledge Base

- **Read aloud to students.**
  This applies to all grades. Include books that students would not be able to read on their own. Choose books that will build background knowledge in a broad spectrum of content and life experiences. Engage students in deep conversations about the text.

- **Give students opportunity to read widely.**
  Provide books that will build a knowledge base with the opportunity to read for at least 30 minutes a day at their instructional reading level.

- **Go on field trips, real or virtual.**
  Field trips provide detailed, interesting information on specific topics. And they are fun. Engage in reflective conversations about the experience.

- **Provide systematic instruction in a content domain.**
  Teach units on specific topics. Provide broad content knowledge through systematic instruction in a specific domain. Don't forget to meet the needs of the kinesthetic learner, who must be actively engaged in discovery activities.

The Shortage of Knowledge

In recent years, there has been a subtle shift in attention to formally teach reading comprehension strategies at the expense of teaching specific, systematic content. Although it is important to teach students certain skills, this approach can potentially rob time from teaching domain specific knowledge. Usually, the reading materials used in these strategy units are isolated texts that have minimal impact on the knowledge base (Palincsar & Duke 2004; Walsh 2003). For example, if students read a single story about Abraham Lincoln, the impact on acquisition of background knowledge will be limited unless it is well integrated into a unit on American history (Catts 2009). To be most effective, it needs to be taught in context of a knowledge domain.

How much time is spent on isolated reading stories and texts? How much time is spent on teaching a specific domain of knowledge? Assess how time is allotted in your classroom to each of these. If you are teaching mainly isolated texts with little detailed systematic content, one immediate remedy is to group books by content area and teach a systematic, detailed unit on a topic. In each subject area, integrate picture books, stories, biographies, historical fiction, and informational texts to enable students to build solid schemata for that topic. It is appropriate to use isolated stories, but not to the exclusion of teaching detailed systematic content.

Connecting to What You Know

It is not enough to have background knowledge. We must know that the knowledge we have applies to the text at hand. Although students may have some background in a topic or a related subject, they might not realize what they are reading is related to what they already know. The following paragraph illustrates this. I assure you that you have all the background knowledge to understand this paragraph.

> If the balloons popped, the sound wouldn't be able to carry since everything would be too far away from the correct floor. A closed window would also prevent the sound from carrying, since most buildings tend to be well insulated. Since the whole operation depends on a steady flow of electricity, a break in the middle of the wire would also cause problems. Of course, the fellow could shout, but the human voice is not loud enough to carry that far. An additional problem is that a string could break on the instrument. Then there could be no accompaniment to the message. It is clear that the best situation would involve less distance. Then there would be fewer potential problems. With face-to-face contact, the least number of things could go wrong.
>
> —Bransford and Johnson
> *Contextual prerequisites for understanding,* 1972, p. 719

You can read all of the words. You even know what the words mean. And you have the background knowledge to understand this paragraph, but why is it difficult to read? It feels out of context. The sentences seem random. Turn to the end of the chapter to see the picture that goes with this paragraph. Then read the paragraph again. You will see it is a well-organized and well-written description.

What was the problem? You had the background knowledge, but you did not know what knowledge to bring to the text. This happens with students, especially poor comprehenders. Once that background knowledge has been associated with the text, they are able to understand.

> "Activation of background schema knowledge is a fundamental aspect of comprehension."
>
> —Carol Westby
> *Assessing and remediating text comprehension problems,*
> 2005, p. 161

Strategies That Activate Prior Knowledge

Which strategies work best to activate prior knowledge, and when should they be used? Direct instruction on background knowledge and activating knowledge already known before reading can significantly improve comprehension (Strangman & Hall n.d.).. To do this, design an introductory activity that intentionally leads students to think about the knowledge base required for understanding the text. It can be an activity that may take only a couple of minutes or it may take an entire class period. It may be a single question asked before a story or a video or it may be an extended activity with more than one component. The following are examples of introductory activities that require using background knowledge. For each of these, it is important to find ways to engage each student in the process so each one activates his or her prior knowledge.

Research has shown that activities that require individual response are more effective than those that are done as a group. The learners who need it most are least likely to pay attention while a group responds. Also, students may passively listen to others express their knowledge, but never activate their own.

Activities Requiring an Individual Response

- **Write a journal response to a question or statement.**
  Provide a quote, a statement or a question that will require students to think of their prior knowledge to answer it. After drawing, let them compare their pictures with a partner and revise it. After reading, students can draw a final picture or diagram as a project.

- **Write prediction or opinion logs.**
  Students write or discuss predictions of a text based on title or pictures. Older students can write opinions about a topic before reading about it.

- **Write all you know about . . .**
  Give students one minute to write all they know about a topic. Then have them turn to a neighbor and compare notes for two minutes. For example, students might be asked to write all they know about volcanoes, or oceans or George Washington, or farms.

- **Draw a picture or diagram of . . .**
Have students draw something from memory to see how much they know and do not know. Let them revise it later. For example, students could draw a volcano and label all of the parts or draw a map of a country and identify three important features or draw a plant cell and label all the parts. After drawing, let them compare their pictures with a partner and revise it. After reading, students can draw a final picture or diagram as a project.

- **Respond to a list of statements.**
Have students select responses to a list of statements about the content before reading. After reading, they revise their answers or complete the response. These statements can take a variety of forms. For example, these can be true or false based in scientific fact or not based on scientific fact, statements that reflect two viewpoints with each statement attributed to a particular viewpoint, or statements that are my opinion and after reading identify the statements that reflect the author's opinion. The knowledge base of the student is identified and refined.

Activities Completed in Groups

- **Solve a problem.**
Present a problem, real or imagined, to solve that will require using the targeted background knowledge. Through the process students often recognize what they know and what they don't know.

- **Pretend you are . . .**
Have students assume an identity and look at a situation through that perspective. To create that perspective, they will have to pull from their knowledge base.

- **Conduct an experiment or demonstrate a phenomenon.**
Most experiments and demonstrations are conducted *after* the lesson to exhibit the content learned. However, by conducting the experiment before reading, students can think about their own background knowledge and identify holes in their understanding.

- **Develop an analogy.**
Build a concept by comparing it to something known. For example, students can identify all the components needed to run a manufacturing company of a particular type such as a chocolate factory. Then, as students read, the analogy is extended to the workings of a cell.

- **Develop a graphic organizer.**
Graphic organizers can be developed by students working in groups of two or three or by the entire class. Be sure to engage each student in the process. Most graphic organizers are a work in progress. Even if they are developed before reading, they often need tweaked during reading and revised after reading. Types of organizers include:
  - Venn diagrams or T charts that compare and contrast ideas
  - KWL that identifies what students know, what they want to know and after instruction, what they have learned
  - Structured overviews that organizes information in such a way that the main ideas with their relationships are visually apparent.
  - Concept, semantic, or vocabulary maps that explore interrelatedness of concepts, ideas, or words

- Process or sequence charts that represent steps in a process or a sequence of time
- Linear arrays that show shades of difference between concepts or words
- **Engage in extension activities.**
  In both reading and content area texts, there are often suggestions for extension activities. Using these *before* reading will increase comprehension of the text because they use prior knowledge and extend the knowledge base.

Don't Forget the Kinesthetic Learner

Always keep the kinesthetic learner in mind. These are the students who usually struggle most in school because they do not learn well by reading, writing, and listening. They are also the students who were too busy to pay attention to general knowledge unless someone has peaked their interest. Writing at whiteboards, manipulating objects and cards, and completing projects are important ways for them to learn. They need to see the big picture so systematic knowledge is appealing to them rather than isolated bits and pieces. Graphic organizers help them see concepts as a whole. Since most of them think in pictures and three-dimensionally, movies, pictures, and diagrams are helpful. Choose strategies for developing or activating knowledge that will maximize their potential.

Summary

Three Indispensable Prerequisites for Reading Comprehension
• Possess a knowledge base.
• Know meanings of words.
• Understand structures of text.
Strategies to Build Knowledge Base
• Read aloud to students.
• Give students opportunity to read widely.
• Go on field trips, real or virtual.
• Provide systematic instruction in a content domain.
Strategies That Activate Prior Knowledge
Individual responses
• Write a journal response to a question or statement .
• Write prediction or opinion logs.
• Write all you know about. . .
• Draw a picture or diagram of. . . .
• Respond to a list of statements.
Group responses
• Solve a problem.
• Pretend you are . . .
• Conduct an experiment or demonstrate a phenomenon.
• Develop an analogy.
• Develop a graphic organizer.
• Engage in extension activities.

The Serenade

The paragraph is found on page 189.

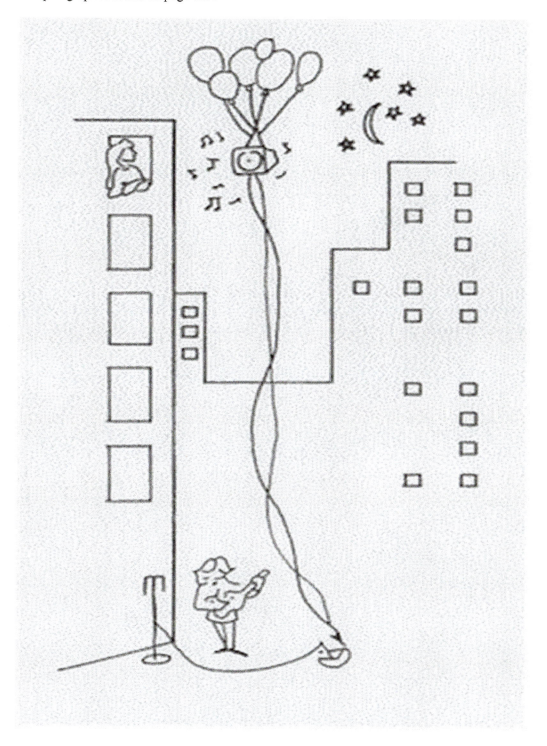

Reprinted from *Contextual Prerequisites for Understanding: Some Investigations of Comprehension and Recall* (1972), Elsevier Science Limited.

Chapter 15

The Meaning of Words

Vocabulary and background knowledge are inseparable twins. You usually don't have one without the other. To describe knowledge, we use vocabulary. The more specific and detailed the content area, the more technical the words used to communicate that knowledge.

Indispensable Prerequisite #2: Understanding the Meaning of Words

Remember the paragraph on scope calibrators in Chapter 14? Besides of a lack of general understanding of the concepts, many of the words were also unknown.

How do we gain vocabulary? If a teacher focuses on 10 to 12 words per week over the 36 weeks of school, only 300 to 400 words can be taught. That is in stark contrast to the number of new words students encounter each year. Nagy & Herman (1987) estimated that students in grades 3 to 9 read 15,000 to 30,000 unfamiliar words per year and learn approximately 750 to 1,500 of those words. Adams (1990) estimated students learn about 3,000 new words per year. These vocabulary words are learned through reading. It is obvious we can't teach all the words students need to know.

> "Research has shown that children who read even ten minutes a day outside of school experience substantially higher rates of vocabulary growth between second and fifth grade than children who do little or no reading."
>
> —Anderson & Nagy
> *The vocabulary conundrum*, 1992, p. 46

The Volume of Reading Directly Impacts Vocabulary Acquisition

The more a student reads, the more encounters there will be with unfamiliar words and the more new words the student will learn. The student who reads less will learn fewer words.

Poor readers have two strikes against them. They do not read as much as proficient readers, and what they do read they have difficulty understanding. Poor readers who must engage all of working memory to figure how to read individual words will stall in vocabulary development and knowledge base because they cannot pay attention to the meaning of words.

Students who are even one or two grade levels behind in reading are thousands of words behind in vocabulary If they are given the tools and can finally read accurately and fluently, the negative effects of the lack of vocabulary and background knowledge will continue to impact reading comprehension unless steps are taken to remediate these areas.

Catching Them Up

Students who have poor background knowledge and vocabulary development will have difficulty comprehending texts even after they learn to read accurately and fluently. It is overwhelming to think how to catch them up since they are thousands of words behind other students. What can be done? First, don't let them get further behind. Then plan activities that will help them gain vocabulary skills. Here are six suggestions:

1. Make sure they are reading at least 30 minutes a day at their instructional level and engaged in deep conversations about the texts they read.

2. Plan systematic, detailed instruction in content areas to grow their knowledge base.

3. Integrate literature with content area texts. Reading both stories and explanations on a topic builds background knowledge and vocabulary more rapidly because the one supports the other. Stories provide a real life context for the new words and concepts and the expository text brings detailed explanation of those ideas.

4. Choose texts for which students already have a knowledge base. If they know nothing about the topic, they will flounder and learn little from the text. Take the foundation of their current knowledge and build new understanding on it.

5. Be strategic in planning vocabulary activities that will develop concepts and provide exposure to the most words possible. Graphic organizers that use many related words, synonyms, and antonyms provide both visual imagery and concept development.

6. Use high-quality, high-interest picture books that contain myriads of pictures, vocabulary words, and diagrams related to one topic. Picture dictionaries are also helpful.

Meet My Students

Lewis

Lewis was a sixth grader when I began working with him. Like many remedial readers that come to me, he was reading at a third-grade level. After 42 hours of instruction in phonemic awareness and a phoneme-based phonics, Lewis was reading above grade level but he couldn't understand anything he read. Why not? He did not listen to recorded books, no one read to him, and he did not engage in meaningful conversations about books or experiences. His knowledge base and vocabulary growth stalled during the years that he could not read. He was thousands of words behind.

As we worked together, I discovered he did not understand some of the fundamental concepts an average student would know. He did not know what a farmhouse was, or a lamb, or many concepts that should have been common knowledge by his age. He was so deficient in background knowledge and vocabulary that even though he could read accurately and fluently, he had no idea what he had read.

To address this problem, he did two things. He checked out specific picture books at the library that contained hundreds of pictures and diagrams related to one topic. These books had high-quality content and were geared to keep the interest of even adults. These books not only introduced a broad spectrum of vocabulary with vivid imagery, but also taught a systematic, detailed content on a subject. In addition, he also checked out picture dictionaries. He enjoyed these even as an older reader. Both of these types of books helped him build a mental image of many words that did not depend on written definitions.

The second activity involved looking at text structure and developing a summary sentence using a sentence frame for each paragraph he read. This strategy will be explained in the next section. At first, gleaning information from text was foreign to him, but within a short time, he could pick out the key ideas in texts. The reading world began to open up for Lewis and after a few sessions with him, he understood for the first time how to gain meaning from text and how to find the answers when he did not know.

Peder

Some poor readers can't read but they can still comprehend. How do they manage? They have gained incredible vocabulary and background knowledge by listening to others read and by engaging in meaningful conversations with adults.

Peder was a sixth grade student who could not read a first-grade primer. In fact, he could not read or "sound out" the simplest words. There was no identifiable reason for his inability to read, although he was critically ill when he was five years old and spent months recovering. In order to remain at grade level, all of his schoolwork had to be read to him. In his leisure, he listened to recorded historical fiction.

During 42 one-hour sessions spread over eight months, he gained phonemic awareness by manipulating chips and sound cards, learned the Real Rules of English through spelling on the whiteboard, and became skilled at decoding both small and big words. By the end of eight months, he was reading young adult literature such as *Lord of the Rings*. He couldn't be without his books. He stashed them under the seat of the family van so he could squeeze in reading every spare moment.

The Importance of Listening Vocabulary

Unlike Lewis, Peder never stalled in his knowledge base and vocabulary development so when he did learn to read, he understood what he read. Listening to books on tape and engaging in meaningful discussions about them kept him growing in these areas.

This informs us how to maintain vocabulary and knowledge growth in students with deficient abilities in reading. Until they learn the essential skills, introduce these students to specific related vocabulary and systematic, detailed content through means other than reading:

- Listening to audio books
- Listening to others read grade-level or above-grade-level materials
- Engaging in learning activities that don't require a lot of reading, such as field trips, movie clips, building projects, and problem solving
- Participating in deep conversations about ideas and content

These activities will help them continue to develop these proficiencies indispensable to comprehension until they can read on their own.

CAUTION: These activities cannot take the place of their own reading at the instructional level at least 30 minutes a day.

Impact of Listening Vocabulary on Comprehension

Researchers refer to four types of vocabulary:

1. *Listening*—the words I understand when listening to others
2. *Speaking*—the words I use when talking with others
3. *Reading*—the words I understand when reading
4. *Writing*—the words I use when writing

Which type of vocabulary is the smallest? Our speaking vocabulary. We use a limited number of words when speaking to others, although we can understand, read, and even write many more words. For example, our writing vocabulary is larger and contains words we would never use in speaking. How often do you use *therefore, thus,* and *hence* when you are speaking? When writing, we have more time to choose words from our listening vocabulary, but while speaking we use words that immediately come to mind.

Which type of vocabulary is the largest? Our listening vocabulary is by far the largest. We may understand words that are spoken to us, but not use them ourselves, recognize them in print, and definitely not use them in writing.

Which type of vocabulary impacts reading comprehension? Our listening vocabulary impacts our ability to understand text, decode multisyllable words, and decode exceptional words (Hoover & Grough 1990).

- **Listening vocabulary helps us understand text.**
  If students are skilled at reading words and have a good listening vocabulary, they will be able to understand text. Although it contains words they never use while speaking or writing, they know what those words mean and can interpret the meaning of the text.

- **Listening vocabulary helps us decode big words.**

  Knowing how to pronounce multisyllable words can present a problem. The pronunciation gets tricky because vowels can change from long to short or short to long and the stressed syllable can change when prefixes and suffixes are added. How do you pronounce *nationality*? The base word *nation* has a long vowel sound with the stress on the first syllable. The word *nationality* has a short vowel sound with the stress on the third syllable. If the word is in my listening vocabulary, although, I have never written, spoken, or read it before, I can tell from the context that the word is *nationality*. If it is not in my listening vocabulary, my only other option is to have someone tell me the word or skip it. I most likely will not look it up in a dictionary to find the pronunciation.

- **Listening vocabulary helps us decode exception words.**

  There are words that break all the rules. For example, the word *yacht* would be impossible to "sound out." However, if the word is in my listening vocabulary I could say "y-a –ch-t," realize it is close to a word I already know that fits the context of rich people sailing on the ocean, and pronounce it correctly. I commonly hear students say, "I didn't know that was what the word looked like." They knew the word; they had just never seen it in print before.

  Young children use this process to adjust the pronunciation of common words like *said* and *there*. The word *there* might momentarily be pronounced *theer*, but quickly adjusted to the correct pronunciation. Students with good listening vocabulary skills are more likely to vary the pronunciation of an unknown word to read it correctly.

> Poor comprehenders scored near the 20th percentile in listening vocabulary.
>
> —Adolf, Catts, & Weismer
> *Language Deficits in Poor Comprehenders*
> 2006, p. 284

Helping Students Build Vocabulary Knowledge

Since most of vocabulary is gained incidentally, it might seem pointless to attempt direct instruction in vocabulary. However, researchers have found that teaching vocabulary makes a dramatic difference in reading comprehension (Stahl & Fairbanks 1986; Bryant, Goodwin, Bryant, & Higgins 2003; Marzano 2004). In an analysis of research on vocabulary instruction, Stahl and Fairbanks (1986) found a difference in the test scores of students with equal background knowledge and equal reading ability but varied vocabulary instruction. Students who received instruction in words related to the content scored 33 percentile points over those who received no instruction.

Notice in Table 15.1 that instruction on vocabulary related to content was much more beneficial than instruction in words from isolated lists. From this, we know that the best vocabulary instruction is tied to the current texts being read.

Table 15.1 Impact of Different Types of Vocabulary Instruction on Test Scores

Impact of Vocabulary Instruction on Test Scores		
Test Scores with No Vocabulary Instruction	Test Scores with Typical Vocabulary Instruction from High Frequency Word Lists	Test Scores with Vocabulary Instruction on Words Related to Content Being Read
50th percentile	62nd percentile	83rd percentile

From statistics in Stahl and Fairbanks (1986)

> Instruction on vocabulary related to content is much more beneficial than instruction in words from isolated lists.

Remember, vocabulary and content knowledge are inseparable twins. To do a good job teaching vocabulary, the concept around the term must be developed and connected to prior knowledge. What better way to do this than through the context of teaching systematic, detailed content? The word will be embedded in a web of ideas with other vocabulary words that support each other in meaning. A term that is connected to content will be used in a variety of ways over a period of time as students study the topic, providing the extended contact with the word that students need.

In contrast, words introduced in an isolated text will usually not be connected well to prior knowledge and have only a one-time exposure. Because the words are not well integrated into a knowledge base, it is difficult for students to remember and use them. If the single text, however, is a chapter book, then all of the advantages of teaching systematic, detailed content apply. Students are spending extended time with ideas and vocabulary as they read the story.

Table 15.2 shows the differences in impact on vocabulary development for the two approaches. This does not mean isolated stories should not be read. They need to be read, but there is definite value in teaching texts that revolve around a topic or theme. Series books and novels such as the *Box Car Mysteries, The Chronicles of Narnia,* or *Lord of the Rings* also provide repetition of specific vocabulary and structure that help vocabulary development.

Table 15.2 The Advantage of Teaching Vocabulary within Context

Clusters of Books on a Topic or Theme	Isolated Story or Expository Text
• Repeated use of specific vocabulary.	• Single or limited use of specific vocabulary.
• Varied exposure over time.	• One-time exposure.
• Concepts around the words are well developed within the context of the topic.	• It is more difficult to develop unknown concepts surrounding the words.
• Strong connection to prior knowledge is established when introducing the topic.	• It is more difficult to connect to prior knowledge due to time constraints.
• Several words are related to the content and to each other.	• Words might not be related, so an effort must be made to categorize words, such as feelings of characters or names of places.

Although we can only teach a fraction of the words student must know, strategic vocabulary instruction helps students understand how words and concepts are related across different contexts, increases background knowledge, and, in turn, increases reading comprehension. It also stimulates enthusiasm about words and encourages students to attend to meanings within texts. We want students to enjoy learning new words and how to use them creatively.

The Poorest Way to Teach Vocabulary

So how do we teach vocabulary? We are all familiar with the dictionary approach to teaching vocabulary. This is what the student is asked to do:

1. Look up a word in a dictionary.
2. Write the definition.
3. Write a sentence using the word.

This is the poorest way to teach vocabulary. The dictionary is invaluable when used appropriately to see variations in meanings, pronunciations, and even parts of speech, but it often cannot produce an understanding of a totally unknown word.

Let's assume you have never seen or even heard of a cow, a mirror, or parasites. You go to the dictionary to look up the meanings.

---

cow:
- The full grown female of any bovine, or oxlike animal or of certain other animals the male of which is called a bull, such as with the elephant, the moose, and the whale.
- A domestic bovine animal without regard to age or sex; found in barns and pastures.

mirror:
- Any surface that is capable of reflecting enough light without scattering it so that it shows an image of any object placed in front of it.

parasites:
- Living things that feed on other living things.

What problems could I have in gaining understanding with these definitions? What are some of the *problems* with looking at definitions?

- **I don't know the words that define it.**
  - What is "bovine," anyway?
  - I have no idea what they mean by light reflecting without being scattered.
  - Is a lion a parasite because it eats a deer?
- **Because the definition didn't help much, I can't picture it.**
- **I could not use it meaningfully in a sentence.**

What do we need to truly understand the definitions of these words?

High-quality Vocabulary Instruction

We learn vocabulary best through context and imagery. The concept of the word must be developed and related to what we already know before we can understand its meaning. We cannot learn isolated words that are not connected to our experience or knowledge base. That is why learning vocabulary words from lists of high frequency words is not as effective as learning words related to the current text.

Since vocabulary is closely related to background knowledge, many of the same strategies used to develop the knowledge base can be used to teach vocabulary.

Strategically Choose Vocabulary Words

You will teach only a fraction of the vocabulary words students need to learn so choose words that are essential to understanding the concepts that represent critical content. If the word is a part of a web of concepts with related words, the whole set of words will be easier to learn. Isolated words are more difficult to teach and remember.

Develop the Concept and Connect It to Prior Knowledge

One of the reasons dictionary definitions are so hard to understand is they only present isolated phrases to define the word. Without context, it is not easy to wrap our minds around the meaning. The sentence example usually does not provide much additional understanding. In order to grasp the meaning of a word, we need to hear it used within some kind of conceptual framework. That is why so much vocabulary is learned through reading, because the word comes within the context of a story or a description.

For the words you have chosen, identify whether students understand the concepts related to the word. Will you be teaching a new word for a new concept or a new word for a known concept? Is it a new meaning or an enriched meaning for a known word? These are important considerations as you identify the background knowledge students bring to this word. Engage them in discovery activities that help them relate the concept to what they already know. Use pictures, diagrams, models, movie clips, demonstrations, synonyms, antonyms, examples, and related words to develop the concepts and connect to prior knowledge.

Provide a Definition Using Everyday Language

Define the word using words students already know. Make it simple. Let them help you refine the definition. Find synonyms and antonyms and provide examples and nonexamples to deepen understanding. This process of comparing and contrasting clarifies meaning so students know what it is and what it is not.

Use the Words

Often, teachers will teach vocabulary but never use the words themselves. Learning vocabulary is often an exercise in memorization rather than a meaningful activity. Model the definition within the context of a sentence or story and then use it yourself in informal conversations and in class discussions with students. As you use the words, students will hear them multiple times within context, which will validate their understanding.

Provide Some Kind of Imagery

Words that produce mental images are easier to remember than those that produce either low images or no images (Marzano 2004; Beck, McKeown, & Kucan 2002). That means we need to provide some type of representation that helps students form a mental image such as a picture, a drawing, an object, a diagram, a personal experience, or demonstration. In studies, these types of nonlinguistic techniques produced vocabulary gains that were 37 percentile points higher than strategies that verbally reviewed definitions and 31 percentile points higher than asking students to generate sentences that demonstrated as understanding of vocabulary words (Marzano 2004).

Some words represent tangible objects so a picture, model, drawing, or even the actual object will produce a mental image that will solidify the meaning. In the paragraph you read on the scope calibrator in Chapter 14, many of the words were unknown. However, if someone brought in a scope calibrator and demonstrated how to use it, you would have a depth of understanding that words could not convey. The mental image produced by seeing the object and the process would provide you with the "definitions" you needed.

If the word is a description or an abstract word, sometimes it is possible to bring in a picture that conveys the meaning. Words such as *beautiful, loyal,* and *sloppy* can often be portrayed through pictures. Be sure to include pictures that describe the opposite to bring clarity to the meaning. If a word describes a process, a drawing or diagram will produce the mental image needed.

Not all words lend themselves to pictures or drawings. If the word is an action word, sometimes it is possible to act it out or use gestures. Include acting out the antonyms so understanding is refined. With some words, you can only use the antonyms, related words, and life examples. If you can help students connect the word to a personal experience, they can demonstrate it through their own drawing (see Figure 15.1).

Figure 15.1   Examples of Vocabulary Words from a Second-Grade Student

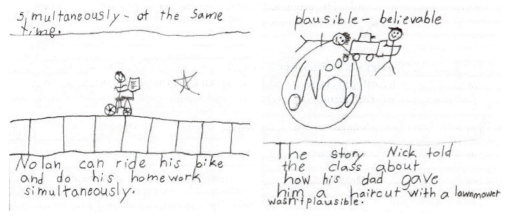

Use Graphic Organizers to Categorize Words and Show Relationships

The same types of graphic organizers used to organize and bring up prior knowledge are valuable in developing vocabulary. They help students construct a schemata related to the words and see relationships between words. Use concept maps, Venn diagrams, T-charts, structured overviews, and linear arrays to compare and classify concepts, related words, synonyms, and antonyms. Additional types of graphic organizers include the semantic analysis matrix, categorization activities, and scavenger hunts.

Matrix for Semantic Feature Analysis

A matrix explores words of similar meaning. Choose a group of related words or concepts and place them on a matrix. Working in groups, students then decide which box is appropriate to check.

Example: What type of fasteners will you use for each of these materials? Why?					
	Wood	**Sheet Metal**	**Machined Metals**	**Dissimilar Material**	**Polymers**
Nails					
Screws					
Natural glue					
Synthetic adhesive					
Machined bolts and nuts					
Pop rivets					

Categorization Activities/ Scavenger Hunt

Provide students with a group of words or concepts related to a topic to group by use, kind, and so on. You can give students the names of the categories or let them choose their own and justify the decision. After categorizing the words, students find pictures, models, or objects that represent the words. The group with the most items wins the scavenger hunt.

Categorize the following words. Decide on which categories you will use. There must be at least three items in a category. Label the name of the category. Then find a picture or object to go with each word. Each picture or object is worth ten points.			
cirrus	rainbow	stratus	frost
cumulus	wind vane	barometer	snow
fog	rain gauge	cyclone	thermometer
hurricane	tornado	blizzard	lightning

Provide Repeated and Varied Exposure to the Words

Writing assignments, projects, and problem-solving activities that require use of the new vocabulary will help students assimilate the words into long-term memory. Words have many nuances in their definitions that cannot be understood outside of meaningful contexts.

Games such as Taboo, Jeopardy, and Charades provide practice while helping students understand synonyms and contexts. Choose words and let students write the games.

Beyond Definitions

When we speak of vocabulary, we mean more than just vocabulary definitions. It extends to figures of speech, idioms, understanding the role of prefixes and suffixes in changing meaning, and nuances in meanings (Hoover & Gough 1990).

Word Roots, Prefixes, and Suffixes

Teaching prefixes, suffixes, and Latin and Greek roots is one way to expand vocabulary with the least amount of work. As students engage in word-building activities associated with learning the spellings of the phonemes, they are also adding prefixes and suffixes to the words. It is important for students to understand what these affixes mean and how they change the meaning of words. Talk about the meanings of these words as students construct them. By adding the prefixes and suffixes, they are learning six to seven additional words for every root word.

Instruction in affixes begins with the first words they learn to spell and read. Because students are adding the prefixes and suffixes themselves, they begin to recognize the root words and affixes in words and understand how meanings are changed. This basic understanding of words exponentially aids their vocabulary development.

Value of Teaching Latin and Greek Roots

Eighty percent of the words in our language and most technical words found in math and science have some basis in Latin or Greek. Become acquainted with these roots so you recognize them in words and can use them to extend the vocabulary knowledge of your students. Even these words are best taught within the context of the word-building activities and texts rather than isolated lists. When students encounter a word with a Latin or Greek root, generate a list of words with the same root. Students may be able to help with creating this list. Even two or three associated words will help students remember the root. For example, if students encounter the word *triangle,* the root *tri* means "three." So *tripod* means three feet and *tricycle* means three circles. For fun, give students challenge words to see if they can figure out the meaning simply by using the root. Make a game of it. Give teams a list of words to decipher.

Students as young as grade 1 can begin to learn the simple roots. They don't have to wait until fourth or fifth grade. The key is choosing common words they encounter in reading and word building.

Figures of Speech and Idioms

In contrast to the straightforward literal meanings of common words, figures of speech imply something different than what the words say. Our language is full of them. This was brought home to me in one of my college classes. The professor or students would joke around, making comments or telling funny stories. Everyone would laugh. Everyone, that is, except my Japanese friend, who spoke impeccable English but had no idea what was said. She would lean over, puzzled, and ask for an interpretation. I realized then how many idioms and figures of speech we use in daily conversation. Often, we don't mean what we say.

Young children are literal-minded, and until about age eight or nine, they are developmentally unable to fully understand many figures of speech and idioms. Books like *Amelia Bedelia* begin to bridge the gap in understanding and some fun activities benefit students, but formal instruction in all types of figures of speech should be delayed until grade 4. At that time, identify the figures of speech used in the texts that students are reading and provide specific instruction in both the type of figure of speech and how to interpret the meaning (see Figure 15.2).

Figure 15.2 Figures of Speech

Figures of Speech

Simile

Comparison of two unlike things using the words "like" or "as."

"The cake was as light as a feather."

Metaphor:

A direct comparison of two things that are not alike by writing as if one is the other.

"The road was a ribbon stretching to the horizon."

Allegory:

A prolonged metaphor. A story that is, in total, a comparison.

Personification

Attributing to an inanimate object or an abstract idea the characteristics of a human being.

"The wind wailed and moaned."

Ono-mat-o-poeia

Using words with sounds that suggest their meaning.

hissed, screeched

Hyperbole

An exaggeration used for special effect.

"I could eat a hundred hamburgers."

Euphemism

Milder expression that will not be offensive for one that is stronger and may seem harsh or offensive.

"He passed away last night."

Irony

An expression or outcome of plot in which the result is deserved but their meaning is contrary to what is expected. The ogre in *Puss in Boots* chooses to show his power by turning himself into a mouse.

Idiom

An expression that means something different than what the individual words mean.

"Sarah kept her eye on the baby."

An idiom is a commonly used expression that means something other than the meanings of its individual words. They are so familiar that most people do not even recognize them as such. Each must be learned as a separate expression with a definite meaning because they are not formed according to any rules. As with all vocabulary, teach them in the context of the texts students are reading. Most idioms will be found in stories and news articles. Table 15.3 gives some examples of idioms.

Table 15.3 Examples of Common Idioms

Idiom	Meaning	Idiom	Meaning
taking root	becoming established	fly the coop	leave
show up	come or arrive	How come?	Why?
on hand	present	face the music	assume the consequences
out of hand	unmanageable	pitch in	help
keep your eye on	watch carefully	piece of cake	easy task

The Complexity of Reading Comprehension

By now, the complexity of reading comprehension should be hitting home. We have only looked at two prerequisites skills needed to be able to read text and gain meaning. Both a knowledge base and vocabulary develop over time and have the best gains through extensive reading with conversations about those texts. In the next chapter, we will look at the last prerequisite that affects the ability to glean meaning from texts.

Summary

High-quality Vocabulary Instruction
• Strategically choose vocabulary words.
• Develop the concept and connect it to prior knowledge.
• Use the words.
• Provide some kind of imagery.
• Use graphic organizers to categorize words and show relationships.
• Provide repeated and varied exposure to the words.

Chapter 16

Mysteries of the Text Itself

The third prerequisite for proficient reading comprehension is understanding the structures found in text. The importance of this cannot be underestimated. Having a solid background knowledge and required vocabulary related to the text is not enough. Students will still be lost if they do not understand how text is organized.

Indispensable Prerequisite #3: Understanding Text Structures

So what is text structure? There are three types of structure that impact the reader, and all are important (see Figure 16.1).

Figure 16.1 Why Text Structure Is Important

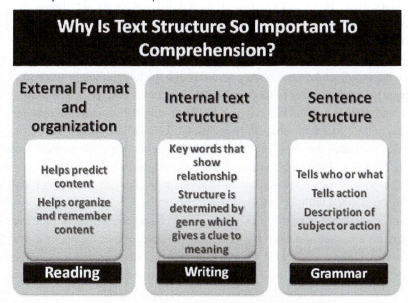

External Text Structure

This is what the text looks like. A novel looks entirely different than a textbook in layout and in components. Almost everything differs—from the type of fonts to the layout of the table of contents. Understanding the purposes of each part of the layout helps students predict, organize, and remember content. If they have only been acquainted with stories, they have no idea that the book has a glossary and the bold headings have meaning that can help them interpret content.

Internal Text Structure

What kind of text is it? Is it mystery, romance, or adventure? What kind of paragraph or essay is it? Persuasive, descriptive, or news report? Text structures tell us what is important. Each form has a unique structure with key words or phrases that inform the reader what ideas are important and how to find them. Internal text structure is so valuable that when students do not have sufficient background knowledge in a topic, they can depend on their knowledge of text structure to help them comprehend (Cataldo and Oakhill 2000).

Sentence Structure

Who or what is doing what action? When? Where? Why? How?

Understanding the parts of speech and the parts of a sentence help the reader identify specific information. Adults who cannot pick out the subject or verb of a sentence have difficulty understanding the meaning of the text. Teaching grammar is a critical piece in reading comprehension.

External Text Structure

Texts vary but essentially fall into two main categories: narrative and expository. *Narrative* is a story, usually with a setting, characters, and plot; *expository* informs, describes, or persuades (see Table 16.1). The external structural differences are significant and have an impact on comprehension.

Narrative text is usually fiction with characters, setting, and plot, but may also be a nonfiction narrative such as a biography. Due to the nature of the content, a reader must start at the beginning and consecutively read through the text, although some readers read the last page to see the ending before they get there. The text includes descriptions, events, emotions, and dialogue and is laid out on a full page with the same font throughout. The only breaks in the text are the chapter divisions. Occasionally, a sketch or a picture is included that enhances the story line. The table of contents lists a short chapter title with the page numbers. There may be a preface and an epilogue that the reader may or may not read. The purpose of the text is usually for enjoyment, so any unknown or difficult words can usually be skipped without consequence.

Expository texts are quite different. There are no characters, setting, or plot. Instead, it is repository of factual information on a topic, which usually allows the reader to start at any point in the text. Often teachers skip around in a textbook, selecting the topics and sequence that fits their purposes. The layout is entirely different from a narrative text. It has headings, subheadings, columns, and fonts of various sizes and types. The table of contents is often de-

Table 16.1 Differences between Narrative and Expository Text

Narrative	Expository
Content	Content
• Fiction (imaginative) or nonfiction.	• Nonfiction.
• Story has characters, setting, action.	• Informational.
• Emotions and feelings are included.	• Straight facts are the focus; any narrative is used to illustrate the point.
• Readers must start at the beginning.	• Readers might be able to start anywhere.
• Includes dialogue.	
Layout	Layout
• Full page, straight text.	• Headings, subheadings, columns.
• Same font throughout.	• Bold, italics, various sizes of fonts.
• Pictures help tell the story.	• Maps, drawings, charts, diagrams, photographs that explain information.
• If there is a table of contents, it includes straight chapters.	• Table of contents includes detailed outline.
• Might have preface, epilogue.	• Index, glossary, maps, extra tools.
Vocabulary	Vocabulary
• Often, it doesn't matter if readers know meaning of words.	• Dense vocabulary concepts; technical words.
	• Need to know meaning of the words.

tailed with not only chapter titles but also subheading titles. It might also be divided into sections. Within the text, there may be tables and figures that show drawings, charts, diagrams, and photographs that explain information. Included are additional sections, such as chapter summaries, a glossary, maps, appendices, a bibliography, and an index that are not found in a narrative text. Dense vocabulary concepts and technical words related to the content require students to know the meaning of the words. They cannot be skipped as in a narrative text.

Children come to school with almost five years of experience with stories. They know that stories have characters, settings, sequence, and plots. They might not know the names of each of these components, but they can readily pick them out of a movie or a story read from a book. They know what to expect. Most of their experience through grade 3 will also be with story, with typically little exposure to expository text.

When they enter grade 4, for the first time, many of the texts that teach science, social studies, history, and other content areas are expository. Students don't know the structure or the components so they do not know how or what they are to find within the text. This lack of knowledge of text structure will hamper their reading comprehension.

Introducing Students to Expository Text

Young children benefit from being introduced to expository text early, with an explanation of the layout. Discuss each component of the text that differs from a story. These early expository texts will not necessarily look like the later textbooks, but they will have bold headings, pictures, and other characteristics that differ from a story. Students will become comfortable looking for information other than the elements of a story.

When students are older and begin using expository texts to learn content, they need to be introduced to their textbook and shown how to use it. In most cases, the teacher hands out a new text and asks students to turn to a page to begin reading. Students do not become acquainted with the book. Have you ever discovered near the end of a course that there was a table or a glossary that would have been helpful but you did not know it was there? Every text is different, so engage students in discovery of the format of each text. To maximize independent learning, students need to know the organization and content of their textbook before they use it.

Parts of the Text

What do students need to know about each part of the text when they first receive it? Table 16.2 details the content and purposes of each part of a text and what students need to be directed to do. We cannot assume they understand where these parts are found or how they are to be used unless we guide them.

Introducing Students to a Textbook

How do you introduce a text to students? Many of the following activities can be used with multiples sections or chapters.

Table 16.2 Exploring the Parts of a Textbook

Part of Text	Content and Purpose	What Students Need to Do
Table of contents	• Summarizes the major concepts and ideas to be covered in the course. • Helps bring up prior knowledge. • May arouse curiosity.	Many students do not read the table of contents unless directed to do so.
Appendix	• Provides additional information and support materials. • Provides more detail than can be found in the main part of the textbook.	Encourage students to identify the content in the appendices.
Index	• A way to find specific information or additional information related to the topics.	Guide students in how to use the index to find "lost" information.
Glossary	• Summarizes key terms and concepts. Often, words in bold are found in the glossary.	Show students how the words in the glossary relate to the words in bold in the text.
Other resources	• Resources are specific for the subject area such as maps, math tables, time-lines, or biographies.	Identify and show how to use all the other resources in the text.
Chapter introductions, summaries, and questions	• Provide an overview of the contents of the chapter for easy review.	Show student the resources for reviewing the chapter.
Headings and subheadings	• Divides content into chunks and tells what the section is about. • Subheadings become the important points under the heading.	Show students how to turn headings and subheading into questions and then locate the information.
Chart, graphs, diagraphs, pictures	• Provides visual description of content.	Encourage students to look at the pictures and read the captions. For some reason, students can feel guilty for taking too much time to look at the visuals in a text.

- **Take 15 minutes to look at pictures and diagrams and read the captions.**
  For some reason, many students can feel guilty for taking too much time to look at the visuals in a text. Encourage students to look at the pictures and read the captions. *What seems interesting? Choose three you like best. How will they help you understand the topic?*

- **Read the table of contents.**
  High-achieving students read the table of contents and peruse the entire book before they ever begin reading. They have an overview of the topic and know what resources are found in the text. Guide students through doing what good students do. Many students do not read the table of contents unless directed to do so. *What topics seem most interesting to you? Choose a topic you know most about. Write down everything you know about that topic. How many units/sections are there? How many chapters?*

- **Find all the special resources in the book.**
  Guide students in finding all the resources in the text. Show them how to use the index to find "lost" information. Demonstrate how the words in the glossary relate to the words in bold in the text. Have them identify the content in the appendices. Identify and show them how to use all the other resources in the text such as maps or other tables of information. *What are the resources? How will they be helpful to you?*

- **Look at the layout of chapters.**
  Chapters are broken into sections with headings and subheadings. Guide students in looking at the chapter they will be reading. Have students read the first paragraph of the chapter and the summary at the end. *What do you predict you will learn in this chapter?* Then have students read all of the bold headings in the first section. *What do you predict is in this section?* Show students how to turn headings and subheading into questions and then locate the information. Ask students to turn the first two of the headings into questions. *What kind of information do you expect to find under these headings?* Have students read the section to find the answer to the question they formed. *How well did the heading predict the content? Look at the questions at the end of the chapter. Guess the answers to the questions.*

- **Have students complete a textbook scavenger hunt.**
  Figure 16.2 illustrates an example of a scavenger hunt.

The goal of these activities is to help students understand external text structure. It will then become one of the supports for comprehending content.

Internal Text Structure

If we say external text structure is bewildering, the internal structure is even more so. Students who can follow narratives may be confused by expository text because it has no plot line to support comprehension. To compound the problem, expository text comes in many types, each with its own structure, signal words, and purpose. That's not all. A single text, a single chapter, a single article will contain multiple types.

Figure 16.2 Textbook Scavenger Hunt

Textbook Scavenger Hunt Example

Let's look at your new science textbook. What's in it? Circle the correct location for each of these parts.

Index ....front back not in the book
Appendix ....front back not in the book
Tips on Using the Book..front back not in the book
Atlas ....front back not in the book
Table of Content...front back not in the book

Now let's look at the chapters in your book. Do they have. . .
an introduction? ....yes no
a summary? ....yes no
major headings in bold? ....yes no
a list of vocabulary words?..yes no
a pronunciation guide for difficult words? ....yes no
any special sections that are not a part of the chapter itself?........................yes no

Now let's use some of these special sections in your book to answer these questions.

1. How many chapters are in the book?   _____

2. What are the names of the two special sections?

_____   _____

3. On what pages is a discussion of cellular digestion?   _____

4. What is the appropriate English system equivalent to a liter? _____

5. Define dermis. _____

6. Name the part of the book where these students can quickly and easily find the answers to their questions.

Student Question	Part of Book
Kala forgot how long a meter is.	
Tom wondered if this science book mentions Gregor Mendel's work.	
Kevin couldn't remember what *commensalism* meant.	
Margi wondered if she was going to study genetics this year.	

Table 16.3 Expository Words and Their Purpose

Type of Text Structure	Purpose
Personal narrative	To tell a personal story
Descriptive	To describe
Informational	To inform
Sequence/how-to	To show steps or sequence
Compare/contrast	To show similarities and differences
Cause and effect	To tell why
Persuasive	To convince
Problem/solution	To provide a solution
News story	To report the facts

Comprehension depends on understanding structure. The way a text is organized impacts the way students will search for meaning within the text (Dymock 1998; Hess 2008). If students are reading a story, they search for the character, setting, and events. They know there will be a problem and anticipate how it will be resolved. They also know the purpose is to entertain. Likewise, if they are reading a comparison essay, they will search for all the ways the subjects are alike. They know the purpose is to compare.

Each of the types of expository text in Table 16.3 has a different purpose and is organized in a unique way to accomplish that purpose. Unfortunately, the author does not outright tell the reader what that purpose is. Instead, signal words and phrases, as well as the way the text is organized, inform the reader of the purpose.

Monitoring Comprehension

Monitoring comprehension is an integral part of reading. It involves making decisions that help maintain or increase the level of comprehension. *What is this saying? Am I getting it?* Understanding text structure helps students with this monitoring (Kinnune & Vauras 1998). Each organizational pattern suggests particular ideas that will be addressed within the text. If it is a persuasive piece, then students know they are looking for pro and con arguments. If it is a cause-and-effect article, they are looking for both the cause and the effects. Proficient readers are able to read, looking for the key points of the text. When the expected information is not there, they stop and reread. They know what should be in the text just as they know that characters, settings, and events are elements in a story. When they are asked to recount what they have read, their summaries reflect the text organization.

If students do not know these structures, they have no idea what elements should be present and so are not searching for that information. They have no way to monitor their comprehension or to prioritize text information. They simply do not have to tools to assess their understanding.

Teaching Internal Text Structure

How do students gain an understanding of text structure? They learn the genre of story over a period of nearly eight years with repeated exposures through books and movies.

Meaningful conversations about the elements in story solidify the understanding of its structure. This is not so with expository text. Students may have minimal exposure until they reach grade 4, where suddenly they are expected to know how to read and comprehend it in order to learn content area subjects. We must bridge that gap by engaging students in a meaningful way in a relatively short amount of time.

Another hurdle in teaching internal text structure is the way it is implemented. Almost all texts use multiple types, and those types may change from paragraph to paragraph. If we attempt to teach it by having students look at text, we find how confusing it is to unravel the intertwined structures. In addition, many textbooks are not well written. Awards are given for the best stories and so they tend to be better written. We have yet to see awards for the best textbook in science or social studies. The bottom line is that it is difficult, if not impossible, to effectively teach internal text structure by looking at text. Some have succeeded by carefully choosing well-written individual paragraphs, but those have been specifically written to teach text structures.

We go back to the same principles used in teaching students to read words. "In order for a child to understand something, he must construct it himself, he must reinvent it" (Piaget 1972, cited in Chomsky 1979, p. 49). The key word is *construct*. One powerful way to teach text structure is to have students plan and write different types of paragraphs themselves. They are producing a product using the concepts and principles of each genre. As soon as students are able to write a sentence, they can learn how to plan and organize text structures appropriate for their grade level.

The skills needed for understanding internal text structure are best removed from reading instruction to writing instruction. We need to use a kinesthetic approach, guide students to construct understanding, and allow them to monitor their learning. *Constructing* means that they must produce and that means writing. We then make the leap back to reading, and through carefully written questions, guide students in understanding the text.

Once students learn the genre, they can also use writing as a way to summarize the text. They use their knowledge of text structure to understand and respond to what they have read. The connection between writing and reading comes full circle (see Figure 16.3). First, students learn the genre through writing, then gain information from a text based on their understanding of the structure, and finally, respond to the ideas found in the text through writing.

Figure 16.3 The Writing and Reading Connection

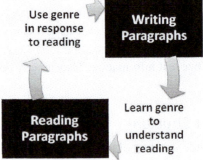

The other means of teaching text structure is more subtle. Using well-planned questions that reflect the text structure, teachers can guide students in finding information within the text. Students will discover the purpose of the author and the details that support the conclusions. The details of this questioning strategy will be discussed later.

Sentence Structure and Grammar

Traditionally, grammar was taught as an isolated skill apart from reading and writing, but because of the skill and drill nature of instruction, its value was questioned and it disappeared from the school curriculum. However, its necessity soon became evident. Research showed that students with poor comprehension skills scored in the 30th percentile in grammatical understanding. They did not understand the structure of sentences and it was impacting reading comprehension (Adolf 2006). To understand who or what a topic is about, what is happening, or how these are described, students must be able to pick out the subject, verb, and descriptors in a sentence.

One of the problems that plagued the traditional approach to teaching grammar was the disconnect with real reading and writing. Students could rattle off definitions of the parts of speech or complete a worksheet where they were required to identify them but had no idea how to find those in their own writing or in the writing of others. It was not practical. They didn't use that knowledge to aid them in reading comprehension or to revise their own writing.

Why Must We Teach Grammar?

Understanding the terms of grammar provides a concrete way to refer to words and discuss how they are used. Imagine walking into a room but having no name for the chair, or the table, or the carpet. We would be pointing or calling it "that." We need to have a way to talk about words and how they are used in sentences. As we will see later, there is no way to have a conversation on the revision of writing without knowing the names of the parts of speech and the structure of sentences.

When teaching students how to write, we need to be able to give a reason why the sentence should be revised. We must be able to say the verb and the noun don't agree, or the participles or gerunds are dangling, or the sentence structure is not parallel. Grammatical knowledge becomes a valuable tool in the hands of students when they are writing. They can look at the nouns and verbs in their sentences and determine the effectiveness of their word choices. They can scrutinize their work to see if verb tenses are correct and if modifiers come where they belong. Without this knowledge, they have no way to make those decisions.

Grammar explicitly teaches the structure of the language, which is helpful for students coming from low literacy backgrounds or who are just learning English. The way words are ordered in sentences differs from language to language. If you have learned other languages, you know how valuable understanding grammar and word order are to proficient understanding (see Table 16.4).

Table 16.4 How Grammar Impacts Reading and Writing

Writing	Reading comprehension
• Informs correct structure	• Helps reader find facts
• Used to revise writing	• Helps reader make inferences

What Do We Need to Know?

Secure a good grammar handbook to use as a reference. It will guide you in understanding the parts of speech, the function of words within a sentence, sentence structure, and punctuation.

Eight Parts of Speech

There are eight parts of speech, which can be represented by a single word, a clause, or a phrase (see Table 16.5). For example, prepositional phrases can act as adjectives or adverbs and clauses can act as nouns. This knowledge is important when determining word order in writing because modifiers need placed as close as possible to the word they are modifying. Students need to know these well enough that they can identify them in their own writing and in the writing of others.

The parts of speech must be learned apart from individual words because a word may serve as different parts of speech. For example, the word *light* can be a noun (Please turn on the *light*), a verb (Did the bird *light* on the telephone wire?), or an adjective (The feather was *light*). The word *home* can be a noun (He bought a new *home*) or it can be an adverb (He went *home*). How it is used in a sentence determines what part of speech it is. Students cannot rely on just remembering that a particular word is a certain part of speech.

If you need help in identifying what part of speech a word is, the dictionary will tell you with examples of its function within a sentence.

Function of Words within a Sentence

Some parts of speech may serve more than one function within a sentence. For example, a noun can be the subject, direct object, indirect object, object of the preposition, or noun of direct address. Understanding the function of a word within a sentence helps the reader know the meaning of the sentence. Is the noun causing the action, receiving the action, or a description of the action? The student has to be able to do more than just read the word. Look at the word *man* in these sentences.

The *man* ran across the street.

The girl gave the *man* a gift.

The dog ran from the *man*.

Knowing how to read the word *man* is not sufficient for understanding the meaning of these sentences.

When it comes to functions of words, what do students need to know?

Table 16.5 Parts of Speech

	Definition	How Used
Noun	Person, place, thing, or idea. Answers the question: *who or what.*	Subject, direct object, indirect object, object of the preposition, noun of direct address. All clauses must have a noun.
Pronoun	Takes the place of a noun. Kinds: • personal (you, he, us) • indefinite (everyone, anyone) • relative (who, whose, which, that) • reflexive (_self & _selves, such as, himself, herself, yourself) • Interrogative (who, whose, whom, which, what) • demonstrative (this that, these, those)	Used in the same way as a noun can be used.
Adjective	Answers the questions: *What kind?* *What color?* *What size?* *What shape?* *How many?*	Modifies a noun Includes the articles, *a, an, the*
Verb	Kinds: action or linking Action: *run, jump, eat, throw, sleep, write* Linking: *is, was, were, am, are, was, taste, smell, appear, seem, sound, become*	All clauses must have a verb Phrases have only a verb and not a noun. Right now, I . . . (Present) Yesterday, I. . . . (Past) Tomorrow, I. . . . (Future)
Adverb	Answers the questions: *When?* *Where?* *How?*	Modifies a verb, adjective, or adverb
Conjunctions	Coordinating: and, but, or, for, either–or Subordinating: *although, until, when, since, if, as, because*	Connects two clauses—independent & independent or independent & dependent
Preposition	Shows position: *to, from, with, through, over, under, on, down, around, up, by, for, above, etc.*	Always occurs with an object (a noun or pronoun). These prepositional phrases may act as adjectives or adverbs within the sentence. Almost all prepositional phrases act as adverbs.
Interjections	Express feelings: *ouch, wow, yea, oh, yes, no, etc.*	Usually set off by commas or by an exclamation mark.

- The parts of a sentence
- The functions of a noun (and pronouns) within a sentence
- The functions of phrases
- The functions of clauses

Correct Sentence Structure

A few rules govern how words are placed in a sentence and which form of the word is to be used. For example, if the subject is plural, then the verb must be plural. If the paragraph begins with the present tense of the verb, then it must continue with present tense. If the antecedent of a pronoun is singular, then the pronoun must be singular.

What do students need to know?

- The difference between independent and dependent clauses and how they are used
- How to make the subject and verb agree in number
- How to use a consistent verb tense
- How to make the pronoun and its antecedent agree in number
- Where to place modifiers
- How to write parallel structure
- How to eliminate dangling modifiers

Punctuation

Beginning writers often forget end punctuation and do not know how to use the other types. Students need to be taught when and how to use periods, question marks, exclamation marks, commas, semicolons, colons, and hyphens.

If students have a working knowledge of these components, they will be able to revise their own writing and to identify them in texts.

Teaching Grammar

Application of grammatical knowledge to both writing and reading is essential, which means we must use the principles of learning transfer:

- Teach concepts rather than rote facts.
- Engage students in monitoring their own learning.
- Show students how to apply those concepts to new situations.

We also want to teach using the principles of the zone of proximal development (Vygotsky 1978), providing students with some help so they can do more and perform better than they can independently. A part of speech or concept is introduced in a lesson and then

Table 16.6 Suggested Order of Introduction of Parts of Speech

Part of Speech/Concept	Number of Weeks	Part of Speech/Concept	Number of Weeks
• Common nouns/ articles	2–3 weeks	• Action verbs—other tenses	2–3 weeks
• Proper nouns	1–2 weeks	• Coordinating conjunctions	1–2 weeks
• Adjectives	2–3 weeks	• Prepositions	2–3 weeks
• Action verbs—simple tense	2–3 weeks	• Pronouns	2–3 weeks
• Sentence parts	1–3 weeks	• Linking verbs	2–3 weeks
• Adverbs	2–3 weeks	• Interjections	1–2 weeks

practiced for one to three weeks with as much help as needed until most students have a high rate of accuracy. A new topic can then be introduced.

Table 16.6 is a suggested order of introduction of the parts of speech. For older students, additional sentence structure topics will need to be taught. Review the standards for your grade level to identify what concepts you need to teach.

The method explained here has been used successfully with students in all grades, 1 to 12. Only the sentences and the depth of knowledge are appropriately adjusted for the grade level. For example, first-grade students do not learn about introductory phrases, but fourth grade students do. Also, the number of weeks on a single topic will vary according to age and ability.

Each grammar lesson introduces or reviews a part of speech or a sentence structure using a sequence of four activities, which are taught two to three times a week for 10 to 20 minutes:

Activity #1: Discover or review the part of speech or sentence structure.

Activity #2: Engage students in oral response games.

Activity #3: Use grammar cards to kinesthetically engage students.

Activity #4: Connect grammar to writing.

Activity #1: Discover or Review the Part of Speech or Sentence Structure

Children who are English speakers enter school with a fairly sophisticated understanding of sentence structure. They know all of the parts of speech and know where they occur in a sentence, although they do not know their names. In this activity, we build on the prior knowledge of sentence structure that students already possess, drawing out the definitions from the students. After they have constructed their understanding of the part of speech, we provide the name of the part of speech.

CAUTION: Limit teacher talk to asking the questions and then giving the final definition. Students will learn this through the activities and not through your explanation and examples.

Procedure:

- The teacher writes a target sentence on the board or overhead.
- Students read the sentence together.
- Students work with this sentence to define the part of speech, guided by questions from the teacher.
- After students verbalize the characteristics, the teacher provides the name and standard definition.

For example, in the first lesson, students explain to the teacher that all of the words are people, places, things, or animals. The teacher then tells students that we call these *nouns.*

If a new concept is *not* being introduced, in this part of the lesson simply ask students for definition of concepts previously taught. For example, "What is a noun?" "What is a verb?" It should take no longer than 30 seconds to 1 minute.

Activity #2: Engage Students in Oral Response Games

This activity requires every student to think of an example of the part of speech within 30 seconds. The teacher then moves from student to student as rapidly as possible, with each giving his or her word. If the group is large, not every student might have an opportunity to speak for each request. Some examples are:

Think of a word that is a noun. You have 30 seconds to think of one.

Think of a word that is a noun that is a place.

Think of a word that is a noun that is a thing.

Think of a word that is an action verb.

Think of a word that could describe a chair.

Think of a word that describes the action verb run.

I will give you the name of a common noun and you give me a proper noun.

Procedure:

- You have 30 seconds to think of a word that. . . .
- Students reply in rapid order, one by one.
- The entire activity takes one to two minutes.

Activity #3: Use Grammar Cards to Kinesthetically Engage Students

This is a kinesthetic, constructivist approach that engages students in translating words in a sentence to the parts of speech. Students reconstruct a sentence by laying down a colored card that represents the part of speech for each word. As they play the game, they must think about broad concepts such as, "An article is always followed by a noun," "All prepositions are followed by nouns," or "All sentences have verbs." They also monitor their own learning because they are able to change their cards to the correct color and order as the correct answers are given.

Each student will need a set of grammar cards in order to play the games. They receive only the cards that represent the parts of speech they have learned. As they learn a new part of speech, a new color is added to the set. If you have students in your class who are color-blind, then write the name of the color on the cards.

Grammar Cards
Create 2″ × 3″ grammar cards from colored construction paper.
Place in individual bags for easy distribution.

Number	Color	Part of Speech		Number	Color	Part of Speech
8	Black	"I don't know"		4	Pink	pronoun
6	Red	noun		4	Yellow	conjunction
8	Orange	adjective/article		4	White	preposition
5	Blue	verb		5	Green	adverbs
				2	Purple	interjections

Procedure:

- Choose three sentences that will demonstrate the parts of speech that have been learned. Not every sentence has to have all components. Where will you find your sentences? You can create your own or lift them from grade level texts or materials.

- Write one sentence on the board or overhead.

- Students do not copy the sentence. They merely lay down a card for every word in the sentence. If they are not sure or the part of speech has not been taught, they use the black card. For example, for the sentence *A lady drove the car,* students would lay down the following cards.

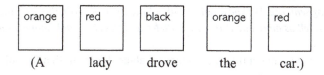

orange	red	black	orange	red
(A	lady	drove	the	car.)

- After students lay out the cards, ask one student to "read" the cards, saying the color first and then the part of speech. As the student gives the answers, the others "fix" their cards so they have the correct colors in the correct order. Using the previous example, the student would read "orange/article, red/noun, black/I don't know, orange/article, and red/noun."

- Now have students look at the sentence and do three or four activities related to what they are learning. This will give more refined practice in analyzing and manipulate the parts of speech. Ask individual students to respond. Keep it very fast-paced. Engage in no teacher talk unless a student needs help. Here are some examples of activities students can do with the sentence. Choose only three or four.

- What are the articles? What do they tell you? ("A noun is coming! A noun is coming!") What are the nouns?
- What are the nouns in the sentence?
- Change a common noun to a proper noun.
- What are the adjectives? What nouns are the adjectives modifying (describing)?
- What is the verb? What tense is it? Let's say the tenses.
- Change the tense of the verb and identify that tense.
- What are the telegraphic parts of the sentence?
- What are the adverbs? What words are they modifying (describing)?
- Add an adjective or an adverb.
- Use this procedure with the other two sentences.

When students understand the routine of this activity, it will take about ten minutes.

Activity #4: Connect Grammar to Writing—Guided Revision

During or just after grammar instruction, students can begin looking at their own writing using their new skills. At least three times a week, have students write or revise based on their knowledge of sentence structure. Through the process of guided revision, help them make specific revisions to their work.

- **Give students a sentence or paragraph to revise, giving specific directions.**
  Even first grade students can make the most amazing revisions.

Example 1: After teaching nouns and adjectives

Write the sentence for students to view. *The truck stopped.*
  This is a boring sentence. We know nothing about the truck. Rewrite this sentence, but add one or two words that tell us more about the truck. (Refer to size, color, kind, shape, number/amount, whose, which one).
  Have students read some of their new sentences aloud. Point out that the adjectives help create a picture in your mind.

Example 2: After teaching nouns, adjectives, and action verbs

Write the sentence for students to view. *The rabbit is in the field.*
  This is a boring sentence. We know nothing about the rabbit. It just is. Rewrite this sentence, but add two or three words that will paint a picture in our minds. Change the verb to an action verb.
  Have students read some of their new sentences aloud. Point out that the adjectives help create a picture in your mind.

- **Have students make specific revisions in their own writing.**
  If students practice with a single sentence as in the previous examples, they are more comfortable making revisions with their own writing.

Example 1: After teaching nouns and adjectives

Have students take out their piece of writing and guide them through the process.
  Underline all the nouns. They may not find all of the nouns in their writing, but that is okay. Make sure the ones they have underlined are actually nouns.
  Look at your nouns. How can you make your writing more interesting?
  Can you replace one noun with a more exact noun?
  Can you add an adjective to describe the noun?
  Have students make one revision and then share it with a partner.

Example 2: After teaching nouns, adjectives, and action verb

Have students take their own sentences and paragraphs and underline the noun once and the verb twice. They may not find all of the nouns or verbs in their writing but that is okay. Make sure the ones they have underlined are actually nouns and verbs.
  Have them look for the verbs *is, was, were, am,* and *are.* If they are not followed by an action verb, circle them.

How can you make your writing more interesting?

Try to change the circled verbs to action verbs,

Have you used the best action verb? For example, rather than *went,* could they use a more specific word such as *walk, run, drive, ride,* etc.?

Look at the nouns. Do you need to replace one with a more exact noun?

Can you add an adjective to describe the noun?

Have students make one revision and then share it with a partner.

- **On assigned writing, require a specific part of speech or sentence structure.**

Example 1: After teaching nouns, adjectives, and adverbs

Use each one of the five vocabulary words in a sentence. Use at least two adjectives and one adverb in your sentences. You may use these in any of the sentences you choose.

Example 2: After teaching conjunctions

When you write your paragraph (specific assignment), include at least one subordinating conjunction.

The first lesson that introduces nouns and articles is found on page 226. Other lessons that introduce the parts of speech are found in Appendix C. These lessons introduce the part of speech and need to be followed by practice lessons that contain the four activities of a grammar lesson.

Using this approach to teaching grammar is engaging for students while producing high achievement results in grammatical knowledge and in the ability to apply that knowledge to reading and writing.

Lesson 1: Common Nouns and Articles

Target Sentence	***The man sat on a chair at the house.***
Guided Discovery 1	• *Think of a word that you can use instead of man. You have 30 seconds.* List under *man*. • *How are all these word alike?* (people, animals)
Guided Discovery 2	• *Think of a word that you can use instead of chair. You have 30 seconds.* List under *chair*. • *How are all these words alike?* (things)
Guided Discovery 3	• *Think of a word that you can use instead of house. You have 30 seconds.* List under *house*. • *How are all these words alike?* (places)
Guided Discovery 4	• *Let's use one of these words instead of sat.* • *Why doesn't the word work instead of sat? (Certain words must come in a particular place in a sentence.)* Try interchanging some of the words with the word *sat* in the sentence. Do a few examples so students can see that you need one type of word in certain positions in the sentence
Definition	• All these words are called nouns. A noun is a person, a place, or a thing.
Oral Response	• *You have 30 seconds to think of a word that is a person. It can't be a name.* (Have students respond rapidly, one right after another.) • *You have 30 seconds to think of a word that is a place. It can't be a name.* (Have students respond rapidly one right after another.) • *You have 30 seconds to think of a word that is a thing.* (Have students respond rapidly one right after another.)
Guided Discovery 5	• *What are the nouns in this sentence?* man, chair, house • *What comes before each noun?* a or the • *What is the difference in meaning between the chair and a chair?*
Definition	a, an, *and* the *are articles that mark nouns. They tell us, "A noun is coming! A noun is coming!" Sometimes the noun doesn't come right after the article, but it does come soon after the article.*
Grammar Cards	Give students a set of cards with black, red, and orange. • Lay out a card for each word in this sentence. The lady drove the car. Have one student "read" the cards, saying the color and the speech part. *What are the nouns? What are the articles? What do the articles tell you?* Continue with two more sentences.

Connecting Text Structure to Writing

Text and sentence structure are not only critical skills that assist reading comprehension but also become an essential foundation for skilled writing. We will see the integral relationship between reading and writing in the next chapters and how they support each other.

Summary

Three Types of Text Structure

• External text structure—Taught during reading
  • Helps predict content
  • Helps organize and remember content
• Internal text structure—Taught during writing
  • Key words that show relationships
  • Structure is determined by genre which gives a clue to meaning
• Sentence structure—Taught during grammar
  • Tells who or what
  • Tells action or state
  • Description of subject action or state

Four Components of a Grammar Lesson
Activity #1: Discover or review the part of speech or sentence structure.
Activity #2: Engage students in oral response games.
Activity #3: Use grammar cards to kinesthetically engage students.
Activity #4: Connect grammar to writing.

What Writing Is All About

When you think of writing in school, what comes to your mind? Book reports, your "My Summer Vacation" essay, stories, or a research paper? For most of us, our memories of writing are not pleasant. We were assigned the task but not given much guidance on how to complete it. In fact, many times writing was only assigned and not taught. The focus was on the end product. We either dreaded it or accepted it as a part of school life.

My own view of writing changed when one teacher took the time to teach us *how* to write (see Figure 17.1). Both the process and the end product were important. We were taught how to plan, revise, edit, and produce a final piece. We learned not only text formats but also proper grammatical structures using Strunk and White's *The Elements of Style*. This invaluable small amount of time revolutionized my thinking about writing.

One year I was assigned to teach Writing Workshop twice a week to grades 4, 5, and 6. In this workshop, students were taught genre, grammatical structures, and how to think about writing. Most of the time was spent in actual writing. Students could choose to write

Figure 17.1   Framework for Teaching Reading

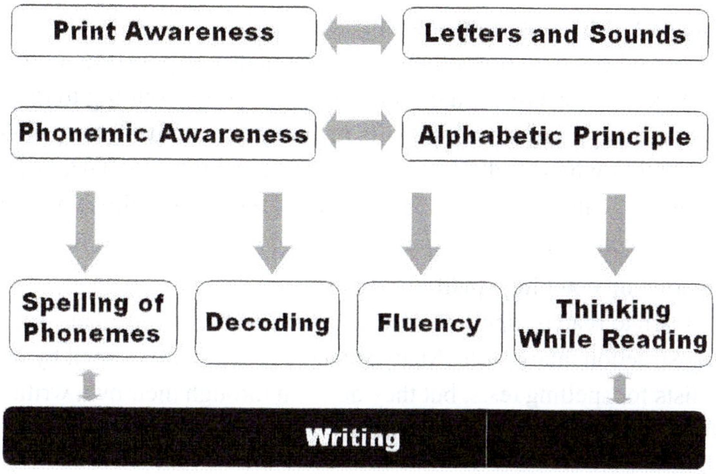

on *any* topic (it had to be appropriate) using any genre that had been taught. Every three weeks, they had to produce a final piece. Students kept record of all their writing and the time spent on a particular piece. They always had in mind that at some point, they had to choose a piece that they could revise, edit, and prepare for a final product. Sometimes, they had only one piece of writing and they took it through the entire process to final draft. Other times, they had three or four pieces, but chose to complete the one they liked best.

Students loved the class. Their comments were amazing. They thought and talked about their writing when they were at lunch, at recess, or talking with friends. They learned to spell—they loved the fact that they learned spell. They loved to write. They announced, "I am an author!" Some of these students were at risk learners and yet they progressed and glowed in the light of their achievements. I found writing can be a positive, life-changing experience.

In order to teach writing, you will need to know what to teach, and how to guide students through the process of writing.

Writing Is for More than Just Learning to Write

Writing is not just an end in itself. The value in writing extends to all of the language arts.

- **It is a means for learning internal text structure.**
  One of the foundational prerequisites for reading comprehension is understanding internal text structure. The most effective way to teach this is through writing instruction. Students construct their understanding of the different genres through writing their own pieces that reflect those structures.

- **It is a means for refining grammatical and sentence structure knowledge.**
  Writing provides a tangible way to manipulate words into correct order with correct usage. Students become brilliant writers. Those who are learning the English language or who come from literacy-deprived environments benefit from explicitly paying attention to structure.

- **It is a means for developing thinking.**
  Students learn how to express themselves logically, supporting their ideas with details. They may be expressing their own ideas or responding to the ideas of others. Either way, they develop skills to communicate what they understand effectively. "Only when students can articulate in writing the basic principles they are learning . . . can we be sure that they are internalizing those principals in an intellectually coherent way" (Sparks 2005, xvii).

- **It is a means for teaching spelling.**
  Students learn to read by spelling, but learn to spell by writing. This is where real spelling instruction takes place. Many students do not learn to spell by memorizing spelling lists for spelling tests, but they do learn through their own writing if they make their own corrections and revisions.

Table 17.1   How Skills Are Applied to Both Reading and Writing

Writing	Reading Comprehension
Choose purpose that establishes text organization.	Identify text organization that reveals purpose.
Understand text structure to design coherent writing.	Understand text structure to find facts and make inferences.
Choose audience.	Identify audience.
Use graphic organizer to plan important ideas.	Use graphic organizer to identify important ideas.

- **It is a means of expanding vocabulary.**
  Writing gives an opportunity to use words from our listening vocabulary and not just speaking vocabulary. By actually using the words we hear but don't speak, our vocabulary expands.

- **It is a means of learning skills that can be used for reading comprehension.**
  Skills acquired in learning to write can be used in reverse to comprehend text. In writing, students engage in constructing and monitoring, essential for transfer of learning. These skills can then be applied to reading comprehension. Attempts to teach students these same competencies through reading comprehension alone often fail because students are not engaged in the construction process. It is a much more challenging task to look at someone else's writing and try to reconstruct what the author did. However, if students have gone through the writing process themselves, it is much easier to spot those same processes when reading. The relationship between writing and reading is shown in Table 17.1.

Guidelines That Apply to All Writing

If we are to accomplish all that writing has to offer, then we must follow some important guidelines. These apply to *all* writing in the classroom except journal writing.

- **Writing needs to be taught and not just assigned.**
  Any time writing is assigned but not taught, the value of writing plummets. Sadly, almost all writing in American classrooms is assigned and not taught.

  Teach students the genre they will need to use in your class. Give students the tools to do a good job. A little class time set apart for this type of instruction pays huge dividends.

- **Develop in students the habit of thinking: plan–write–revise–edit.**
  This is the thinking we want students to use for all writing, including worksheets and tests in all subject areas. They need to know how to plan–write–revise–edit. If students go through this process for only some types of assignments, it sends a mixed message about writing and students compartmentalize this thinking for only those special occasions.

  Post it in the classroom. You will need to teach students exactly what to do for each step. No writing, except journal writing, should escape this thinking.

- **Have students write only as much as they can successfully revise and edit.**
  We usually have students write too much. Before I learned this principle, my students would write and write and write. There were so many errors and so many parts that had to be revised that it was impossible to make the corrections. If I asked students to look at their work, they became discouraged at the insurmountable task. Neither the students nor I enjoyed it. I wanted to go through the plan–write–revise–edit process, but the length of the writing prohibited it.

  So how long should the piece be? Just long enough for students to revise and edit it in a reasonable amount of time. The better writers they become, the longer the piece can be (see Figure 17.2). Start with one sentence. When students can write the perfect sentence, teach them how to write one paragraph. When students can write one paragraph with few or no errors, teach them how to write three paragraphs, then five paragraphs, and finally longer reports. As students learn the skills, they make fewer and fewer errors so in the end a five paragraph essay had no more errors than the one sentence or one paragraph did at the beginning.

- **Provide feedback throughout the entire writing process.**
  How does this differ from what is often done in the classroom? Many times, writing is assigned with very little feedback offered to students during the process. The teacher correcting errors after writing is completed is not teaching writing. Using the principles of the zone of proximal development (ZPD), we provide as much feedback as needed until students can perform the task independently.

  Feedback is also an indispensable part of writing. Only in classrooms is this omitted. This is due to the "testing" mindset, which says the teacher explains and the students show they know. Professional writers receive feedback from multiple sources before their final revision goes into print. Part of developing good writing habits in students is providing feedback and showing them how to use that feedback to improve their writing.

- **Expect students to apply the writing skills to all writing in all subject areas.**
  The standard remains the same no matter what students are writing. We don't want students to compartmentalize their thinking about writing and relegate it only to "writing time." We need to look at all writing in the classroom in all subjects—even that done on worksheets or answering questions at the end of the chapter.

Figure 17.2 Sequence of Writing Assignments

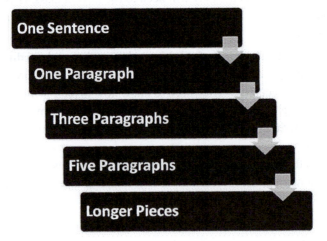

One Sentence

One Paragraph

Three Paragraphs

Five Paragraphs

Longer Pieces

- **Show students how to apply the mechanics of writing to their own writing.**
  First of all, they must learn grammar, capitalization, and punctuation in such a way that it transfers to their own writing. They must be engaged in applying this knowledge to word choice, sentence structure, spelling, punctuation, and capitalization. We expect them to use the grammar they have learned.

- **Give time to write every day.**
  If students are to be skilled writers, they need to practice often. They do not have to write for long periods of time, but they do have to write. And whatever they write must be self-corrected using their knowledge of grammar, capitalization, and punctuation.

> Professional writers experience near panic at the thought of missing one day of writing. They know that if they miss a day it will take enormous effort to get their minds back on the trail of productive thought.
>
> When writers write every day, they compose even when they are not writing.
>
> —Donald Graves,
> *A Fresh Look at Writing*, p. 104

- **As much as possible, give students choices in what they write.**
  Dishonest writing is not good writing. It is difficult to write what you do not feel or what you do not know. Give as much choice as possible even when assigning for a particular purpose. Offer choices in viewpoint, audience, genre, and/or topic. For example, if students must write on the causes of Civil War, they can be given a choice of the audience, genre, or viewpoint. Rather than just write a report, they could write a formal treatise, news article, magazine article, letter to a friend, or diary. They could write it from the viewpoint of the North or the South, making sure they bring in the viewpoint of the other. Be creative in the possible ways to design written assignments so students have choices.

Figure 17.3 compares the traditional approach to writing with the approach taken by real writers. Note how the focus is on self-direction, self-correction, and self-motivation when the authors choose what they want to write about.

Figure 17.3   Comparison between Approaches to Writing

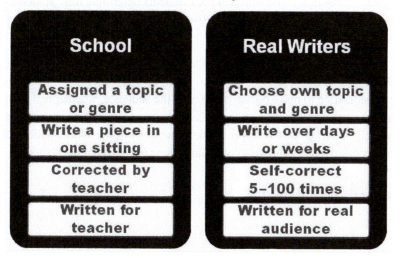

Plan–Write–Revise–Edit: A Habit of Thinking

We want to approach writing from a different perspective. In many classrooms, the teacher assigns a report, a letter, an essay, or story. Students complete the assignment, hand it in to the teacher, and the teacher grades it, noting any errors. What do students do with the paper when it is returned? They look at the grade and will either scan the noted errors or just crumple it up and throw it away. What have students learned about writing? Very little. They may have gained some content knowledge through the process, but the potential value of the assignment has been overlooked.

Whether students are responding to a question in a text or writing an original essay, we want them to get in the habit of thinking through the writing process. If they do it enough, it will become second nature.

So what should we teach and expect students to be able to do in each part of the thinking process? Table 17.2 describes a better process of writing.

Planning

What do students need to think about when they are planning their writing? What do they need to know? Without instruction, they will not know how to plan.

Purpose

What is the purpose of the piece of writing? The purpose will determine the type of text (genre). As we saw, each type of text has a specific purpose and a specific organization.

> **purpose → type of text → organization of text**

For example, if the purpose is to persuade, it precludes a persuasive text that has a specific organization. If the purpose is to tell why, it requires a cause-and-effect structure with a specific organization. In order for students to write, they need to know both the purpose of the writing and understand the structure of the genre. That needs to be explicitly taught.

If students are responding to questions in a text, they need to determine the purpose so they can structure the response properly with the correct organization. Instruction in identifying key words in the question will help students determine this. Students should not be expected to know how to answer questions in a text without explicit direction on how to do so.

Audience

The other consideration to make during planning is the audience, whether real or imaginary. It makes a difference whether the audience is a classmate, a city commissioner, a teacher, a Northern merchant during the Civil War, or the community of the World Wide Web. Both content and perspective are adjusted to communicate to the needs of the audience.

> **audience → content → perspective**

Table 17.2 The Write Way of Thinking

	What to Do	Focus	What Students Need to Know	How to Teach
Plan ↓	Generate and organize ideas.	Ideas Organization Audience	Internal text structures How to write a response to questions	Use oral sentences and paragraphs. Organize writing with graphic organizers. Develop paragraph frames. Organize thoughts in outlines.
Write ↓	Write. Read aloud. Use self-check list. Make obvious corrections.	Voice	Word spacing Indent paragraph Special formats for letters, poems, and others	Write every other line. Write with big spaces between words. Write with wide margins. Teach how to form letters properly.
Revise ↓	Add or delete. Rearrange. Replace words.	Word Choice Sentence Fluency	Grammar Sentence structure Unique characteristics of the genre	Teach the parts of speech. Teach sentence structure. Guide step by step through the revision process.
Edit ↓	Correct spelling. Correct punctuation. Correct capitalization.	Conventions	Capitalization Punctuation Spelling How to use a dictionary	Consider dictation of words and sentences. Use games to teach dictionary skills.
Publish ➡	1. Individual book 2. Classroom book 3. On the web 4. Hand in to teacher only		5. On walls of classroom or hall 6. Portfolio of final drafts 7. Letter or article to community 8. Newsletter to students or parents	

Ideas

Without ideas, there is no coherent writing. Ideas, or what to say, come from reading and personal experience. The assigned topic may require research or it may entail brainstorming personal perspectives and experience.

ideas → research or reading or personal experience

Organize Writing: Graphic Organizers

What can we do to help students organize their writing? First of all, we must teach them the different types of texts with their specific organization. Graphic organizers that reflect the text structure aid students in identifying the ideas that are important. For example, a Herringbone identifies the information for a sentence, a Venn diagram shows how two things are alike and different, a flow chart shows sequence, a matrix identifies characteristics. These are particularly helpful for the kinesthetic learner who must see the big picture displayed succinctly. When planning a writing assignment, choose graphic organizers that will best reflect the organization for the particular genre.

text structure	→	oral sentences or paragraphs	→	graphic organizers	→	paragraph frames	→	organizational outlines

Organize Writing: Paragraph Frames

Paragraph frames provide a "fill in the blank" structure that supports students while they are learning the organization of a type of paragraph. They have been successfully used with primary grade students as well as students through high school who struggle with writing (Nichols 1980; Cudd & Roberts 1989). Any student who does not know how to structure a paragraph will benefit. The following is an example of paragraph frame for a sequential paragraph on how paper is made.

I learned many interesting things about how paper is made. First, _____
_____. Next, _____
_____. Finally, _____.
After this, _____.

You can develop your own paragraph frames to fit the needs of your topic and the text genre you are teaching. Provide the initial statement for students and the key words commonly used in the succeeding sentences. Sometimes it is appropriate to leave blanks in the initial sentence. For example, in a comparison paragraph, the first sentence might read: "_____ and _____ are alike in many ways."

How do you use them to help students plan? First students need to know the specific structure of the genre, identify the ideas, and arrange them on a graphic organizer. The information from the graphic organizer can then be transferred to the paragraph frame. Support students through the entire process, asking questions, modeling, and guiding. Use the principles of the zone of proximal development, providing as much help as needed until students can complete them independently.

After completing the frame, students should *always* recopy the paragraph or paragraphs so the paragraph appears just as if they had written it completely on their own. This way, they must pay attention to capitalization, punctuation, and formatting.

Organize Writing: Organizational Outlines

As students become more sophisticated in their understanding of the text structures, they may not use the graphic organizers or need the paragraph frames, but may only use a written organizational outline. It might look like this for the previous sequential paragraph.

1. How paper is made
   a. Step 1 (two- or three-word description)
   b. Step 2 (two- or three-word description)
   c. Step 3 (two- or three-word description)
2. What happens after it is completed

Writing

Students are now ready to write. Require good writing and good form. This might mean showing them how properly form letters, leave spaces between words, or indent a paragraph. To have high expectations is a sign of caring.

Although you expect them to write well, students must have the mindset that this is the first try. Have them write every other line and leave wide margins. This leaves room to revise and edit. If they are responding to questions from a text or on a test, they will, of course, not be making the same type of revisions so they do not need to leave those kinds of spaces.

After writing, all students need to do a quick self-check. If they are writing answers to questions, this might be all the revising and editing that is done. Provide students with a permanent checklist that is appropriate for their skill level. This will be readily available whenever they write.

The following sample includes a list of common errors that are made by writers of all ages. I used this list for my first graders as well as my eighth graders. Whisper reading or reading aloud is essential for all of us. It allows us to see mistakes that we otherwise "fix" when we read silently. If students are having difficulty with dangling modifiers, parallel structure, or other structural elements, add these to the checklist.

Check your work
- Read your sentence or paragraph in a whisper voice.
- Did you leave out any words?
- Does it make sense?
- Is there a capital letter at the beginning of each sentence?
- Is there a capital letter at the beginning of all names?
- Are there capital letters where they should not be?
- Is there end punctuation at the end of each sentence?
- Underline each word you are not sure how to spell. Look them up in a dictionary.
- Correct any other mistakes you find.

Revising

What is revision? It is making changes to words, forms of words, and sentence structure. It can include adding, deleting, replacing, or rearranging words, a process that requires knowledge and thought. General instructions to make revisions to improve word choices and meaning are not sufficient. Students need to know exactly what to do and how to do it.

What do students need to know in order to revise their work? They need to pull in their knowledge of grammar. If it has been taught properly, they already know the tie between grammar and writing through the mini-activities they have done. Any additional information on unique components of text, such as how to add conversation to a story, can be taught during writing.

Guided Revision Revisited

Students are guided step by step through the revision process, looking for specific words and making specific revisions. The focus of revision is on sentence fluency and on making word choices that convey exact meaning or build a mental picture. The teacher must determine what will be the most productive revisions based on the age and ability of the students and the type and length of the piece of writing. If students know only nouns and adjectives, then that will be the focus of the revision. If students know all the parts of speech and sentence structures such as introductory phrases, then the focus will be determined by the need of students. Focus the revision on whatever errors students are consistently making. For example, if students are consistently using bland words such as nice, go, have, and lots, have them underline those words and replace them.

The length of the writing will guide in determining the amount of time spent on revision. If it is one sentence or one paragraph, revision can be done in a few minutes. If it is five or more paragraphs, you may choose to have students revise over two or three days with a different focus on each day. Remember, the pieces they are writing are short enough that they can be revised easily.

Guided revision was modeled in the activities in Chapter 16 to tie grammar to writing. The entire process can be completed in 5 to 20 minutes:

- Students take out their writing and underline, double underline, circle, box, or place a check mark on the target words or section. It is not important that they find every instance in their paper. This will take only one or two minutes.
- The teacher directs them to make specific changes. In some instances, examples of the focus must be introduced and discussed. For example, if students are to rewrite the first sentence of their story to grab the reader's attention, then they need to hear good examples and then immediately apply the instruction to their own story. If they are to use third-party conversation or indirect description to describe their character, then they need to see and hear examples of it and then immediately apply it. Table 17.3 provides examples of some of the types of revisions that can be made.
- Once students have identified the target words or section and made an initial correction, they can share those with a partner for more ideas. This will take only a few minutes.
- Have students read *before* and *after* sentences to the class. This is always an encouragement to everyone in the class.

Figure 17.4 provides a guideline for revising stories.

Table 17.3 Types of Guided Revision

Underline the nouns once.	Change to a more exact noun or add an adjective.
Double underline the verbs *is, am, are, was, were* that are not helping verbs.	Change them to action verbs.
Double underline all the action verbs.	Change any action verbs to more exact or interesting verbs.
Circle every *and*	If it is at the beginning of a sentence, cross it out. If it is connecting two sentences, change it to a subordinating conjunction such as while, since, etc.
Underline the beginning of every sentence.	If any of them begin the same way, change them so they begin differently.
Whisper read your piece. Does it flow easily?	If every sentence begins with the same word, is the same length, or even contains the same words, it will not flow. Make the necessary changes.
Look for repeated words. Underline.	What word can you substitute? Use a thesaurus.
Put a check mark by the description of your character.	Rather than you describe the character, how can you have their words or actions describe them OR how can you have another character describe them in a conversation?
Put check marks where you have told the audience of the time and place.	Make the descriptions more vivid by adding adjectives and using more exact nouns or use the conversation of the characters to give that information.

Figure 17.4 Revising Stories

Revising Stories

Procedure for teaching the elements of a story:

- In one to two minutes, explain the element.
- Read two or three examples from actual stories that illustrate the element.
- Have students find the element in their own story.
- Give them time to make revisions on the spot.

Example of an element to teach:

- Discuss ways characters can be described in a story.
  - Direct description of the character
  - Actions that reveal what the character is like
  - Listening in on conversations
  - Thinking process and feelings of a character
- Read and show examples of the element to students.
- Now look at your story. How did you tell us about your characters?
  - Did you describe them?
  - Did you describe their actions?
  - Do I know what they are like by the way they talk?
  - Does someone in your story talk to someone else about them?
- Find where your characters are described.
  - What can you change to make your story better?
  - How can you change the way your characters are introduced?

Figure 17.5 Game to Generate Alternate Words

Game to Generate Alternate Words

Procedure:

- There are four people on a team. Students choose or teacher assigns who will take these positions.
  - A messenger takes the answers to the team seated next to them.
  - A secretary will be responsible for NEATLY writing the answers. In order to get credit, the other team MUST be able to read your writing.
  - A reader will read the answers of the other team.
  - A leader will lead the discussion of the group.
- The teacher will give a word and the team has one minute to generate as many words as possible that could be used in place of it to give a more exact meaning.
- The teacher will say STOP and all pencils go down. There is absolute silence while the messenger takes the list to the team next to them.
- Each team will check the words and give 1 point for each acceptable word.
- The team with the most words wins or receives points.
- Four or five rounds of this game can be completed at one time.

Suggested words and possible substitutions:

- walk: saunter, stride, stroll, tromp, lope, hike, jaunt, march, pace, traipse, tramp, ramble
- find: locate, spot, see, detect, stumble upon, track down, uncover, notice
- said: add, affirm, announce, answer, claim, suggest, express, pronounce, relate, remark, state
- went: advanced, journeyed, departed, escaped, fled, traveled, drove, skipped, rode
- has: owns, holds, acquires, occupies, possesses, retains
- children: kids, baby, toddler, adolescent, infant, descendant, teenager, squirt, tot
- street: lane, road, avenue, roadway, route, drive, parkway, trail, court, boulevard

Use interesting introductory words and connectors to show relationship rather than just the words *and* and *but*.

Generate a list of interesting connector or introductory words: while, since, before, after, during, yet, however, instead, therefore, besides, furthermore, although, if until, as soon as, when, nevertheless, consequently, moreover, on the other hand, indeed, and in fact.

Activities that Support Revision

Students need ideas on word choices. How will they know how to choose a more exact word? Games can help them generate lists that can then be posted in the classroom (see Figure 17.5). Even first-grade students can generate a short list of substitute words. Once they understand the possibilities, they are motivated to find their own substitutions through a thesaurus. This also provides an opportunity to talk about nuances in meanings of the words.

Word lists such as the following can be posted in the classroom to help students with word choice. These words should be avoided in writing.

nice	say	go	get	big
very	said	got	pretty	some
like	eat	see	good	bad

Editing

How does editing differ from revision? Rather than looking at word choice and structure, students focus on the conventions of spelling, capitalization, and punctuation. Although they have been introduced to these conventions during reading, vocabulary, and grammar, this is where they learn to implement what they know. Guide students in finding the errors in their writing. The self-evaluation done right after the first draft will catch some of the errors, but there are usually more. At this point, if students cannot find them, either have students check each other's work or locate the errors yourself. Use standard editing marks to indicate what needs to be corrected. *Always* let students make their own corrections. If you do it for them, they will not learn from their mistakes.

Over time, when students must correct their errors, they begin to see them before anyone points them out. After they make the error, they self-correct, using the correct spelling, punctuation, and capitalization. Eventually, these kinds of errors will be less common as they learn to write correctly.

No matter what writing students do, except for journal writing, have them edit their work and make corrections. This includes worksheets or simple one-sentence assignments. It will exponentially increase their skills in spelling, punctuation, and capitalization. Figure 17.6 shows the long-term effects of self-correction.

Publishing

Find creative ways to exhibit student work. It will encourage them to take pride in their writing. Some of the options include:

- Create an individual book.
- Create a classroom book.
- Publish on the web.
- Display on the walls of classroom or hall.

Figure 17.6   The Long-term Results of Self-correction

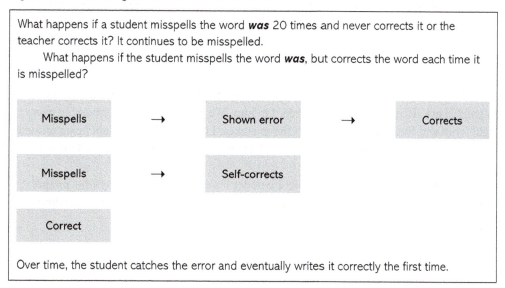

What happens if a student misspells the word ***was*** 20 times and never corrects it or the teacher corrects it? It continues to be misspelled.

What happens if the student misspells the word ***was***, but corrects the word each time it is misspelled?

| Misspells | → | Shown error | → | Corrects |

| Misspells | → | Self-corrects |

| Correct |

Over time, the student catches the error and eventually writes it correctly the first time.

- Compile a portfolio of final drafts.
- Send a letter or article to community members.
- Publish a newsletter for students or parents.

Meet My Student

John

The first time I met John was in the resource room late in September. He was in third grade and spent two hours in the morning working on language skills.

"I can't read. I'm dumb," he seriously announces to me as we begin work. I point out the story that he read to me perfectly the day before. It does not convince him.

"Would you like to write on the chalkboard?" I ask. His eyes light up and he gives a nod. I suggest that he writes a sentence on the board. We will "fix" it together, and then he could write it on a large sheet of construction paper and draw a picture to go with it.

His serious expression returns. "I can't spell. I'm dumb. I can't write anything."

We discuss some of the things he could write about and the way he could say it. I am very reassuring and supportive in my tone of voice and in my words. Suddenly, he has an idea. He writes: "Thir is a mnster undr mi bed."

"I can read your sentence, John. I know exactly what you wrote!" I am smiling. He grins.

I read it to him. "That is a very good sentence, John. Should we fix it so you can write it on the paper and draw a picture?" He nods, very pleased with himself.

We go through the sentence word by word, discussing every thing that is right and discussing what can be changed. He makes the corrections with very little help. He grins. He has felt tremendous achievement.

I get the construction paper out for him and his sullen expression returns. "I can't draw. I'm dumb." He carefully writes his sentence. He makes a few marks on the paper under his sentence.

"It looks like a very scary monster to me! I like it!" He colors, although he is still looking as if he is unsure. However, he is pleased enough to find a place to display his work when it is finished.

The next day, John comes into the resource room and the first thing he says is, "Can I write another sentence on the board?"

Without any hesitation he writes: "I wnt on a vakasun."

I feel very pleased that he has enough courage to take the risk to write. "May I read it to you?" I ask. He grins and nods. I read it to him. We fix the sentence, discussing every right word and figuring out how to fix the mistakes. I commend him for not being afraid of using vacation even though it is a long word. He is happy. He has experienced many successes in one sentence.

John draws another wonderful picture under his sentence. He displays this picture, too, looking as if the sense of achievement has totally changed his outlook on reading and writing.

Teaching Writing

We have only talked about the process of writing. Now we must look at the specific structure of each genre and how to teach it.

Summary

The Value of Writing
Writing is a means . . . • For learning internal text structure • For refining grammatical and sentence structure knowledge • For developing thinking • For teaching spelling • Of expanding vocabulary • Of learning skills that can be used for reading comprehension
Guidelines That Apply to All Writing *Except* Journals
• Writing needs to be taught and not just assigned. • Develop in students the habit of thinking: plan–write–revise–edit. • Have students write only as much as they can successfully revise and edit. • Provide feedback throughout the entire writing process. • Expect students to apply the writing skills to all writing in all subject areas. • Show students how to apply the mechanics of writing to their own writing. • Give time to write every day. • As much as possible, give student choice in what they write.
Plan–Write–Revise–Edit: A Habit of Thinking
Planning • Purpose determines type of text and the organization of that text. • Audience determines content and perspective. • Ideas come from reading and personal experience • Organize writing: Graphic organizers that reflect text structure organize ideas. • Organize writing: Paragraph frames support learning a text structure. • Organize writing: Organizational outlines organizes ideas. **Writing** • Write every other line and leave wide margins. • Complete the self-check. **Revising** • Use guided revision. **Editing** • Focus on the conventions of spelling, capitalization, and punctuation. **Publishing** • Find creative ways to exhibit student work.

Chapter 18

Teaching Writing versus Assigning Writing

Unfortunately, writing is assigned but rarely taught. Students are given cursory instructions on a topic and format, and that is all: "Write a report on Abraham Lincoln." They write, turn in their papers, and receive grades. And in that process, we have missed the incalculable impact writing could have on thinking, spelling, vocabulary, and reading comprehension.

Quality writing instruction is sequenced, explicit, and thorough. We begin with the rudimentary structure of the sentence before we teach them how to write a paragraph. We teach only one type of paragraph at a time, providing multiple experiences with that genre that include examining the elements of the structure, orally producing a paragraph, planning, writing, self-checking, revising, and editing. We use the principles of the zone of proximal development (ZPD) to provide all the support and help necessary for students to become proficient at the independent level. Once students have mastered a particular genre of paragraph, we teach them how to expand that same framework into a three- or five-paragraph essay. Instruction is not haphazard but organized and detailed. Every step of the way, students are taught all they need to know with ongoing feedback.

The Perfect Sentence

We begin by teaching the sentence. The detail and the amount of time spent on this will be determined by the age and ability of the student. At all grade levels, including college, there will be students who do not know the difference between a sentence and an incomplete sentence. All remedial readers, no matter what their age, must spend some time getting acquainted with the sentence.

Learning about the Sentence

What is a sentence? Providing a definition is not sufficient. If we want information to transfer, students must engage in developing a definition. Kindergarten and first-grade students will need the most help from you, but students in other grades should be able to construct a definition, providing examples and nonexamples. Once students have defined it, demonstrate the differences. This is an example:

"A sentence is a complete thought. It tells us who or what and tells us something about the person, place or thing.

"If I come up to you and say, '*a yellow cat*,' (actually approach a student and say a *yellow cat*) you have no idea what I am talking about. But if I say, 'My brother gave me a yellow cat for my birthday,' then you understand. It is a complete idea.

"Every sentence begins with a capital letter and ends with a period, question mark, or exclamation point."

This idea is reinforced through asking questions every time students write until they no longer make the errors. "What does every sentence begin with? What comes at the end of every sentence?"

After demonstrating, students must apply the information to new situations. The use of oral activities provides a way for students to practice rapidly with immediate feedback. Instead of using worksheets that rob from valuable writing time, have them respond to oral sentences and nonsentences with thumbs up or thumbs down or with a response card that indicates yes or no. Ask them to explain why they answered as they did. Adjust the difficulty of the sentences and nonsentences for the grade level. For example, what a first-grade student will mistake for a sentence differs from what a high school student mistakes as a sentence. You can lift examples from student work or find sentences and nonsentences in materials for that grade level.

The activity in Figure 18.1 takes only two or three minutes and tells you exactly who understands the concept and who doesn't. For those who do not "get it," provide extra practice spread over a few days.

Constructing Oral Sentences

Another activity that is helpful for young children or for those learning the language is creating oral sentences (see Figure 18.2). Students make up a sentence using a vocabulary or spelling word. For example, for the word *store*, the student might say, "*My mom went to the store.*"

Figure 18.1   Activity: Is it a Sentence?

Is It a Sentence?

Students show thumbs up or thumbs down OR red card = no; green card = yes.

After the response, ask,

Why do you say it is a sentence?

Why do you say it is not a sentence?

Sample sentences:

- the huge whale
- The little lamb ran up to the fence.
- seemed like a friendly dog
- She explained how to get to the park.
- Come find the treasure.
- ate quickly

Figure 18.2 Constructing Oral Sentences

Oral Sentences

- Teach students that a sentence gives complete information.
- Give examples of complete and incomplete sentences by using the vocabulary/spelling words or words from the story.
- Give students a vocabulary word or ask a question. Have them make up a sentence. Have students *extend* their oral sentences by asking **when, who, what, where, why,** and **how.**

Figure 18.3 Assignment Ideas for a Single Sentence

Assignment Ideas for Writing a Single Sentence

- Copy a single sentence and draw a picture to go with it.
- Write a single sentence from a vocabulary word.
- Write a single sentence from a picture using the sentence frame.
- Write a single sentence about the story.
- Write a single sentence to describe a person, place, or thing.
- Write a single sentence in answer to a single question.
- Write a single question and answer it with a single sentence.

By asking *what, where, when, why,* and *how* questions, you can help students extend the sentence. "When did she go to the store?" *"This morning, my mom went to the store."* "Why did she go to the store?" *"This morning, my mom went to the store to get milk."*

The strategy can also be used to answer questions on a story. Students become confident in their ability to create a meaningful sentence.

Planning the Sentence

Write sentences as a class before asking students to write their own. If students are young, you may need to do three or four before students are comfortable with the process. Grades 2 and up can usually write independently after one class experience. Some remedial students of all ages will need to spend more time planning sentences.

Start with a word, a picture, a story, or an experience (see Figure 18.3). Words can come from spelling or vocabulary lists. Pictures may be those you have cut from magazines or those from a text. A story provides a description of a character, a setting, or plot summary. A personal experience is described with one sentence.

Generating Ideas for a Sentence

- Think of three things you know about this person, place, or thing.
- Use who, what, when, where, why, how.
- Use how it looks, smells, feels, sounds, and/or tastes to help you think of ideas.
- Use short words to make a list.
- Fill in a sentence frame. Use one word or a phrase in each box. Sometimes, one or more of the boxes is not applicable to the sentence.

The Sentence Frame

Who?	What?	When?
Where?	Why?	How?

Writing the Sentence

Instruct students to convert their sentence frame to a sentence:

- Using the words in the boxes, craft a well-written sentence.
- The words might have to be rearranged.
- Leave spaces between words. Use the self-check list to fix any mistakes.
- Find out how to spell words you don't know.

Students of all ages using this frame can write funny, interesting, incredible sentences. This frame not only is useful in writing a creative sentence but also can guide students in writing a summary of a paragraph or a story they have read. Remedial students benefit from using this frame to identify key ideas in a passage. Lewis from Chapter 16 used it to gain comprehension from a passage. He completed one of these on every paragraph he read, and eventually for a whole story.

Revising the Sentence

These are the key questions to ask when revising a single sentence:

- Are all the words in the right place?
- Could I use a better word?
- Could I tell more?
- Did I need to tell who, what, when, where, why, and how?

As students learn the parts of speech, use guided revision to revise the single sentence.

Editing the Sentence

There is not much to edit, but students might have missed an error in their self-check. Capitalization, punctuation, and spelling are the focus. Word spacing might also need to be corrected. Peers or the teacher might have to point out the error. Let the student make the correction.

Publishing the Sentence

Not all sentences will be published, but some will. Rewrite the sentence using good form and neatness. Here are some possible ways to publish:

- On a sentence strip tacked/pasted to a large class poster
- On a sentence strip pasted to a construction paper background
- On a sentence strip placed under the picture it describes
- Placed in a portfolio
- Placed in a class book

Supporting Apprehensive Writers

For students who do not like to read and write, it is best to start with very short assignments. We don't want to do too much too soon. Writing a single question with a single-sentence answer on something they are reading is a comfortable way to start. When giving the following assignment, model the process for students. They need to see you think about a book, ask a question, write out the question, and then write out the answer in a complete sentence. They need to interact with you as they orally think of a question and orally answer it. Assign only one of the three types of questions at a time.

The "What" question
Pretend you are the teacher.
Write *one* good **"what"** question about your book. "What . . . ?"
Then answer your question in a complete sentence.

The "How" question
Pretend you are the teacher.
Write *one* good **"how"** question about your book. "How . . . ?"
Then answer your question in a complete sentence.

The "Why" question
Pretend you are the teacher.
Write *one* good **"why"** question about your book. "Why . . . ?"
Then answer your question in a complete sentence.

The purpose is to ensure success at every level. These assignments help students *begin* to think about what they are reading as well as help them develop writing skills. For each assignment, students need to go through the plan–write–revise–edit process. The goal is a perfect question and a perfect answer. Once students successfully write questions and answers, they are ready to proceed to paragraphs.

The Single Paragraph

Understanding the elements of the single paragraph is necessary not only for writing, but also for reading comprehension. In order to glean information from text, the internal structure must be recognized. Learning the organization of paragraphs is best done by constructing them rather than observing. Although seeing models of well-constructed paragraphs is important, models are usually not sufficient. We can watch someone bake a cake and see a wonderful cake, but only until we bake one ourselves do we grasp the details.

So, how is a paragraph constructed? All paragraphs except the comparison/contrast and the news story have a similar format. The kind of information that goes into each piece will differ from paragraph genre to paragraph genre. Once students learn the structure for one genre, that skill can be transferred to the other types. Of all the paragraphs, the persuasive is possibly the most difficult to write because it requires critical thinking.

The Basic Structure of a Paragraph

The following is the basic structure of a paragraph. Most genres will follow this form with slight differences in the type of information that goes into each section.

The Basic Paragraph Structure

Thesis statement

- Supporting detail 1
- Supporting detail 2
- Supporting detail 3

Concluding sentence

Look at the basic structure of each of these paragraphs in Figure 18.4. See how each compares to the basic structure, but notice the subtle differences. What is included in the beginning and concluding statement will differ, as well as the type of information that supports those statements.

Figure 18.4 Basic Structure of Paragraphs

Personal Narrative	Descriptive	Informational
To tell a personal story	*To describe*	*To inform*
Thesis statement	Thesis statement	Thesis statement
• 3 descriptions of event	• 3 descriptions	• 3 detail/support/reasons
Thesis statement stated backward	Thesis statement stated backward	Thesis statement stated backward
Sequence/How-to	**Compare/Contrast**	**Problem/Solution**
To show steps or sequence	*To show similarities and differences*	*To provide a solution*
State the topic or product	Statement of two things compared or contrasted or both	Statement of problem
• List the steps or sequence in order	• Similarities and/or	• 3 solutions
State the final product	• Differences	Summary of solution in relationship to problem
	Restating two things	
Persuasive	**Cause and Effect**	**News Story**
To convince	*To tell why*	*To report the facts*
Opinion statement	Explain the result	Lead—summary (who, what, when, where, why , how)
• 3 arguments with counterarguments	• 3 causes	• 3 facts in descending order of importance
Final conclusion	Summary of relationship of effect to causes	
Arguments are placed in ascending order of importance.	The outline would be opposite if the focus is on effects.	

Review your state standards to determine what paragraph types you need to teach at your grade level. You will only need to teach a few each year so you can spend weeks teaching the format of one type. If students write multiple paragraphs using a format across multiple subject areas, it will become second nature. No matter what the grade level, the first experience with the paragraph needs to be with the informational or descriptive paragraphs. They are similar and it is easy to generate ideas for them. If students have not had previous writing instruction, they must have this foundation.

Kindergarten teachers lay the foundation of thinking for each type of paragraph. Although these young children may not write a paragraph, they can verbally create the ideas and support statements for them. For example, they can identify an object and think of three ways to describe it. They can compare and contrast. They can list events or steps in order. This practice will prepare them not only for writing but also for pulling these ideas out of the texts they read.

Planning the Paragraph

The paragraph is planned in the same way that a sentence is planned. Once the type of paragraph is identified, then the audience is determined. Both of those will influence the information and ideas that will be gathered.

- **Generate ideas for an informational paragraph.**
  - Choose the topic or idea.
  - Make a list of three things you know about the person, place, thing, or idea.
  - Use who, what, when, where, why, and how.
  - Use how it looks, smells, feels, sounds, and/or tastes to help think of ideas.
  - Use short words to make a list.
- **Choose a graphic organizer.**
  Use a graphic organizer that will arrange the ideas. Venn diagrams, T-charts, a metric, sequence and flow charts, timelines, and tables are some examples.
- **Use a paragraph frame, if necessary.**
  Design a paragraph frame that will support students as they are learning the genre. After students become skilled with the paragraph type, they will no longer need a frame.

  It is also helpful to orally rehearse the topic sentence, the three supporting sentences, and the concluding sentence when students are first learning the genre. In essence, you are verbally reciting the paragraph.

  Writing paragraphs as a group also provides a model and support for students as they are learning the particular genres of paragraphs.
- **State your key idea in one sentence.**
  What are you trying to say? What is the important idea? This will be the first sentence in a paragraph and the thesis statement in a longer piece. All good writers are able to state what their writing is about in one sentence, no matter how long it is. This focuses the writing and gives the writer direction on what to include and what not to include in the piece. Novice writers might need the help of the sentence frame to generate this sentence.

Writing, Revising, and Editing the Paragraph

Writing, revising, and editing the paragraph is the same as for the sentence. Revision becomes more sophisticated with more possibilities for improvement.

Run-on Sentences

Now that students are writing multiple sentences, run-on sentences must be addressed. Sometimes it is difficult, if not impossible, for students to tell when a sentence ends and another should begin. When writing, ideas can come all at once. How will they be able to tell? Here are some guidelines for students:

- Read and listen to where you *take a breath* or *where you stop*.
- Then double check by reading it to see if the sentence makes sense. Is it a whole sentence? Does it tell who or what? Does it tell what they did or what they are? This is where knowledge of grammar and the parts of a sentence are helpful.

Both paragraphs in Figure 18.5 were written in December of first grade by two different children in two different classrooms. What do you observe about each piece? What are the differences in the thinking processes required? What are the differences in the skills required? The first paragraph uses the basic paragraph structure, with the first line indented. The second paragraph is more of a worksheet that does not follow a strict paragraph structure. Although the student had to do some planning on ideas, she did not have to plan the organization or provide capitalization at the beginning of sentences. Which assignment taught the student more about writing?

Figure 18.5   Analyzing First-Grade Examples of a Descriptive Paragraph

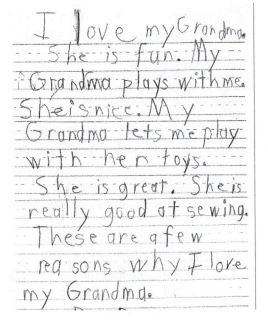

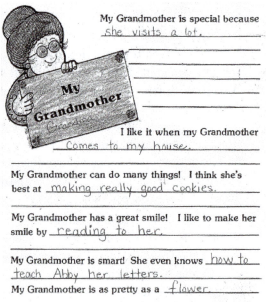

Figure 18.6 Building Blocks of Essays

One Paragraph with Five Sentences		Three Paragraphs		Five Paragraphs
Thesis sentence	1	Introduction—thesis statement, explain, state the 3 ideas/details.	1	Introduction—thesis statement, explain, state the 3 ideas.
Supporting detail 1	2	Three ideas/details are explained, with one support idea for each.	2	Idea 1 is supported by 3 reasons.
Supporting detail 2			3	Idea 2 is supported by 3 reasons.
Supporting detail 3			4	Idea 3 is supported by 3 reasons.
Concluding sentence	3	Conclusion—Restate introduction in reverse order.	5	Conclusion—Restate introduction in reverse order.

The Three- and Five-Paragraph Essay

Once students have mastered a genre, they can easily expand their writing into a three- or five-paragraph essay. In a three-paragraph essay, the topic sentence becomes a whole paragraph, the three supporting details are a paragraph with at least one reason for each, and the last sentence becomes the concluding paragraph. In a five-paragraph essay, each sentence of the one paragraph becomes a paragraph of its own. This is illustrated in Figure 18.6.

Here is a more detailed description of the five-paragraph essay.

The Five-Paragraph Essay

First paragraph
This will include your main point (thesis statement) and the important areas/elements you are going to discuss. It is like an overview of your whole paper.

Paragraphs two, three, and four
Each area/element is a paragraph in your paper. State your point and then tell why you said what you did.

Fifth paragraph
This has the same elements as your first paragraph, but in reverse order! You summarize the areas/elements and then use your main point (thesis statement) as the final sentence.

Be sure to include good transitions from one paragraph to another. You can use words like *next, second, after, another.*

An outline of your paper will look something like this:

I. Thesis statement
   A. Supporting statement
   B. Identification of areas/elements
II. Area/Element 1
   A. Supporting detail 1
   B. Supporting detail 2
   C. Supporting detail 3
III. Area/Element 2
   A. Supporting detail 1
   B. Supporting detail 2
   C. Supporting detail 3

IV. Area/Element 3
   A. Supporting detail 1
   B. Supporting detail 2
   C. Supporting detail 3
V. Summary statement
   A. Summary of areas/elements
   B. Thesis statement reworded

How to Answer Questions from a Textbook

Students must answer questions found in textbooks and on tests but are not usually taught how to do so. It remains a mystery to them. The following is a simple process that will help them become confident in responding if they have been taught to write a paragraph and can turn it into a three- or five-paragraph essay:

1. Read the question and determine what it is asking. The question will often give a clue as to the type of response that is required. Are you to explain? Compare? Describe? Analyze and support your ideas?

2. Write a thesis statement using *exact words* from the question as part of the statement.

3. Write two or three support sentences that tell why you said what you did.

4. A conclusion sentence may or may not be necessary.

Examples of Questions and Answers from a Text

Question: How do you think <u>Esperanza did staying home with the babies</u>?

Answer: <u>Esperanza did very well for her first time babysitting</u>. She gave the babies rice water to calm their stomachs. She also put blankets over their heads to protect them from the dust storm.

Question: <u>If you had to care for two babies all day long</u>, how well do you think you would do?

Answer: <u>If I had to care for two babies all day long</u>, I probably wouldn't do too well. I don't know what babies need and they cry when I hold them.

Note how the answers contain some of the words from the question and have two ideas that support the main thesis.

Older students will often be expected to provide a well-written paragraph, if not a three-paragraph essay, in answer to questions. In order to do that, they will go through the steps of planning and organizing a paragraph. Students who have learned the genres can recognize what type of paragraph to write. The question will often give a clue as to the type of response that is required. Notice in Table 18.1 that key words in the question or essay will inform students how to structure their response.

Table 18.1 Using Key Words to Identify How to Answer Questions

Words Used in Essay Prompts	Paragraph Type
Explain why	Cause and effect
Trace	Sequence
Discuss or describe	Descriptive
Summarize	Informational
Compare or contrast	Compare and contrast
Analyze	Persuasive

Writing Stories

Stories need the same kind of planning that paragraphs do. The level of preparation for writing will vary, depending on the age level. At minimum, students who provide a title and a brief synopsis of the story before writing do much better than students who just start writing. I have copies of amazing stories that young children have written when they have followed this process (Melton 1985).

The type of stories written depends on the age of the student. Before eight or nine years old, children are not usually developmentally ready to write a story with a plot and character development. Instead, their stories are more like a series of events.

The plan–write–revise–edit thinking needs to be used with stories. There is a great opportunity for growth in understanding narrative when students can revise their beginning sentence to grab the readers' attention, learn the different ways to communicate a setting, add conversation, or describe a character using various means. This is accomplished through guided revision where you provide examples and then allow students to make the appropriate changes on the spot.

Journals

Journals have been mentioned only in the context of escaping the plan–write–revise–edit way of thinking. That is because they usually serve a different purpose than other writing. They are useful in motivating students to think and write about ideas before they are ready to organize them. In my classrooms, students had time to write in a journal on any topic of their choice. It was free writing time.

Invariably when I was teaching kindergarten or first grade, students would ask permission to copy a book into the journal. They intensely work at transferring the printed page into their own writing. They usually do not do this for more than a week or so, but the process helps them construct their own understanding of the conventions of print.

Kindergarten children need to be writing in a journal from the very beginning, even if they are just beginning to learn letters. The conventions of writing on a line, from left to right, and holding a pencil are all beneficial, besides the deep satisfaction it gives them. As the year progresses, the growth is astounding as they move from writing single letters for words to writing whole words that are phonetically correct to spelling words correctly.

Meet My Student

Tammy

Tammy could barely read at a third-grade level, although she was a junior in high school. In order to function in school, she had to have someone read all her textbooks to her. Her committed parents and teachers made sure that happened. She was friendly, outgoing, and seemed to take her lack of ability to read in stride, an unusual characteristic for such a poor reader. Whatever she decided to do, she put her full mind to it.

After 45 hours of research-based reading instruction that spanned over seven months, Tammy was reading at grade level. According to the Woodcock Reading Master Tests, she had gained nine grade levels in reading during that time. Her commitment to reading at least an hour a daily instead of the required 30 minutes certainly played a part in attaining those dramatic gains. During that time, she also began writing, using the plan–write–revise–edit way of thinking. At first, she only wrote one question and a one-sentence answer. Soon she was writing a single paragraph with the support of a graphic organizer and paragraph frame. In the end, she could write a paragraph and became a top-notch speller.

Comprehending Text

We are finally ready to talk about reading comprehension. The prerequisite skills of background knowledge, vocabulary, and text structure have been addressed. In the next chapter, we will look at what it takes to gain meaning from text.

Summary

The Sequence of Writing Assignments
• Single sentence
• One paragraph
• Three-paragraph essay
• Five-paragraph essay
• Longer pieces

The Basic Paragraph Structure
Thesis statement
• Supporting detail 1
• Supporting detail 2
• Supporting detail 3
Concluding sentence

The Five-Paragraph Essay
First paragraph (overview):
• Thesis statement.
• Identify important areas/elements you are going to discuss.
Paragraphs two, three, and four:
• Each area/element is a paragraph in your paper.
• State your point and then tell why you said what you did with supporting ideas.
Fifth paragraph:
• Same elements as the first paragraph, but in reverse order.
• Final sentence is the thesis statement restated.

Getting Meaning from Text

W̲e have come full circle back to reading comprehension after looking in depth at the three prerequisites for reading comprehension. Weaknesses in background knowledge, vocabulary, or understanding text structure can hinder comprehension. It is a poignant reminder of the interrelatedness of all the language arts—reading, writing, speaking, and listening. All contribute to proficiency in reading.

Now we must get down to the business of thinking while reading (see Figure 19.1). How do we get meaning from text?

Figure 19.1   Framework for Teaching Reading

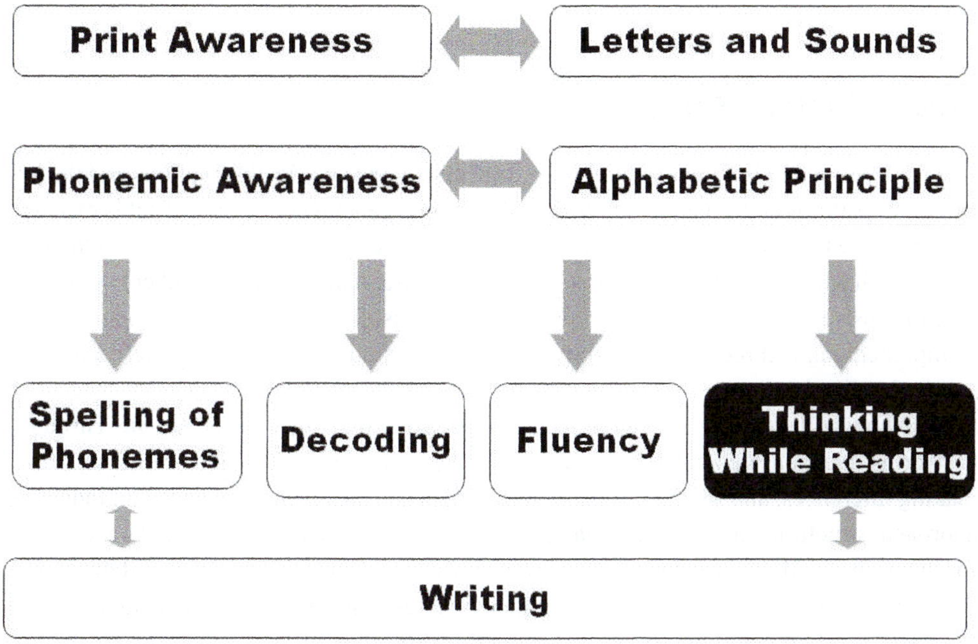

How to Approach a Text: Strategy versus Content

There are two basic approaches to teaching reading comprehension: We can teach strategies or we can focus on content. The *strategy approach* focuses on procedures such as visualizing, think-alouds, and summarizing. The *content approach* uses inductive investigation of the text itself to uncover meaning. Research on the comparison of these two approaches is unexpected in that it runs counter to what we have thought. The research in this area points to the content approach as the most effective (Afflerbach & Johnston 1984; Catts 2009; McKeown & Gentilucci 2007; McKeown, Beck, & Blake 2009). So what does this mean?

This does *not* mean that students do not visualize. Remember from Chapter 14 how background knowledge about Abraham Lincoln involuntarily produced visual images? It does not mean students do not engage in think-alouds. We all do that as we read, questioning and monitoring our understanding. It also does not mean we do not summarize. However, as Catts (2009) pointed out, summarization is more a result of comprehension rather than the means to comprehension. To summarize a passage adequately, you must first comprehend it. What it does mean is that students must focus on the content in order to gain meaning.

To understand why the content approach might trump the strategies approach, we must go back to the concept of working memory and the limitation of elements we can think about at one time. If mental energy is allocated to calling up strategies, adequate resources might not be available for understanding the text. Research suggests that focusing on strategies may distract from comprehension (McKoewn 2007). We want to put all of our resources into developing critical thinking skills and comprehension of text. Then the visualization, thinking aloud, and summaries will come as a result.

The Inductive Approach

Inductive reasoning is a kind of thinking that begins with specific observations and the detection of patterns and organization that leads to some general conclusion. That is exactly what we do when we comprehend a text. We analyze the specific components and then draw conclusions. A *deductive* approach is the opposite. It assumes the teacher is going to give the answers. But to comprehend text, students must find the answers for themselves. Comprehending text requires the ability to *inductively* find the facts, make inferences, and see the implications.

So how will students learn an inductive approach? Students must be *taught*. Through answering questions generated by the teacher, they will acquire the skills of finding facts, making inferences, and seeing implications. This means the teacher must take an inductive approach, structuring assignments that guide students to discover answers and concepts for themselves. All the principles of learning apply here. Students construct and monitor their own learning and apply concepts, guided by questions the teacher has written. Over time, students will begin to process text using this procedure.

Questions: The Heart of the Inductive Approach

I keep six honest serving-men
    (They taught me all I knew);
Their names are What and Why and When
    And How and Where and Who.
—Rudyard Kipling

Well-written questions guide students in discovering the text. As students respond to those questions, they soon begin asking themselves those same types of questions as they read. It becomes a way of thinking.

Teachers ask many questions throughout the day, but most have not been prepared ahead of time, let alone written down. In order to become a first-class inductive teacher, you must develop the habit of writing out both your questions *and* a phrase that answers it. There are many reasons for doing this:

- High-quality questions take thought. They usually are not generated "on the fly."
- It takes practice to write questions of this caliber, and that practice can only come through writing out your questions and honing them until they do the work they are intended to do.
- Questions need to be sequenced to guide thinking from literal facts to higher levels of thinking. It is impossible to track that sequence without writing them down.
- A question might sound wonderful, deep, and thought-provoking, but it has no answer. I don't know how many questions I have written that lead nowhere. You only discover this by jotting down the answer yourself.
- Questions may also sound admirable, but only require a one-word answer. Those are often not caught unless you answer them yourself.

If you take the time to learn the skill of questioning, it will pay enormous dividends in the cognitive development of your students.

Qualities of a Good Question

So what does an excellent question look like? There are some rules that govern the basic structure of questions.

- **Good questions start with *who, what, when, where, how,* or *why.***
  Ask mainly "*What . . . ?*" "*How . . . ?*" or "*Why . . . ?*"
  It is amazing that teachers will write "questions" that begin with *explain, discuss,* or *find.* Those are statements and not questions and will not develop inductive thinking. They carry a message of "Give me the answer," rather than "Find the answer."

- **Avoid yes/no questions. These start with *do, can, will, is,* and *are.***
  These are the kind of questions we are prone to ask when we haven't prepared ahead of time. Keep in mind that the real answer to this type of question is *yes* or *no.* Because of this, such questions can produce some negative results:
  - A teacher can lose control of a classroom by asking two or three yes/no questions in a row. If students are vocalizing the answer all once, behavior can become disruptive. Students feel the teacher has given permission for them to talk.
  - The discussion falls flat. There is nothing to discuss.
  - These tend to be narrow, funneling the answer in a particular direction. Sometimes the teacher will try to recoup this type of question by tacking on "Why?" or "Why not?" However, if the entire question is reworded to begin properly, the question becomes broader and more thoughtful. It becomes a much better question.

- **Avoid simple questions that require only a one- or two-word answer.**
  Unless you are scaffolding the investigation process for novice readers who are having difficulty locating the basic information, this type of question is insulting to the intelligence of the student. If the topic is on atoms and the question is asked, "What is the topic about?" no one feels like answering it. Attention wanders when questions require little or no thought.

- **Do not add extra words such as, "Who can tell me . . ." or "Does anyone know . . . ?"**
  We fall into the trap of using this type of question when we have not prepared. First of all, it is a yes/no question, and students may be inclined to just answer yes or no. The major downfall of this type of question, though, is the effect it has on a discussion. It slows the pace considerably, dragging down the interest of students. The real question is halfway thorough the sentence. You've said twice as much as you needed to say.

  A gifted high school teacher used a wide variety of strategies in her classroom, but tried to engage students in discussion without preparation. Invariably, her questions contained this extra verbiage. When she began writing out her questions, both the pace and the quality of the discussions dramatically improved.

The Essence of Inductive Thinking

Inductive thinking begins with observations and searching for patterns, sequence, cause, and comparisons. Based on those observations, inferences are made that eventually lead to conclusions. This model for inductive thinking provides a structure that informs us of the type of questions that should be asked.

Finding Facts

What are the facts? Inductive thinking is based on identifying the facts of the passage observing patterns, sequence, causes, comparisons, and contrasts.

Making Inferences

We do not stop at facts. As the famous teacher Agassiz said, "Facts are stupid things." He pressed his students to make observations based on the facts ("The Student" n.d.).

What do the facts tell me? Making inferences requires putting the facts together to gain further insights. It also demands bringing prior knowledge to bear on the facts. If I have no prior experience or knowledge of bum lambs, I can make no inference when the full-grown sheep comes running up to the girl to be petted. But from my background knowledge, I know that this girl bottle fed and cared for this sheep when it was just a lamb. That is the only instance when an adult sheep would exhibit this behavior.

Students who struggle with making inferences may be suffering from a lack of background knowledge. Texts must be carefully chosen that have elements within their experience or that are close enough that additional background knowledge can be easily supplied before reading.

Seeing Implications

Based on what has been discovered in the text, students can form an opinion, draw conclusion, or make applications.

Translating the Tools into Inductive Thinking

Sometimes the line between finding facts, making inferences, and seeing implications is extremely thin. For example, if students are looking for repetition in a text, at what point are they finding just the facts and when does it converge into making an inference? Sometimes it is difficult to tell the difference between an inference and a conclusion. For purposes of teaching meaning, it does not matter. We only need to make sure we are addressing all three facets of inductive thought in the lesson (see Figure 19.2).

Figure 19.2   The Essence of Inductive Thinking

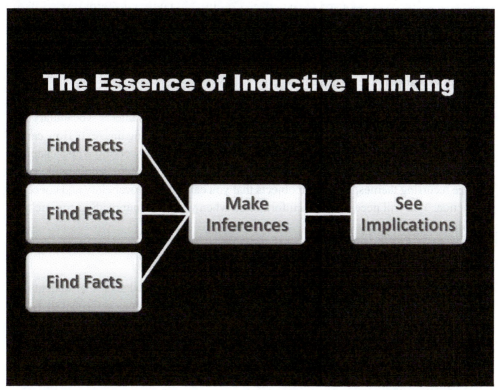

At what level, do we start using the inductive approach? From the very beginning. Preschool children can learn at their developmental level how to answer simple questions, make simple inferences, and form an opinion on texts that are read to them. When students read the first sentence, they can begin to approach it from an inductive perspective. We already ask these young students questions. It will only require that we be more purposeful in what questions we ask.

Preparing Questions to Develop Inductive Thought

The task of developing inductive thought depends on you, and a foundational piece is honing your ability to create and ask well-designed questions. Don't depend on questions that accompany texts because they are usually designed to test rather than to develop thought processes. There have been times that there is not one question I would ask.

In order to write questions, you will need to first identify the content yourself. Divide a page into two columns. In the first column, identify the information, and in the second column turn that information into well-structured questions. The Guidelines for Planning and Writing Questions (Table 19.1) will help you do this. Be careful to avoid yes/no and simple-answer questions.

Find the Facts

In the left column, find the facts in the text. Generate a list of statements that tell who, what, when, where, why, and how. Look for repetition of words, phrases, or ideas, patterns, sequences, causes and effects, things that are like, and things that differ. You may see a sequence or reoccurring characteristics of an individual. You are pulling together the facts from the text.

Catalog the facts in some way in order to see relationships and choose a graphic organizer that will display the significant facts.

At this same time, *on a separate sheet of paper,* note words that students might have difficulty decoding or words or concepts that might not be in the students' vocabulary or knowledge base. What prior knowledge is critical for understanding this text? How can this prior knowledge be brought to the students' attention? When working with a chapter book, record this information chapter by chapter. When you look at the whole book, you will see recurring themes, ideas, and objects that you can use for vocabulary and concept instruction. You will need all of this information when you plan your reading comprehension lesson.

Make Inferences

Generate statements of inference based on the facts and the knowledge base of students. Read between the lines. You are pulling the facts together to see things in the text that are not explicitly stated, but are implied. What are the facts telling me? What does it mean? Keep in mind that inferences require the reader to bring prior knowledge to bear on the text.

To help you look for inferences, compare and contrast this text to other situations or texts, analyze character traits, identify cause and effect, interpret motivation, interpret feeling or mood, perceive relationships, identify humor, look at the significance of repetition, patterns, or sequence, and interpret similarities and differences.

See Implications

Generate statements that reflect your opinion or the conclusions you draw. What do you think? How has this been a situation like yours or those of your students? How is this like someone or something else I know? What is the message? Why is it important?

Write Your Questions

Now you are ready to write a sequence of well-thought-out questions that will lead your students through the text, guiding them to find the facts, make inferences, and see the implications. Turn your statements into questions, writing questions at all three levels. Make sure your literal questions require thought and combine facts, although the information is found right in the text. Use the guidelines for writing questions.

Two Sets of Questions

Two different first-grade teachers prepared to teach the following story about two frogs. The first teacher had a general idea of what she wanted students to look at and asked her questions "on the fly." The second teacher wrote out the key questions (and answers) for the story. What is the difference in content, wording, and intent of the questions? What would be the difference in the effect on class discussion?

Two Frogs and the Well

Two frogs lived by a big pond. One summer it was so hot the pond dried up. There was no more water. They needed to find a drink. They hopped and hopped to find water. Soon they came to a deep well with some water in it.

"I want to jump in," said one frog. "I want a drink."

"No! No!" cried the other frog. "This well is too deep. We can jump into the well, but can we jump out of the well?"

—Adapted from *Aesop's* Fables

Question Set #1	Question Set #2
1. How many frogs were there?	1. Why did the frogs have to leave the pond? (Literal question)
2. Can you tell me why the pond dried up?	
	2. How would the dry pond affect the frogs? (Inferential)
3. What was in the well that the frogs wanted?	3. Why did one frog want to jump into the well? (Literal question)
4. Does anyone know why the first frog wanted to jump into the well?	4. What did the second frog think would happen if they jumped into the well? (Inferential question)
5. Do you think the second frog was right? Why or why not?	5. Why do you think it would be easier to jump into a well than to get out of a well? (Analytical question)
	6. Both frogs made a decision. Which decision was better? What made it better? (Analytical question)

Table 19.1 Guidelines for Planning and Writing Questions

Guidelines for Planning and Writing Questions	
Find the Facts	**Literal Questions**
• Generate a list of statements that tell who, what, when, where, why, how.	• The answers can be lifted from the text. CAUTION: *Literal* does not mean one word or simple answers. Write literal questions that provoke thought.
• Look for repetition of words, phrases, or ideas, patterns, sequences, causes and effects, things that are like, and things that differ.	• Turn your statements into questions. Write questions that combine facts. Help students find repetition, patterns, sequence, cause and effect, comparison and contrast.
• Catalog facts in some way in order to see relationships.	• Knowledge of text and sentence structures enable students to find pertinent information.
• Choose a graphic organizer that will display the significant facts.	
Make Inferences	**Inferential Questions**
• Generate statements of inferences. Pull facts together to make inferences based on the facts and knowledge base. Read between the lines.	• The answers will be found by reading between the lines. The answers cannot be lifted directly from the text.
• What are the facts telling me? What does it mean? What is the text saying but not explicitly saying? Interpret the text.	• Turn your statements into questions. Write questions that lead students to inferences based on the facts.
• Compare and contrast this text to other situations or texts. Analyze character traits, identify cause and effect, interpret motivation, interpret feeling or mood, perceive relationships, identify humor, look at the significance of repetition, patterns, or sequence, and interpret similarities and differences.	• Example generic questions: ◦ What do the responses tell you about motivations? feelings? ◦ What do the actions and responses tell you about the character? about relationships? ◦ What do the facts tell you about the time or setting? ◦ Why is something humorous?
See Implications	**Analytic Questions**
• Generate statements. What do you think?	The answers will be found beyond the text.
• Form opinions: ◦ How has this been a situation like mine? ◦ How is this like someone or something else I know?	Write "what do you think?" questions.
• Make applications and draw conclusions:	
• What is the message? Why is it important?	

One of the obstacles in developing a reading lesson using inductive thought is the quality of the text. Sometimes you will have texts that have no substance but are merely a series of events with little impact. If that is the case, choose something else. We don't want to dull the minds of students with that kind of text.

Designing a Reading Comprehension Lesson

We are ready to put all of the reading comprehension pieces together into a lesson format that can be used for all kinds of texts for any grade level. Our goal is to step up the quality of reading and writing, moving from a language arts and crafts curriculum to meaningful interaction with text that fosters proficiency. Most of the time will be spent in reading and writing, with some time left over for meaningful discussions before, during, and after reading.

Choose texts that are at the instructional reading level of students. This becomes an issue if you have students reading below grade level, but yet you are required to use the grade level text. If students go ahead and read the text, all of the problems associated with reading texts at the frustration level occur. It is actually harmful in many ways to the student. The other solution is to read the text to the student, but then the student is robbed of the reading experience and the much-needed time reading. The best solution is to have texts that students can read at their instructional level.

Comprehension of a text is dependent on background knowledge, so choose texts that are not completely removed from the experience of the learners. This will become evident as you plan your lesson. If there are too many vocabulary words and too many unknown concepts, you know the text is not suitable for your students. If the text is embedded in a unit, then the hurdles of vocabulary and background knowledge can possibly be overcome because those topics will be revisited more than once. You can take more time to build that vocabulary and knowledge.

Before Reading: The Setup

You have already identified the vocabulary, difficult words to read, and the prior knowledge required to read the passage when you generated your questions. Choose an activity that ties vocabulary and knowledge base together. Activities to teach vocabulary and bring up prior knowledge are found in earlier chapters. Write questions to accompany these activities that will arouse curiosity and focus student attention on the text. These will come from the questions you generated when planning the inductive lesson.

For any words difficult to read, have students decode them. Talk about any spellings they do not know.

During Reading: Inductive Thinking Skills

Students read the text silently to themselves first and then, the same day or the next day, they read the text aloud in small groups with the teacher. Choral reading and reader's theater are used for reading. During this time, the teacher guides students by asking the questions generated on the text. This develops inductive thinking in the students as they have conversations about the text. Students may later read the text aloud with a partner.

After Reading: Writing Response

Here are some ways students can demonstrate an understanding of the text.

A Title

What title could you give this section in three words or less? What new title could you give to the story?

A Sentence

Use the sentence frame to generate ideas of who, what, when, where, why, and how. Then write a well-constructed sentence that conveys the main idea of this section or story. Use the self-check list, revision, and editing on the sentence.

One or More Paragraphs

Choose a writing assignment, using the genres students have learned. Whether students are reading expository or narrative texts, an isolated text or several chapters, writing assignments can be designed that encourage thought and understanding. Give students some choices in topics, audience, and/or genre. Have them complete the plan-write-revise-edit process so they gain maximum benefit from the assignment. They will not only be thoughtfully interacting with their text but also developing all the skills associated with writing.

Table 19.4 shows examples of writing assignments that are tied to the story *The Empty Pot* by Demi. They can be designed to target a specific idea, person, or event. These assignments can also be adapted to require a single paragraph, three-paragraph essay, or five-paragraph essay. Be sure students have had previous instruction and practice on the genre chosen. The examples give only a few suggestion out of a wide range of possibilities in designing writing assignments that are connected to text.

Example of a Reading Comprehension Lesson

A reading comprehension lesson can be designed with narrative or expository text for any grade level (see Table 19.3). Table 19.2 shows the process in developing the lesson using a story adapted from *Aesop's Fables*.

The Donkey and His Load

A merchant loaded a donkey with heavy bags of salt. As the donkey crossed a bridge on the way home, he slipped and fell into the water. When the donkey got out of the water, his load was lighter. The water had washed away the salt in the bags. This pleased the donkey.

The next day, the merchant loaded him with bags of sponges. When the donkey came to the same stream he thought, "If I fall in, my load gets lighter."

He fell into water, but his load did not get lighter. The sponges soaked up water. His load became almost too heavy to carry.

—Adapted from *Aesop's* Fables

Table 19.2 Preparing and Implementing a Lesson Based on "The Donkey and His Load"

Preparing a Reading Comprehension Lesson	Implementing a Reading Comprehension Lesson
Before Reading: The Setup	
Vocabulary words: *merchant, sponges, thought, salt* Associate prior knowledge: • What a donkey looks like. • Semi trucks carry goods. Know required vocabulary and possess knowledge base: • What happens to salt in water. • What happens to sponges in water. • Merchants use donkeys to carry loads. Related books/units: • Explore science unit on solutions/"things that dissolve."	Introductory questions: • How does the grocery store get its groceries? How do they get there? (semi trucks) • How do all stores get the things they are going to sell? (come by trucks) • We use trucks to haul goods. But not every country does that. How are these goods carried? *Show clips or pictures of donkeys carrying big loads.* Read the words: *merchant, sponges, thought, salt* • What is a merchant? • What is a sponge? (show one to the class; let them touch and feel it) What happens when you put it in water? (demonstrate if necessary) • What happens to salt when you put it in water? (demonstrate if necessary) *In our story, a donkey carries goods for a merchant.*
During Reading: Inductive Thinking Skills	
Facts • Donkey carries salt but falls into the water. • His load becomes lighter. • Donkey carries sponges and purposely falls into the water. • His load becomes heavier. **Make Inferences** • Donkey was surprised the first time. • Donkey wanted a lighter load. • Donkey didn't know the difference in what water would do to salt and what it would do to sponges. **See Implications** • Donkey was trying to get out of carrying a heavy load. • Donkey didn't stop to think how this affected the merchant.	Students read story silently. Questions for discussion when reading aloud together. • What kinds of goods did the merchant have the donkey carry? • What do you think he was going to do with the salt and sponges? • What happens the first time the donkey falls into the water? the second time? Why was it different each time? • Why do you think the donkey purposely fell into the water the second time? • How do you think his falling into the water affected the merchant? • How would you describe the donkey?
After Reading: Writing Response	
	Using the sentence frame, write one sentence that tells what the story is about.

Table 19.3 Preparing and Implementing a Reading Comprehension Lesson

Preparing a Reading Comprehension Lesson	Implementing a Reading Comprehension Lesson
Before Reading: The Setup	**Before Reading: The Setup**
Words: • *What words might students have difficulty decoding?* Look for words that have unusual phoneme spellings, words that have spellings students have not learned, words students don't usually read, and "big" words. Associate prior knowledge: • *What prior knowledge is critical for understanding this text? How can this prior knowledge be brought to the students' attention?* Know required vocabulary and possess knowledge base: • *What words or concepts might not be in the students' vocabulary or knowledge base?* Generate a list of texts, both narrative and informational, related to this text: • *What texts would enhance and extend the vocabulary and knowledge base?*	• Choose an activity that ties vocabulary and knowledge base together. You will need to ask one or two questions to generate information. Activities to teach vocabulary and bring up prior knowledge are found in earlier chapters. • Show difficult words. Have students decode them. Talk about any spellings they do not know. • Ask one or two questions about the text that will arouse curiosity and focus student attention on the text. These will come from the questions you generated when planning the inductive lesson.
During Reading: Inductive Thinking Skills	**During Reading: Inductive Thinking Skills**
The questions you generated can be asked during reading or after reading. • Find the facts: *Who, what, when, where, why, how?* • Make inferences: *What are the facts saying? What does it mean?* • See implications: *What conclusions or applications can be made?*	• Students read text silently to themselves. • The same day or the next day, students read the text aloud in small groups with the teacher. Choral reading and reader's theater are used for reading. • During this time, the teacher guides students by asking the questions generated on the text. This develops inductive thinking in the students as they have conversations about the text. • Optional, students read the text aloud with a partner.
After Reading: Writing Response	**After Reading: Writing Response**
• Have students write a sentence, paragraph, story, or essay. Young children will include a drawing.	• Choose a writing assignment for students, using the genres they have learned. Give students some choices in topics, audience, and/or genre. • Complete the plan-write-revise-edit process.

Table 19.4 Sample Writing Assignments

Here are two sample writing assignments that can be used as a response to *The Empty Pot*. More are found in Appendix D.

Cause-and-Effect Paragraph	Persuasive Paragraph
Write a cause-and-effect paragraph using *The Empty Pot*. PLAN: 1. Brainstorm possible ideas—why the seed didn't grow; why Ping was chosen emperor. 2. Choose an event in Ping's life that had a cause or that was an effect. 3. Decide on the audience. 4. Gather information. List the causes with their effects and/or list the effects with their causes. | Cause	Effects
	| 5. The first sentence will tell what cause (or effect) you are talking about. After a cause, list its effects OR after an effect, list its causes. 6. The last sentence will be a summary of why it happened or what was the cause. WRITE.	Write a persuasive paragraph using *The Empty Pot*. PLAN: 1. Brainstorm ideas. 2. Choose an issue to convince someone. 3. Decide on the audience. 4. Gather information on both sides of the issue. Decide on your position. 5. Make a chart, grouping the disadvantages for the opposite position and the advantages for your position. Put them in order from least important to most important. 6. The first position tells your position. Next, list the problems (disadvantages) of the opposite position with examples to support. Then list the advantages of your position. 7. End with the most important reason. WRITE.

Writing and Reading

Our goal is to provide students with the tools they need to become proficient readers and writers and then design classroom instruction that engages students in using those tools in a meaningful way. In the last chapter, we will focus on principles of teaching that will help you put it all together.

Summary

Qualities of a Good Question
• Good questions start with *who, what, when, where, how,* and *why.* Ask mainly *"What . . . ?" "How . . . ?" or "Why . . . ?"*
• Avoid yes/no questions. These start with *do, can, will, is,* and *are.*
• Avoid simple questions that require only a one- or two-word answer.
• Do not add extra words such as: *"Who can tell me . . ."* or *"Does anyone know . . . ?"*

The Essence of Inductive Thinking
• Find the facts; *Who, what, when, where, why, how?*
• Make inferences: *What are the facts saying? What does it mean?*
• See implications: *What conclusions or applications can be made?*

Chapter 20

Putting It All Together

You are the one that can make it happen. Our nation is in a reading crisis with no reversal in sight. We have not changed our paradigm of reading instruction for nearly 100 years. We've added strategies here and there, but the basic philosophy of reading has remained the same. And what we are currently doing is not working. The reading achievement scores tell us that. We need courageous individuals who are willing to take the risk to implement a framework based on research with strategies that have been well proven to produce extraordinary results.

We Can Do It

You are the one who can make the difference in the lives of students. In my own experience with students of all ranges of abilities and disabilities and ages, I have found that the research is correct. It produces results beyond anything we expected. Students *can* learn to read well.

To make the difference, you must believe students can achieve, never giving up hope on any student. Your beliefs about your students will influence your behavior and ultimately their achievement. The well-known research projects by psychologists have proven that teachers' beliefs about their students make a difference. When teachers mistakenly thought their students were in the high-ability group, they were more patient and provided more explanations. Those low-ability students rose to meet the expectations of the teachers, performing just like high-ability students.

When we assume a student who has not learned to read by the end of third grade has little hope of improvement, we doom that student to social, psychological, physical, and financial suffering. I have worked with many high school students who could only read a beginning primer, but ended up reading above grade level. Applying the principles of the research makes the difference. It takes some students longer to learn and some need more practice. Others just need kinesthetic methods to make it all click.

> Your beliefs about the abilities of your students will profoundly influence your behavior and ultimately their achievement.

> All students can learn the next thing to what they already know.

What Students Need

One of the most important needs we all have is the need for a sense of achievement. When it comes to reading and writing, many students have failed so many times that they have internalized failure to the point they feel they *are* a mistake. It becomes their identity. They don't expect to succeed at anything acceptable to society. We hear the words, "I can't," "I'm dumb." The stress of failure snowballs into more stress and failure. But we can turn that around.

> Few people will attempt to perform a task for which they believe they have little opportunity for success.

Using the principles of the zone of proximal development is one way we can do this. Students should always be working at their instructional level with help and support. They not only accomplish more than we or they thought they could, but they also begin to grow in their confidence as we implement errorless learning. They actually have work that is correct for a change. Building success into the lives of students relieves that stress and starts the spiral upward. Success breeds more success and motivation. A sense of accomplishment emerges.

My students always loved dictation because when they found all of their errors—it was a perfect paper. Little successes built on little successes grow into a sense of achievement. Success is motivating. Students who disliked reading and writing now enjoy it because they can actually perform successfully. I think of my student Nate, who ended up getting a college degree in journalism of all things, and Kirby and Josh, who stashed books under seats so they could snatch a little reading time, and Nathan, who chose being a lawyer (just think of the reading) as his career goal. These were the students who hated reading, despised themselves for their failures, and counted on doing not much in life.

> People want to learn everything unless they become discouraged.

Principles of Instruction and Scheduling

Basic principles of instruction will support reading and writing in your classroom. Many of these apply to any subject area, not just reading and writing:

- **Every day, begin at the easiest level—begin with what all can do.**
  Some can do it with a little help. Some can do it with no help. This establishes a comfortable, safe environment for learning. Then gradually increase the difficulty. At no time should the work be at the frustration level for students.
  Meet the needs of students by working in small ability groups, if needed.

- **For students in PreK to grade 3, alternate writing and listening or reading.**
  Reading and writing require the use of the fine muscles in the eye and in the hands. Developmentally, those muscles do not mature completely until age nine or ten. That means students will be at varying levels of ability until that age. Writing and coloring might be uncontrolled, and their eyes will tire easily. It is important in scheduling to alternate the use of fine motor skills and large motor skills so students are not doing too much at once. Some students indicate that they are tired by shaking their hand, but others will just be off task.

- **Pay strict attention to the limits of attention span.**
  Whoever did the research on attention spans did it right. These are invariably true, and the price for not adhering to them is behavioral problems. It is almost impossible for children to stay attentive once the time limit has expired. Once you change the activity or the place, you can begin a new time span.

Preschool	2 to 3 minutes
Kindergarten	5 to 10 minutes
Grades 1 to 3	15 to 20 minutes
Grades 4 and up	Adult

- **Use small-group instruction as much as possible.**
  This is a tall order, but find creative ways to accomplish this. It is important because excellent reading and writing instruction depends on providing immediate feedback and monitoring the level of help students need. You can't do this well in a group of 25 students.

  What are some solutions? Whether these will work will depend on your class size, your class behavior, and your school resources. Decide whether you can divide your class into two or three groups. Have one or two groups working independently while you teach the other group. If your classroom has good routines and student behavior is controlled, you can do this without problems. Otherwise, a parent, an aide, or instructional assistant can supervise the other students while you work with a small group.

  - Identify what activities can be done independently and what activities need supervision.
  - Identify which activities are best done in a small group and which ones can be done with the whole group. Table 20.1 provides some suggestions.

- **Manage your classroom so you have time for individual conferences daily.**
  During this time, you can listen to individual students read or talk with them about their writing for about five to ten minutes. In a two-week period, you should be able

Table 20.1 Activities for Group and Independent Learning

Independent	Teacher-led Small Group	Whole Group
• Silent reading	• Oral reading with inductive questions	• Grammar
• Writing	• Spelling of phonemes/decoding	• Dictation
• Free-choice reading		• Writing instruction
• Free-choice journal writing		• Teacher reads aloud
• Partner reading		

to have a conference with each student. This can be done during journal writing or free-choice reading.

- **Alternate silent reading with oral reading.**
  Have students read a text silently first. You can work with one group while one or two groups are reading silently. Grades 2 and up can read orally with you every other day. This is the time you use the inductive questions to guide the discussion. Students in grades K and 1 need to read orally with you every day.

- **Have students read 30 minutes a day at their instructional level.**
  Fervently guard this time. This is a minimum, even though it is three times as long as the average classroom. Try to double the time to 60 minutes. You can count silent reading, oral reading, and reading done in other subjects. Also, continually monitor reading levels because they can change rapidly.

- **Use the four types of reading almost daily.**
  Use all four types of reading in your classroom because each makes a unique contribution to the reading skills of your students:
  1. Silent reading increases silent reading speed.
  2. Oral reading with the teacher develops inductive thinking and comprehension.
  3. Free-choice reading increases reading enjoyment and fluency.
  4. Teacher reading aloud increases knowledge base and vocabulary.

- **Provide lots and lots of practice using kinesthetic methods.**
  The two-minute activities, individual games, and group games provide ongoing practice, give students feedback to perfect their skills, and provide a way you can monitor their progress. The goal is to close the achievement gap.

- **Know the reading status of your students at all times.**
  For grades K to 3 and poor readers in grades 4 and up, know whether students have phonemic awareness, the ability to represent phonemes with the graphemes, and the ability to decode. Assess the root issues of fluency and comprehension problems.

- **Limit "teacher talk."**
  Students learn more and transfer to real situations better if they construct their own understanding with feedback from you. Teacher explanations often fall on deaf ears. Notice that in this model, most teacher explanations are only one to three minutes long.

Sample Schedule for Primary Grades

Table 20.2 is an example of a daily schedule for primarily grades. Older grades tend to have longer blocks of time allocated to subject areas.

How to Implement These Principles

You can't do everything at once, so where do you start? Begin with phonemic awareness and the phoneme-based phonics. Those are the critical skills for beginning and remedial readers. Know how to assess these and teach these. Use the principles of transfer and keep

Table 20.2 Sample Daily Schedule for Primary Grades

Time	Activities	
	Group 1	**Group 2**
20	Phonemic awareness, spelling of phonemes, decoding	Pencil and paper activities in grammar, reading, writing, vocabulary
20	Pencil and paper activities in grammar, reading, writing, vocabulary	Phonemic awareness, spelling of phonemes, decoding
	Whole Class	
10–15	Grammar and writing instruction grammar cards, writing revisions, intro to new genre	
	Group 1	**Group 2**
15	Oral reading with inductive questions	Writing
15	Writing	Oral reading with inductive questions
Recess		
	Whole Class	
15–20	Immediately engage in free-choice reading or partner reading OR journal writing Individual conferences	
45	Math	
	LUNCH	
15	Immediately read words for dictation when they come into class Dictation	
10–20	Teacher reads aloud	
25	Science/Social Studies	
	Specials—music, art, library, P.E.	

aware of the zone of proximal development. Make sure students are reading 30 minutes a day at the instructional level. As you are comfortable with these, then you can add some of the other strategies. You can use this book as a reference for decoding, fluency, and comprehension issues and address those as you face them. Over time, you can implement the reading comprehension and writing strategies to support the literacy growth of your students.

You have in your hands the tools to turn the literacy crisis around, to change the statistics so almost all students leave school as proficient readers. When we teach reading using the processes the brain uses, we can be successful.

Acting out the Sound

Grapheme		Action
a	say /a/ when scared	Let's pretend we just saw a mouse. Let's throw our hands up and say /a/. Sometimes when you are scared of something, you might throw up your hands and say /a/.
b	beating heart	/b/ reminds me of a beating heart. Let's pretend we are beating hearts and say the sound /b/. (Take the right fist and beat in rhythm against the heart.)
c	camera click	/c/ reminds me of taking a picture with a camera. When I push the button to take the picture, it says /c/. (Pretend to hold a camera to take a picture. Pretend to push the button and say /c/.)
d	shoe in washing machine	/d/ sounds like a tennis shoe in a washing machine, hitting the sides of the washer as it is washing. (Make a wide circle with one arm (the tub of the washing machine). Make a fist with the other hand and make a circular motion inside the tub, hitting the side of the washer with a jerk and saying /d/ as it "hits" the side.)
e	Grandpa can't hear	/e/ reminds me of what a grandpa might say if he can't hear you. Let's put a hand to our ears and say /e/? (Cup one hand around one ear, turn your head a little, and lean forward as if you are trying to hear someone speak.)
f	flying with wings	The /f/ sound reminds me of the sound of wings of a bird as they are flying through the air. (Flap your arms like you are flying and say /f/. It is the sound of the wings whooshing through the air that makes the /f/ sound.)
g	drinking water— gulping	If I am drinking a glass of water fast, sometimes it sounds like /g/. Let's pretend we are drinking water and say /g/. (Pretend to hold a glass up to your mouth and be gulping down the water and say /g//g//g//g//g//g//g/.)
h	out of breath running	/h/ sounds like a runner out of breath after running a long way. Let's pretend we have just finished a long, hard race and say /h/. (Pretend like you are running with your arms moving at your side and saying /h/.)
i	gross or nasty—icky, sticky goo	If we were pulling up icky, sticky goo from our hands, we would say /i/. (Hold one palm out with pretend nasty, gross, icky, goo on it, and with the other hand, pretend you are pulling up the goo and saying /i/.)
j	jumping rope	/j/ reminds me of jumping rope. It is the sound of the rope hitting the ground. (Go through the actions of jumping rope and say /j/ as the rope would hit the ground.)

	Grapheme		Action
k	camera click (same as /k/)		/c/ reminds me of taking a picture with a camera. When I push the button to take the picture, it says /c/. (Pretend to hold a camera to take a picture. Pretend to push the button and say /c/.)
l	beaters on a mixer		/l/ reminds me of an electric mixer, making a cake. Let's pretend we are mixers and say the sound /l/. (Move your fist around in a small, fast circular motion and say /l/. If students are not aware of the sound of an electric mixer, you may have to bring in one and have them "hum" the /l/ with the sound of the motor.)
m	good taste—rub tummy		/m/ reminds me of what we say when we eat something good. What is your favorite food? (Say /m/ and rub our tummies as we say the sound /m/.)
n	racecar driver		/n/ reminds me of a racecar driver. Pretend you are driving a car and say /n/. (Pretend you are gripping the steering wheel of a racecar and driving.)
o	open mouth for doctor		/o/ reminds me of opening my mouth when a doctor wants to look in my throat. Let's pretend we have to say /o/ for the doctor. (Use your index finger as the tongue depressor, open your mouth and point your finger to your open mouth (don't touch it) and say /o/.)
p	popcorn popping		/p/ reminds me of popcorn popping. Let's pretend that popcorn is popping and say /p/. (Flick the fingers of both hands quickly in the air and say /p/p/p/p/p/ as if popcorn were popping.)
q	duck quacking		If you say the /qu/ (sounds like kw) very fast, it sounds like a duck quacking. Let's pretend we are quacking ducks and say /qu//qu/. (Put your thumb and fingers together to form a duck's beak. Move them together and apart to look like a duck quacking.)
r	scary growl of dog (or lion)		/r/ sounds like a growling dog. Let's pretend we are dogs growling and say /r/.
s	snake hissing		/s/ sounds like a snake hissing. Say /s/ as you pretend to be a snake slithering through the grass. (Extend both arms with palms together and make a slithering motion.)
t	clock ticking		Look at the second hand on the clock. See how it moves around. Let's pretend we are the hands of the clock moving in a circle and say /t/. (With arms straight, put the palms of the hands together overhead and then move the full arm in a clockwise motion to the side, down, and then up again.)
u	don't know something		Sometimes I say /u/ when I don't know the answer. I am trying to make up my mind and decide what to do. Do you want a cookie or a piece of cake? (Put your finger to your cheek and look like you don't know the answer as you say /u/.)
v	cell phone vibration		The /v/ sound reminds me of a cell phone that is vibrating. Let's pretend we have a cell phone and say /v/. (Pretend like you have a cell phone in your pocket and it is vibrating. Clutch your hand over your pocket and make it vibrate.)
w	rodeo rope		/w/ reminds me of the sound a rope makes when a cowboy's lasso is twirling over his or her head. Let's pretend we are cowboys twirling ropes and say the sound /w/. (Twirl imaginary lasso above head and say /w/.)
x	open a soda (pop) can		/x/ reminds me opening a can of pop that has been shaken up. Let's pretend to open a can of pop and say /x/. (Hold an imaginary pop can in one hand and as you pretend to open it, say /x/.)

Grapheme		Action
y	karate chop	/y/ reminds me of a karate chop. (Take a karate stance with one hand vertical, palm flat and the other hand horizontal, palm down. then do the chop by moving the horizontal hand quickly away from you.)
z	buzzing bee	/z/ sounds like a buzzing bee. Say /z/ as you pretend to be a bee buzzing around. (Hold your thumb and index finger together and you make zigzag motions and say /z/.)
au	something broke	Let's pretend our pencil just broke and we say /au/. We say /au/ when something happens that we do not like such as having your pencil break in half. (Make the motion of your pencil breaking into two pieces as you say /au/.)
oi	sea lion	Let's pretend we are sea lions slapping our flippers on the water and say /oi/. (Pretend like you are a sea lion, with your arms extended straight in front of you, palms horizontal to the floor. Clap your hands like the flippers hitting the water or ground. You may have to play a sound clip of California sea lions.)
ou	hurt finger	We say /ow/ when we are hurt. Let's pretend we just touched a hot stove with our finger. We say /ow/ when we get hurt. (Pretend you have just touched a hot stove with your finger and quickly lift your finger from the stove and saw /ow/.)
ar	pirate	/ar/ reminds me of a pirate who says /ar/. Let's pretend we are pirates. (Swing the bent arm in front your body and scrunch up your face as you say /ar/.)
sh	quiet	/sh/ reminds me to be very quiet. Let's pretend to tell everyone to be quiet and say /sh/. (Put your forefinger to lips as you say /sh/.)
wh	blowing out birthday candles	/wh/ reminds me of blowing out a candle. Let's pretend we are blowing out a candle and say /wh/. (Lean forward and pretend to blow out candles on a birthday cake.)
th	angry goose	/th/ sounds like an angry goose. (Flap elbows like wings and say /th/.)
th	swarm of bees	Note: this is the voiced sound of /th/ as it occurs at the beginning of *the* and *those*. /th/ sounds like a swarm of bees. (Move open hands, fingers apart in arbitrary motions to look like a swarm of bees and say /th/.)
ch	train	/ch/ reminds me of engine of a train going down the tracks. Let's pretend we are trains and say /ch/. (Move arms at your side like the wheels on a train engine.)
_ng	hitting a gong	/ng/ reminds me of the sound made when someone hits a big gong. Let's pretend to hit a gong and say the sound /ng/. (Pretend to hit a gong by making a striking motion with your hand.)
_s_	sawing wood	Let's pretend we are sawing wood and make the /_s_/ sound as we saw. (Use long arms motions, pretending to saw a huge piece of wood.)
Long a	thumbs and say /ay/ when something is good	If we like something and agree with it, we can say /ay/! (Lift both arms, bent at elbow with thumbs up in the air. Give a strong thumbs up and say /ay/.)
Long e	you draw backward because you just saw a mouse	Let's say /ee/ as we pretend we have seen a mouse. (Draw backward and draw your arms and hands to your body as if afraid.)
Long i	sailor salutes and says "aye, aye"	The sound reminds me of a sailor who is saluting an officer and says, "Aye, aye." (Stand at attention, salute, and say "aye, aye.")

Grapheme		Action
Long o	something is wrong	Sometimes when something happens that I didn't want to happen, I might say "oh! oh!" (Pretend something happened that you did not want to happen. Hit both cheeks with the palms of your hand and say, "oh, oh!")
Long u	something stinks (hold nose)	Pretend you smell a skunk. Hold your nose and say "u_e." (Pretend that you smell a skunk or some other thing that stinks. Hold your nose and emphatically say, "u_e.")
Long oo	turn head both ways as an owl and say "oo."	Let's pretend we are owls and turn our heads completely to the right and then to the left and say /oo/. (Pretend you are an owl. Be very still except turn your head completely to the right and completely to the left as you say /oo/.)
Short oo as is foot	lift something heavy such as a barbell	Let's pretend we are lifting weights over our heads that are almost too heavy for us. We say /oo/ as we struggle to lift it. (Pretend like you are lifting a heavy barbell starting at waist position and lifting it with difficulty over your head. Say the sound /oo/ very slowly like it is almost too heavy to lift.)

Word Workshop Phonics Lesson

►ALPHABETIC PRINCIPLE

There are three main ways to spell the sound /c/. We have learned two spellings, the c and k. Today we will learn another way to spell the sound /c/.

►INTRODUCE THE SOUND /ck/

Write the letters *ck* on the chalkboard. Say the sound /ck/ as you write them. *Remember it never comes at the beginning of a word. it always comes after a short vowel.*

Say the sound and write it in the air three times.

►HOW THE SOUND IS PRODUCED

/c/ is produced at the back of the mouth at the top of the throat.

• How do you make the sound?
• What do you do with your tongue?

►ACTING OUT THE SOUND

Pretend to hold a camera to take a picture. Pretend to push the button and say /c/.

This same action as used for the letter *c*.

/c/ reminds me of taking a picture with a camera. When I push the button to take the picture, it says /c/.

▶ BUILDING WORDS

pick	picks
trick	tricks
sick	
stick	sticks
pack	packs
sack	sacks
stack	stacks
tick	tickėt
	jackėt

The dot reminds
students to say /uh/.

FOR EACH WORD:
Say the word. Use it in a sentence.
- **What sound do you hear at the beginning? in the middle? How do you change** *pick* **to** *picks*? *sip* **to** *sips*? **etc.**
- **Listen carefully for all the sounds in** *trick, stick* **and** *stack*.
- **We can add the sounds /ut/ to words? It is spelled** *et*. **What would we add to** *tick* **to make** *ticket*? *jack* **to make** *jacket*?

- Have students use individual chalkboards or letter tiles to form the words.
- Guide them in spelling the words correctly.
- Have the students read each word after spelling it.

▶ READING WORDS AND SENTENCES

Have the students read the words from a chart and use them in oral sentences and extend them to tell why, when, and how. Have students read the words and sentence.

When we write the exact words someone says, we put special marks, like hands, (cup hands toward each other to demonstrate). These are called quotation marks. What quotation marks do you see? What do those marks tells us?

What comes at the beginning of each sentence? What comes at the end of each sentence? What does the question mark tell us?

▶ SOUND CARD GAME: FIND AND SHOW

Students need the White cards m, s, r, n, and f
Say word. . .Repeat word. . .Find. . .Show. . Sound

Find the sound. . .
        /m/. . ./s/. . ./r/. . ./n/. . ./f/
What sound do you hear at the beginning of...
        fun. . .nose. . .mouse. . .finger. . .song. . .not. . .
        rotten. . .make. . .number. . .slick. . .road
What sound do you hear at the end of...
        sun. . .bluff. . .jam. . .life. . .spoon. . .soar. . .cuff
        line. . .miss. . .deer

Lines 1 - 4, write the sounds. . .
Three ways to spell the sound /c/ in any order.
/k/   /c/   /ck/   /l/

Lines 5 - 8, write the words. . .
man   pick   sack   fill

Write the sentence. . .
He was sick.

Have the answers on the board or overhead.

1. One line at a time, guide students in checking their work against the model.
2. Wait for them to make any corrections.
3. Have them hand in their papers.

Sample Grammar Lessons

Lesson to Introduce Common Nouns and Articles	
Target Sentence	*The man sat on a chair at the house.*
Guided Discovery 1	• *Think of a word that you can use instead of man. You have 30 seconds.* List under *man*. • *How are all these word alike?* (people, animals)
Guided Discovery 2	• *Think of a word that you can use instead of chair. You have 30 seconds.* List under *chair*. • *How are all these words alike?* (things)
Guided Discovery 3	• *Think of a word that you can use instead of house. You have 30 seconds.* List under *house*. • *How are all these words alike?* (places)
Guided Discovery 4	• *Let's use one of these words instead of sat.* • *Why doesn't the word work instead of sat? (Certain words must come in a particular place in a sentence.)* Try interchanging some of the words with the word *sat* in the sentence. Do a few examples so students can see that you need one type of word in certain positions in the sentence
Definition	• *All these words are called nouns. A noun is a person, a place, or a thing.*
Oral Response	• *You have 30 second to think of a word that is a person. It can't be a name.* (Have students respond rapidly, one right after another.) • *You have 30 second to think of a word that is a place. It can't be a name.* (Have students respond rapidly one right after another.) • *You have 30 second to think of a word that is a thing.* (Have students respond rapidly, one right after another.)
Guided Discovery 5	• *What are the nouns in this sentence?* man, chair, house • *What comes before each noun?* a or the • *What is the difference in meaning between the chair and a chair?*
Definition	a, an, *and* the *are articles that mark nouns. They tell us, "A noun is coming! A noun is coming!" Sometimes the noun doesn't come right after the article, but it does come soon after the article.*

Lesson to Introduce Common Nouns and Articles	
Target Sentence	*The man sat on a chair at the house.*
Grammar Cards	Give students a set of cards with black, red, and orange.
	• *Lay out a card for each word in this sentence.*
	The lady drove the car.
	Have one student "read" the cards, saying the color and the speech part.
	What are the nouns? What are the articles? What do the articles tell you?
	Continue with two more sentences.

Lesson to Introduce Proper Nouns				
Target Sentence	*Mr. Brown sat on the chair.*			
Guided Discovery	• *What are the nouns in this sentence?* (Mr. Brown, chair)			
Definition	Mr. Brown is the name of a man.			
	Any name is called a proper noun.			
	All proper nouns are capitalized.			
	The name of the day, month, holiday, restaurant, state, book, person, or pet.			
	All names are proper nouns and are capitalized.			
	Nouns that are not names are called common nouns.			
Oral Response	I will say a common noun and you give me a proper noun for each. Point to different students and have them rapidly, in order, give you a proper noun in place of the common noun.			
	teacher	state	car	day of the week
	boy	month	city	street
	park	holiday	restaurant	girl
	All names have a capital letter.			
Grammar Cards	Give students a set of cards with black, red, and orange.			
	Lay out a card for each word in this sentence. Use only one card for each proper noun even though it may have more than one word.			
	Mr. Johns walked to town.			
	Have one student "read" the cards saying the color and the speech part. Now, the student must indicate whether it is a common or proper noun when "reading" the cards. So it is *"red—proper noun."*			
	What is the proper noun? What is the common noun? What proper noun could you use instead of town?			
	Continue with two more sentences.			

Lesson to Introduce Adjectives	
Target Sentence	*The cat purred.*
Guided Discovery 1	*What do you know about the cat?* You know what it did—purred—but you know nothing about it. *What would you like to know about the cat? What could you know?* List as students tell you. *size, color, kind, shape, number/amount, whose, which one*
Guided Discovery 2	You have 30 seconds to think of one word you could add to this sentence that would tell us more about the cat. (Students will reply with *white, fat, fluffy,* etc.) They might use a pronoun his/her or a possessive noun. These are often referred to as adjectival nouns and pronouns. See the Note to Teachers on Adjectives following this chart.
Definition	These words that tell us more about a noun are called adjectives. We will use our orange cards because articles are a kind of adjective.
Oral Response	For each one of these, give students 30 seconds to think of a word they could use to show this attribute. Point to different students and have them rapidly, in order, give you a word. • *What are some of the different words we could use for size?* • *What are some of the different words we could use for color?* • *What are some of the different words we could use for kind?* • *What are some of the different words we could use for shape?* • *What are some of the different words we could use for number or amount?* • *What are some of the different words we could use for which one or whose?*
Grammar Cards	Give students a set of cards with black, red, and orange. Lay out a card for each word in this sentence. Use only one card for each proper noun even if it has more than one word. *Mrs. Jones baked a chocolate cake for the little neighbor girl.* Have one student "read" the cards saying the color and the speech part. *What is the proper noun? What are the common nouns? What are the adjectives? What words do they describe? What common noun could you use instead of Mrs. Jones? What proper noun could you use instead of little neighbor girl?* Continue with two more sentences.
Revising Writing	Write the sentence for students to view. *The truck stopped.* This is a boring sentence. We know nothing about the truck. Rewrite this sentence, but add one or two words that tell us more about the truck. (Refer to *size, color, kind, shape, number/amount, whose, which one.*) Have students read some of their new sentences aloud. Point out that the adjectives help create a picture in your mind.

(continued)

Lesson to Introduce Adjectives	
Target Sentence	*The cat purred.*
Connecting Grammar to Writing	Have students take their own sentences and paragraphs and underline the noun once. They might not find all of the nouns in their writing, but that is okay. Make sure the ones they have underlined are actually nouns.
	Have them look at the noun.
	How can you make your writing more interesting?
	Can you replace the noun with a more exact noun?
	Can you add an adjective to describe the noun?
	Have students make one revision and then share it with a partner.

Note to Teacher on Adjectives

Unfortunately, English is quite complex when it comes to some of the parts of speech. Adjectives are just such an area. In certain cases, words that are classified as nouns or pronouns are used as adjectives:

- Possessive pronouns are called pronouns but actually act as adjectives within a sentence to show whose. For example, my dog, your coat, his truck, her car.

- Demonstrative pronouns also act as adjectives in sentence. For example, this book, that house, those lights, these dishes.

- Nouns are also used as adjectives. For example, chicken soup, baseball player. These are called attributive nouns, noun adjuncts, or adjectival nouns.

- Possessive nouns also act as adjectives within a sentence to show whose or which one. For example, Sally's bike, the boy's coat, summer's warm wind.

Our purpose in studying grammar is to help students revise and improve writing. Therefore, there is not a lot of stress on the exact terminology of a word. If students provide any of the above words as an example of an adjective, they are correct. In my experience in working with students, if the emphasis is on answering the questions of size, color, shape, kind, amount, which one, this has never been a problem in having them identify the part of speech correctly.

Lesson to Introduce Action Verbs	
Target Sentence	*The girl ran.*
Guided Discovery 1	*What is the sentence about?* the girl
	What did the girl do? ran
	Let's identify the words in the sentence.
	the = definite article/adjective
	girl = common noun
Definition	*There are two kinds of verbs: action and linking*
	Right now, we will only talk about action verbs.
	It tells something someone DOES.
Oral Response	*You have 30 seconds to think of something you can do.*
	Point to different students and have them rapidly, in order, give you a word.

Lesson to Introduce Action Verbs (continued)	
Target Sentence	*The girl ran.*
Definition	Verbs not only tell us what someone or something has done, but it also gives us a clue as to WHEN it was done. The tense of a verb tells us when. (They are learning simple tense).
	We have some words that will help us remember the tense of a verb.
	Right now, I. . . Yesterday, I . . . Tomorrow, I . . .
	Right now is called present tense. It is happening right now.
	Yesterday is called past tense. It happened in the past. It could be five minutes ago, yesterday, or a month ago, a year ago, or many years ago. All we know is that it has already happened.
	Tomorrow is called future tense. It hasn't happened yet, but it is going to happen. It could be in one minute, in one hour, in a year, or in many years ahead. We just know that this is something people think is going to happen.
	Notice we always use the word *will* or *shall* to help us say the future tense. *Will* and *shall* are called a **helping verbs**.
Oral Response	*For each of these words, let's say all of the tenses that tell when.*
	Give the word and then say the tenses together.
	Right now I run. Yesterday I ran. Tomorrow I will run.
	Right now I jump. Yesterday, I jumped. Tomorrow I will jump.
	Right now I call. Yesterday, I called. Tomorrow I will call.
	Right now I go. Yesterday I went. Tomorrow I will go.
	Notice that sometimes we add the _ed to make the past tense and sometimes we completely change the word.
Grammar Cards	Give students a set of cards with black, red, orange, and blue.
	Lay out a card for each word in this sentence. Lay down card for each part of the verb. Sometimes there is a helping verb.
	Mrs. Carter will talk on the phone with Sarah after the long meeting.
	Have one student "read" the cards, saying the color and the speech part.
	For each sentence, have students tell whether the noun is a common or a proper noun, what noun the adjectives describes (modifies), and the tense of the verb.
	What is the proper noun? What are the common nouns? What are the adjectives? What words do they describe? What common noun could you use instead of Mrs. Carter? What is the tense of the verb? Change the tense to past tense.
	Continue with two more sentences.
Group Activity	Give students five to eight sentences written on a sheet of paper. It is best if you use sentences that have previously been used for the grammar card activity.
	Have them change the tense of the verb. They must identify the old tense and the new tense of the verb.
Revising Writing	Write the sentence for students to view. **The rabbit is in the field.**
	This is a boring sentence. We know nothing about the rabbit. It just is. Rewrite this sentence, but add two or three words that will paint a picture in our minds. Change the verb to an action verb.
	Have students read some of their new sentences aloud. Point out that the adjectives help create a picture in your mind.

(continued)

Lesson to Introduce Action Verbs (continued)	
Target Sentence	*The girl ran.*
Connecting Grammar to Writing	Have students take their own sentences and paragraphs and underline the noun once and the verb twice. They might not find all of the nouns or verbs in their writing, but that is okay. Make sure the ones they have underlined are actually nouns and verbs.
	Have them look for the verbs *is, was, were, am,* and *are*. If they are not followed by an action verb, circle them.
	How can you make your writing more interesting?
	Can you change the circled verbs to action verbs?
	Have you used the best action verb?
	For example, rather than "went," they could use a more specific word such as walk, run, drive, ride, etc.
	Look at the nouns. Can you replace one with a more exact noun?
	Can you add an adjective to describe the noun?
	Have students make one revision and then share it with a partner.

Writing Assignments for *The Empty Pot,* by Demi

Write a character sketch of someone in *The Empty Pot.* **PLAN:** 1. Brainstorm ideas. 2. Choose the character. (Ping, one of the children, Emperor) 3. Decide on the audience. 4. Gather information. Choose categories to show the subject's most memorable traits (looks, attitude, feelings, character, what he does, etc.). 5. Add details to each category. Make a cluster diagram to show the traits. The first sentence will introduce the character and why chosen (memorable trait). Next, describe each category with the details. 6. Conclude with your reactions, feelings. **WRITE.**	**Write a news story of an incident in *The Empty Pot.*** **PLAN:** 1. Brainstorm ideas. 2. Choose an event for the news story. 3. Decide on the audience. 4. Gather information. Find the *who, when, where, what, why,* and *how*—use only facts. 5. Make a chart with this information. 6. The first sentence will give as much information as possible to tell what the story is about. The first paragraph will give the most important information. 7. End with the least important facts. Make sure the details are told in order. **WRITE.**

Write a personal narrative from Ping's viewpoint. **PLAN:** 1. Brainstorm ideas of events you could choose from Ping's life (get the seed, plant the seed, go to the palace, OR use the entire story). 2. Choose one of the events. 3. Decide on the audience. 4. Gather information. List the events in order. Add Ping's feelings to these events. Use your imagination. 5. Choose which details to include and which details to leave out.	**Write a descriptive paragraph from Ping's viewpoint.** **PLAN:** 1. Brainstorm things you could describe (Ping's garden, the flowers, Ping himself). 2. Choose what to describe. 3. Decide on the audience. 4. Gather information. List words that would describe. 5. Organize the information on your general structure. 6. The first sentence will tell what you are describing. You can use the sentence frame for this sentence. This sentence will be your key idea. It will summarize what

(continued)

6. The first sentence will tell what the paragraph is about. It should tell who, what, when, where, why, and/or how. You can use the sentence frame for this sentence. It will summarize what you are trying to say.
7. The next sentences will show the order that includes descriptions and feelings.
8. Your last sentence will tell the person's general conclusion.
WRITE.

you are trying to say about what you are describing.
7. The next sentences will use the list of words that you used to describe.
8. Your last sentence will give a general conclusion on what you are describing.
WRITE.

Write a comparison/contrast paragraph using information from *The Empty Pot*.
PLAN:
1. Brainstorm ideas on what you can compare.
2. Choose the two items to compare and contrast.
3. Decide on the audience.
4. Gather information. Make a detailed list of the description of each item.

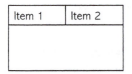

Item 1	Item 2

5. Make a Venn diagram to show the ways these are alike and different.
6. The first sentence will tell what items you are comparing. The next sentences will state ways they are alike first and then ways they are different. Give specific examples to illustrate your point.
7. The last sentence will summarize what you have compared and contrasted.
WRITE.

Write a how-to paragraph using the information from *The Empty Pot*.
PLAN:
1. Brainstorm ideas on what you can describe—perhaps how to plant and take care of a seed.
2. Decide on the audience.
3. Gather information. List the steps to be taken in order.
4. Double-check the list to make sure you have not forgotten a step.
5. The first sentence will tell what the audience is going to learn to do.
6. Make sure the steps are in order. Use words such as *first, second, next, then, last.*
7. Your last sentence will tell the final product.
WRITE.

References

Adams, J. M. (1990). *Beginning to read: Thinking and learning about print.* Cambridge, MA: MIT Press.

Adolf, S., Catts, H., & Weismer, S. (2006, April). Language deficits in poor comprehenders: A case for the simple view of reading. *Journal of Speech, Language, and Hearing, 49,* 278–293.

Afflerbach, P., & Johnston, P. (1984). Research methodology on the use of verbal reports in reading research. *Journal of Reading Behavior, 16,* 307–321.

Allen, K. A., Newhaus, G. F., & Beckwith, M. C. (2005). Alphabet knowledge: Letter recognition, naming, and sequencing. In Birsh, J. R (Ed.), *Multisensory Teaching of Basic Language Skills,* Second Edition (83–112). Baltimore, MD: Paul H. Brooke, Publishing Co.

Allington, R. L. (2000). *What really matters for struggling readers.* New York: Longman Publisher.

Anbar, A. (1984). *Natural Reading Acquisition of Preschool Children.* (Doctoral dissertation, State University of New York at Buffalo).

Anbar, A. (1986). Reading acquisition of preschool children without systematic instruction. *Early Childhood Research Quarterly I,* 69–83.

Anbar, A. (2004). *The Secret of Natural Readers.* Westport, CT: Praeger Publishers

Anderson, R.C. & Nagy, W. E. (1992, Winter). The vocabulary conundrum. *American Educator: The Professional Journal of the American Federation of Teachers, 16*(4), 14–18, 44–47.

Anderson, R. (1994). Role of the reader's schemata in comprehension, learning, and memory. In R. B. Ruddell, M. Rapp, & H. Singer (Eds). *Theoretical models and processes of reading* (4th ed.), pp. 469–481. Newark: DE: International Reading Association.

Anonymous (n.d). The Student, the Fish, and Agassiz. Retrieved from http://www.skidmore.edu/~mmarx/L&EF09/agassiz.pdf.

Ball, E. W., & Blachman, B. A. (1991). Does phoneme awareness training in kindergarten make a difference in early word recognition and developmental spelling? *Reading Research Quarterly, 16* (1), 49–66.

Balmuth, M. (1982). The roots of phonics: A historical introduction, Baltimore, MD: Paul H. Brookes Publishing Co., Inc.

Balmuth, M. (2009). The roots of phonics: A historical introduction, Revised Edition, Baltimore, MD: Paul H. Brookes Publishing Co., Inc.

Beck, I. L., McKeown, M. G. & Kucan, L. (2002). Bringing words to life: Robust vocabulary instruction. New York, NY: Guilford Press.

Bentin, S., & Leshem, H. (1993). On the interaction between phonological awareness and reading acquisition: It's a two-way street. *Annals of Dyslexia, 43,* 125–148.

Bodrova, E., & Leong, D. J. (1996). *Tools of the mind: A Vygotskian approach to early childhood education.* Englewood Cliffs, NJ: Prentice-Hall.

Bradley, L., & Bryant, P. E. (1983). Categorizing sounds and learning to read—a causal connection. *Nature, 30,* 419–421.

Bradley, L., & Bryant, P. E. (1985). *Rhyme and reason in reading and spelling.* Ann Arbor: University of Michigan Press.

Bradley, L., & Bryant, P. E. (1991). Phonological skills before and after learning to read. In *Phonological processes in literacy: A tribute to Isabelle Y. Liberman,* edited by S. A. Brady & D. P. Shankweiler. Hillsdale, NJ: Erlbaum.

Brady, S. A., & Shankweiler, D. P. (Eds.). (1991). *Phonological processes in literacy: A tribute to Isabelle Y. Liberman.* Hillsdale, NJ: Erlbaum.

Bransford, J. D., & Johnson, M. K. (1972, December). Contextual prerequisites for understanding: Some investigators of comprehension and recall. *Journal of Verbal Learning and Verbal Behavior 11*(6), 717–726.

Brown, J. L. (1970, May). You can read faster. *Reader's Digest,* Pleasantville, NY: The Reader's Digest Association.

Bryant, D. P., Goodwin, M., Bryant, B. R., & Higgins, K. (2003). Vocabulary instruction for students with learning disabilities: A review of research. *Learning Disability Quarterly, 26,* 117–128.

Calfee, R., & Henry, M. (1996). Strategy and skill in early reading acquisition. In J. Shimron (Ed), *Literacy and education: essays in memory of Dina Feitelson* (pp. 47–68). Cresskill, NJ: Hampton Press.

Cardoso-Martins. C., Mesquita. T., & Ehri, L. (2011). Letter names and phonological awareness help children to learn letter-sound relations. *Journal of Experimental Child Psychology, 109,* 25–38.

Cataldo, M., & Oakhill, J. (2000). Why are poor comprehenders inefficient searchers: An investigation in the effects of text representation and spatial memory on the ability to locate information in text. *Journal of Educational Psychology, 92* (4), 791–799.

Catts, H. (April 2009). The narrow view of reading promotes a broad view of comprehension. *Language, Speech & Hearing Services in School, 40,* 178–183.

Chomsky, C. (1979). Approaching reading through invented spelling. In Resnick and Weaver (Eds.), *Theory and practice of early reading, Vol. 2.* Hillsdale, NJ: Erlbaum.

Clay, M. M. (1979). *Reading: The patterning of complex behavior.* Auckland, New Zealand: Heinemann.

Coyne, M. D. (2007, April). Supporting vocabulary development. Rhode Island Reading First Conference. Retrieved from http://www.ride .ri.gov/instruction/curriculum/rhodeisland/ ppts/SupportingVocabularyDevelopment.pdf.

Cudd, E. T., & Roberts, L. (1989). Using writing to enhance content area learning in the primary grades. *Reading Teacher, 42* (6), 392–404.

Davis, R. D. (2010). *The Gift of Dyslexia: Why Some of the Smartest People Can't Read and How They Can Learn.* New York, NY: Perigee.

Dochy, F., Segers, M., & Buehl, M. M. (1999). The relation between assessment practices and outcomes of studies: The case of research on prior knowledge. *Review of Educational Research, 69*(2), 145–186.

Durkin, D. (1966). *Children who read early.* New York: Teacher's College Press.

Dymock, S. J. (1998). A comparison study of the effects of text structure training, reading practice, and guided reading on reading comprehension. *National Reading Conference Yearbook, 47,* 90–102.

Ehri, L. C. (1983). A critique of five studies related to letter–name knowledge and learning to read. In *Reading research revisited,* edited by L. M. Gentile, M. L. Kamil, & J. S. Blanchard. Columbus, OH: Merrill.

Ehri, L. C. (1991). Development of the ability to read words. In *Handbook of Reading Research,* edited by R. Barr, M. L. Kamil, P. Mosenthal & P. D. Pearson. New York: Longman.

Fernald, G. (1943). *Remedial techniques in basic school subjects.* New York, NY: McGraw-Hill Book Company, Inc.

Geelan, D. R. (1997, August). Prior knowledge, prior conceptions, prior constructs: What do constructivists really mean, and are they practicing what they Preach? *Australian Science Teachers Journal, 43*(2), 26–28.

Good, R. H., & Kaminski, R. A. (Eds.). (2007). *Dynamic Indicators of Basic Early Literacy Skills* (6th ed.). Eugene, OR: Institute for the Development of Educational Achievement. Retrieved from: http://dibels.uoregon.edu/.

Goodman, K. (1969). Analysis of oral reading miscues: Applied psycholinguistics." In *Language and literacy: The selected writings of Kenneth Goodman,* edited by F. Gollasch. Vol. I. Boston: Routledge & Kegan Paul.

Goodman, K. (1971), *The search called reading.* In Helen M. Robinson (Ed.), *Coordinating Reading instruction.* Glenview, IL: Scott, Foresman, and Company. Quoted in J. J. (2001), *Basic Reading Inventory.* Dubuque, IA: Kendall Hunt Publishing Company.

Goodman, K., & Goodman, Y. (1986). *What's whole in whole language?* Portsmouth, NH: Heinemann.

Goswami, U. C., & Bryant, P. E. (1990). *Phonological skills and learning to read.* East Sussex, BN: Lawrence Erlbaum Associates Ltd, Publishers.

Graves, D. H. (1994). *A fresh look at writing.* Portsmouth, NJ: Heinemann.

Hart, B., & Risley, T. (1995). Meaningful differences in the everyday experience of young American children. ERIC: Document Reproduction Service No.ED387210, p. 256.

Hasbrouck, J. E., & Tindal, G., (1992). Curriculum-based oral reading fluency norms for students in grades 2 through 5. *Teaching Exceptional Children, 24,* 41–44.

Henderson, E. H. (1992). The interface of lexical competence and knowledge of written words. In *Development of orthographic knowledge and the foundations of literacy: A memorial Festschrift of Edmunch H. Henderson,* edited by S. Templeton & D. R. Bear. Hillsdale, NJ: Erlbaum.

Henderson, E. H., & Beers, J. W. (Eds.) (1980). *Developmental and cognitive aspects of learning to spell: A reflection of word knowledge.* Newark, DE: International Reading Association.

Henderson, E. H., & Templeton, S. (1986). A developmental perspective of formal spelling instruction through alphabet, pattern, and meaning. *The Elementary School Journal, 86* (3), 305–316.

Henderson, L., & Chard, J. (1980). The reader's implicit knowledge of orthographic structure. In *Cognitive processes in spelling,* edited by U. Frith. New York: Academic Press.

Henry, M. K. (2005). The history and structure of written English. In Birsh, J. R (Ed.), *Multisensory Teaching of Basic Language Skills,* Second Edition (83–112). Baltimore, MD: Paul H. Brooke, Publishing Co.

Herron, J. (2008, September). Why phonics teaching must change. *Educational Leadership.* Association for Supervision and Curriculum Development. p. 77–81.

Hess, K. K. (2008). Teaching and assessing understanding of text structures across grades. National Center for the Improvement of Educational Assessment. Retrieved from http://www.nciea.org/publications/TextStructures_KH08.pdf.

Honig, B. (2001). *Teaching Our Children to Read.* Thousand Oaks, CA: Corwin Press, Inc.

Honigsfeld, A., & Dunn, R. (2009). Learning-style responsive approaches for teaching typically performing and at-risk adolescents. *The Clearing House, 82*(5), 220–224.

Hoover, W. A., & Gough, P. B. (1990). The simple view of reading. *Reading and Writing: an Interdisciplinary Journal, 2,* 126–160. Netherlands: Kluwer Academic Publishers. Retrieved from http://homepage.psy.utexas.edu/homepage/class/Psy338K/Gough/Chapter7/simple_view.pdf.

Hoover, W. A., & Gough, P. B. (2010). The reading acquisition framework—An overview. Retrieved from http://www.sedl.org/reading/framework/overview.html.

Huey, E. B. (1908). *The psychology and pedagogy of reading.* New York: Macmillan.

Juel, C. (1994a). *Learning to read and write in one elementary school.* New York, NY: Springer–Verlag.

Juel, C. (1994b). Teaching phonics in the context of the integrated language arts. In L. M. Morrow et al. (Eds.). *Integrated Language Arts* (pp. 133–154). Needham Heights, MA: Allyn and Bacon.

Juel, C., & Roper/Schneider, D. (1985). The influence of basal readers on first grade reading. *Reading Research Quarterly, 18,* 134–152.

Killgallon, P. A. (1943). *A study of the relationships among certain pupil adjustments in language situations* (Doctoral dissertation), The Pennsylvania State College. Dissertation Abstracts International, 10, 75.

Kim, Y., Petscher, Y., & Foorman, B. (2010, May). Contributions of phonological awareness and letter–name knowledge to letter–sound acquisition—A cross-classified multilevel model approach. *Journal of Educational Psychology, 102* (2), 313–326.

Kinnune, R., & Vauras, M. (1998). Comprehension monitoring in beginning readers. *Scientific Studies of Reading, 2*(4), 353–375.

Kuhl P., Williams K., & Lacerda, F. (1992). Linguistic experience alters phonetic perception in infants by 6 months of age. *Science, 255*, 606–608.

Kuhl, P. K., Stevens, E., Hayashi, A., Deguchi, T., Kiritanif, S., & Iverson, P. (2006). Infants show a facilitation effect for native language phonetic perception between 6 and 12 months. *Developmental Science, 9*(2), F13–F21.

Lass, B. (1982). Portrait of my son as an early reader. *The Reading Teacher, 36*(1), 20–28.

Lass, B. (1983). Portrait of my son as an early reader II. *The Reading Teacher, 36*(6), 508–515.

Learning Stewards (2011). *Children of the Code.* Retrieved from http://www.childrenofthecode.org/.
I recommend going to this site and watching each of the videos.

Liberman, I. Y., Shankweiler, D., Fischer, F. W., & Carter, B. (1974). Explicit syllable and phoneme segmentation in the young child. *Journal of Experimental Child Psychology. 18*, 201–212.

Liberman, I. Y., Shankweiler, D., & Liberman, A. M. (1989). The alphabetic principle and learning to read. In *Phonology and Reading Disability: Solving the Reading Puzzle*, edited by Shankweiler and Liberman. Ann Arbor: University of Michigan Press.

Linksman (2011). The fine line between ADHD and kinesthetic learners. Association for Comprehensive Neurotherapy. Palm Beach, FL: Retrieved from http://www.latitudes.org/articles/learn01.html.

Marzano, R. J. (2004). *Building background knowledge.* Alexandria, VA: Association for Supervision and Curriculum Development.

McKeown, M. C., Beck, I. L., & Blake, R. (2009). Rethinking reading comprehension instruction: a comparison of instruction for strategies and content approaches. *Reading Research Quarterly, 44*(3), 218–253.

McKeown, R. G., Gentilucci, J. L. (2007, October). Think-Aloud Strategy: Metacognitive development and monitoring comprehension in the middle school second-language classroom. *Journal of Adolescent & Adult Literacy, 51*(2), 136–147.

Melton, D. (1985). *Written and Illustrated by. . .* Kansas City, MO: Landmark Editions, Inc.

Moats, L. (1998, Spring/Summer). Teaching decoding. *American Educator,* 42–49, 95–96.

Moats, L. (2004, October). Relevance of neuroscience to effective education for students with reading and other learning disabilities. *Journal of Child Neurology, 19*(10), 840–845.

Moats (2009). *The challenge of learning to read, 2nd ed.* Longmont, CO: Sopris West Educational Services.

Montessori, M. (1964). *The Montessori method.* New York: Schocken Books.

Morais, J. (1991). Constraints on the development of phonemic awareness. In D. Shankweiler (Ed.), *Phonological processes in literacy: A tribute to Isabelle Y. Liberman* (pp. 5–28). Hillsdale, NJ: Lawrence Erlbaum Associates, Publishers.

Morris, D., & Perney, J. (1984). Developmental spelling as a predictor of first-grade reading. *The Elementary School Journal, 84*(4), 441–457.

Moran, C., & Calfee, R. (1993). Comprehending orthography: Social construction of letter–sound in monolingual and bilingual programs. *Reading and Writing: An Interdisciplinary Journal, 5,* 205–225.

Nagy, W. E., & Herman, P. A. (1987). Breadth and depth of vocabulary knowledge: Implications for acquisition and instruction. In *The nature of vocabulary acquisition*, edited by M. G. McKeown & M. E. Curtis. Hillsdale, NJ: Erlbaum.

Nagy, W. E, & Anderson, R. C. (1984). How many words are there in printed school English? *Reading Research Quarterly, 19*(3), 304–330.

Nation, K. (2005). *Children's Reading Comprehension Difficulties.* In *The Science of Reading*, edited by M. Snowling & C. Hulme. Malden, MA: Blackwell Publishing, Ltd. National Center for Educational Statistics (2011), National Assessment of Educational Progress, Retrieved from http://nces.ed.gov/nationsreportcard/.

NAEP (2002). NAEP oral reading fluency scale, grade 4: 2002. U.S. Department of Education, Institute of Education Sciences, National Center for Education Statistics Retrieved from http://nces.ed.gov/nationsreportcard/studies/ors/scale.asp.

National Institute of Child Health and Human Development (NICHD) (2000). Report of the national reading panel: An evidence-based assessment of the scientific research literature on reading and its implications for reading instruction. NIH Publication No. 00-4754. Washington, DC: U.S. Government Printing Office. Retrieved from http://www.nichd.nih.gov/publications/nrp/smallbook.cfm.

Nichols, J. N. (1980). Using paragraph frames to help remedial high school students with written assignments. *Journal of Reading, 24* (3), 228–231.

Niedelman, M. (1991). Problem solving and transfer. *Journal of Learning Disabilities, 24* (6), 322–329.

Nist, J. (1966). *A structural history of English.* New York, NY: St. Martin's Press.

Palincsar, A. S., & Duke, N. K. (2004). The role of text and text-reader interactions in young children's reading development and achievement. *The Elementary School Journal, 105,* 183–197.

Papanicolaou, A. C., Simos, P. G., & Fletcher, J. M. (2003). Early development and plasticity of neurophysiological processes involved in reading. In *Preventing and Remediating Reading Difficulties: Bringing Science to Scale,* edited by B. F. Foorman. Baltimore, MD: York Press.

Piaget, J. (1972). The principles of genetic epistemology. New York, NY: Basic Books.

Powel, G. (1980, December). A meta-analysis of the effects of "imposed" and "induced" imagery upon word recall. Paper presented at the annual meeting of the Nation Reading Conference, San Diego, CA (ERIC: Document Reproduction Service No. ED 199644).

Presseisen, B. Z. (1995). Critical issue: Building on prior knowledge and meaningful student contexts/cultures. North Central Regional Educational Laboratory. Retrieved from http://www.ncrel.org/sdrs/areas/issues/students/learning/lr100.htm.

Read, C. (1971). Pre-school children's knowledge of English phonology. *Harvard Education Review, 41,* 1–34.

Read, C. (1975). *Children's categorization of speech sounds in English.* Urbana, IL: National Council of Teachers of English.

Reading by Touch (1948, July 12). *Time.* Retrieved from http://www.time.com/time/magazine/article/0,9171,804743-1,00.html\.

Ricketts, J., Bishop, D., & Nation, K. (2008). Investigating orthographic and semantic aspects of word learning in poor comprehenders. *Journal of Research in Reading, 31*(1), 117–135.

Shankweiler, D. (1991). The contribution of Isabell Y. Liberman. In *Phonological processes in literacy: A tribute to Isabelle Y. Liberman,* edited by D. Shankweiler. Hillsdale, NJ: Lawrence Erlbaum Associates, Publishers.

Share, D. L., & Gur, T. (1999). How reading begins: A study of preschoolers' print identification strategies. *Cognition and Instruction. 17*(2), 177–213.

Shaywitz, S. (November 1996). 10 years of brain imaging research shows the brain reads sound by sound. *Scientific American*, pp. 98–104. Retrieved from http://kidsadhd.com/learning/brain.shtml.

Shaywitz, B. A., Shaywitz, S. E., Pugh, K. R., Mencl, W. E., Fulbright, R. K., Skudlarski, P., . . . & Gore, J. C. (2002). Disruption of posterior brain systems for reading in children with developmental dyslexia. *Society of Biological Psychiatry.*

Shaywitz, S. (2003). *Overcoming Dyslexia.* New York, NY: Alfred A. Knopf, a division of Random House, Inc.

Shaywitz, B. A., Shaywitz, S. E., Blachman, B. A., Pugh, K. R., Fulbright, R. K., Skudlarski, P. . . . & Goret, J. C. (May 2004). Development of left occipitotemporal systems for skilled reading in children after a phonologically based intervention. *Biological psychiatry, 255,* pp. 926–933. Found online at http://www.haskins.yale.edu/papers/intervention_biol_psych_200.pdf.

Simos, P. G., Fletcher, J. M., Bergman, E., Breier, J. I., Foorman, B. R., Castillo, E. M., . . . & Papanicolaou, A. C. (April 2002). Dyslexia-specific brain activation profile becomes normal following successful remedial training. *Neurology, 58.*

Sparks, D. (2005). *Leading for results*. Thousand Oaks, CA: National Staff Development Council/Corwin.

Spaulding, R., & North, M. (2003). *Writing road to reading*. New York, NY: Harper Collins Publishers, Inc.

Sporleder, R. (1995). *Early spontaneous readers*. Unpublished manuscript.

Sporleder, R. L. (1998, April). A comparison of three approaches to literacy acquisition: Traditional phonics, whole language, and spelling before reading. Doctoral dissertation Montana State University, Bozeman, Montana.

Sporleder, R. L. (2009). *Phoneme, Phonics, and Language Structure*. Marion, IN.

Sporleder, R. L. (2010). *Word Workshop B*, Revised Edition. Marion, IN.

Stahl, S. A., & Fairbanks, M. M. (1986). The effects of vocabulary instruction: A model-based meta-analysis. *Review of Educational Research, 56*, 72–110.

Strangman, N., & Hall, T. (n.d.). Background knowledge: curriculum enhancement report National Center on Accessing the General Curriculum. Retrieved from http://www.cast.org/system/galleries/download/ncac/ncac_BK.pdf.

Stuart, M., & Coltheart, M. (1989). Does reading develop in a sequence of stages? *Cognition, 30*, 139–181.

Treiman, R., Tincoff, R., & Rodriguez, K., Mouzaki, A., & Francis, D. (1998, December). The foundations of literacy: learning the sounds of letters. *Child Development, 69* (6), 1524–1540.

Uhry, J. K. (2005). Phonemic awareness and reading: research, activities, and instructional materials. In *Multisensory Teaching of Basic Language Skills,* Second Edition, edited by J. R. Birsh. Baltimore, MD: Paul H. Brooke, Publishing Co.

Vellutino, F. R., & Scanlon, D. M. (1987). Phonological coding, phonological awareness, and reading ability: Evidence from a longitudinal and experimental study. *Merrill-Palmer Quarterly, 2*(3), 75–105.

Venezky, R. L. (1970). The structure of English orthography. The Hague, Paris: Mouton.

Vygotsky, L. S. (1978). *Mind in society: The development of higher psychological processes*. Cambridge, MA: Harvard University Press.

Wagner, R. K., & Torgesen, J. K. (1987). The nature of phonological processing and its causal role in the acquisition of reading skills. *Psychological Bulletin, 101* (2), 192–212.

Walsch, K. (2003). Basal readers: The lost opportunity to build the knowledge that propels comprehension. *American Educator, 27*, 24–27.

Westby, C. E. (2005). Assessing and remediating text comprehension problems. In *Language and reading disabilities*, edited by H. W. Catts & A. G. Kahmi. Upper Saddle River, NJ: Pearson Education, Inc.

White, S. (1995, August). Listening to children read aloud: Oral fluency. Washington, DC: National Center for Education Statistics. Retrieved from http://nces.ed.gov/pubs95/web/95762.asp.

Yeh, S. S., & Connell, D. B. (2008). Effects of rhyming, vocabulary and phonemic awareness instruction on phonemic awareness. *Journal of Research in Reading, 31*(2), 243–256.